Lake Chapala

a postcard history

ISBN 978-1-7770381-2-0
First edition 2022, reprinted 2025
Text, captions and maps © 2022 by Tony Burton

Cover design: Peter Shandera and Trevor Burton
Background: vecteezy.com

All rights reserved. Derechos reservados. No part of this book may be reproduced or transmitted in any form or by any means, electronic or mechanical, including photocopying, recording, or by any information storage and retrieval system, without written permission from the publisher.

Any post-print revisions can be found at sombrerobooks.com/?p=7796.

Sombrero Books, Box 4, Ladysmith B.C. V9G 1A1, Canada

LAKE CHAPALA

a postcard history

TONY BURTON

SB
SOMBRERO BOOKS, B.C., CANADA

Contents

Introduction	1
1. Wish you were here: picture postcards in Mexico	3
2. By boat, stagecoach and train	13
3. Chapala at the end of the nineteenth century	25
4. South shore: Tizapán el Alto and La Palma	35
5. Chapala 1900–1920: the golden age of tourism	41
6. East end: Ocotlán and Hotel Ribera Castellanos	61
7. Chapala 1920–1940: opportunities and challenges	71
8. Fishing and environmental change	87
9. Chapala 1940–1960: tourism and redevelopment	103
10. Ajijic: favored by foreigners	119
11. West end: Jocotepec and Roca Azul	131
Acknowledgments	140
Appendix 1. Dating postcards	141
Appendix 2. Index of photographers and publishers	143
Endnotes	144
Bibliography	149
Index	150

Maps

Map 1. The Lake Chapala Region	13
Map 2. Mexican Central Railway	20

"The illustrated postcard has become a true epidemic..."

—El Tiempo Ilustrado, 1909

Currency

Unless otherwise indicated, monetary values throughout the book are expressed in US dollars.

Images

The size and color of images closely match the original postcards. In the interests of quality, most images have been digitally retouched prior to publication.

Captions

Image captions have a date, followed by (where known) the names of the photographer and/or publisher. The use of "?" following a name indicates a tentative attribution. The use of "c. 1905" for a date indicates that the publication date is thought to be within five years of 1905; "c. 1905?" is indicative of a wider time range.

Introduction

What was the Lake Chapala area like in the old days? Previous illustrated books about Lake Chapala with reproductions of old photographs, though visually appealing, have barely scratched the surface of the rich and often intriguing history of the places, buildings and subjects depicted.[1] Lacking any informed commentary on individual images, they fail to connect readers with the historical context.

This book aims to stimulate a deeper appreciation of historical photographs by looking at carefully selected vintage postcards, alongside pertinent information about their photographers, genesis, purpose and implications. Using these images to interpret the cultural landscape and history of Lake Chapala helps reveal their true significance.[2]

The vintage postcards reproduced here were originally published between 1900 and 1960. Though their artistic quality varies greatly, they were published in the belief that they would serve as inexpensive mementoes of a trip to Lake Chapala and as an efficient way to promote the area to friends and family.

Limiting the illustrations to picture postcards brings both advantages and disadvantages. On the one hand, each image shows the specific characteristics of the scenery, people and life of Lake Chapala that a publisher deemed worthy of mass reproduction. On the other hand, they fail to provide a balanced overview of the entire region since some buildings and locations were photographed far more often than others. The south shore is greatly under-represented, and the lake's main island—Mezcala Island—is conspicuous by its absence, despite its immense historical significance.

Even though these irresistible little rectangles of card have been chosen to cover as wide a range of subject matter as possible, they do not fully reflect the numerous aspects of the lake captured on postcards. More than 1200 different vintage postcards of Lake Chapala are currently known, and new ones turn up almost every week.

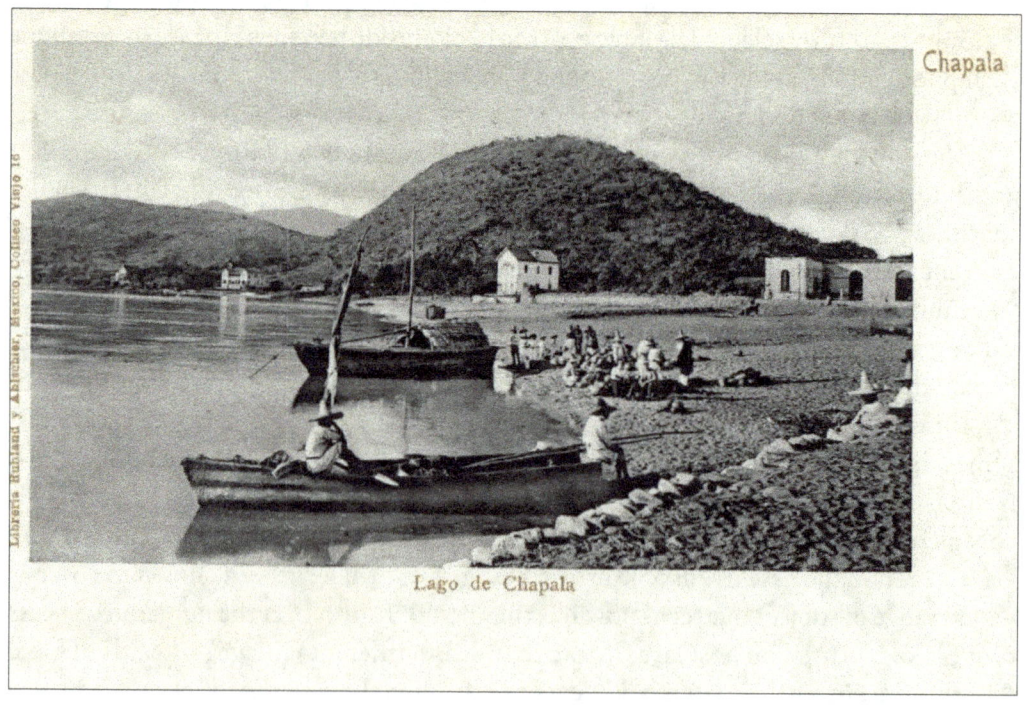

1.1. *Chapala waterfront, c. 1897. W Scott; Ruhland & Ahlschier.*
This postcard of a photograph taken by Winfield Scott was first published in about 1901. The boat in the foreground is alongside the rustic pier. The prominent buildings along the shore are (right to left) the Hotel Arzapalo, Casa Capetillo, Villa Tlalocan and Casa Albión (later known as Villa Josefina). The Hotel Arzapalo was still under construction, which dates this image to 1896 or 1897.

1

Wish you were here: picture postcards in Mexico

Improvements towards the end of the nineteenth century in two key areas of technology—photography and lithography—combined to trigger the introduction of picture postcards. Photography enabled the faithful 'realistic' capture of people, events and places; with better lenses and film, photographers could leave their studios and shoot pictures outdoors. Lithography enabled the rapid, mechanized reproduction of illustrations, including photographs. These developments reduced the difficulties and expense of publishing images in large print runs, and led to a proliferation of both postcards and illustrated magazines.

Mexico's earliest postcards with photographs appeared in 1897 when Correos Mexicanos signed a contract with Ruhland & Ahlschier, a firm owned by two Germans, Emil Ruhland and Max Ahlschier, who had a bookstore in Mexico City.[1] Ruhland & Ahlschier's beautifully produced postcards included several views of Lake Chapala; they served not only as a means of communication but also as inexpensive souvenirs. Precisely when these postcards of Chapala were first published is unclear; the earliest postmark known on a Chapala card is 1901.

Photographers associated with this firm include Americans Winfield Scott (1863–1942) and Charles Betts Waite (1861–1927), two important names in the history of Mexican photography. Scott lived in Mexico, with brief exceptions, from 1895 to 1924, undertaking commissions for railroad companies, and running a ranch near Ocotlán, toward the eastern end of Lake Chapala. He also became a hotelier, first at Hotel Ribera Castellanos and then at the Hotel Arzapalo in Chapala.

Waite set up shop in Mexico City in March 1897 and quickly amassed a vast collection of thousands of images taken all over Mexico, including many superb images of Chapala. After he bought the photographic business of Carmichael and Cox in 1904, and purchased all Scott's "photographic view negatives" in 1908, he advertised that he possessed "the largest assortment of views of any one country in the world."[2]

In Guadalajara the best known Mexican photographer taking postcard views was José María Lupercio, whose images were reproduced by a number of regional and national publishers, including Juan Kaiser. Swiss-born Kaiser (1858–1916), a pioneer of early postcards in Guadalajara, first arrived in Mexico in about 1886 and bought a

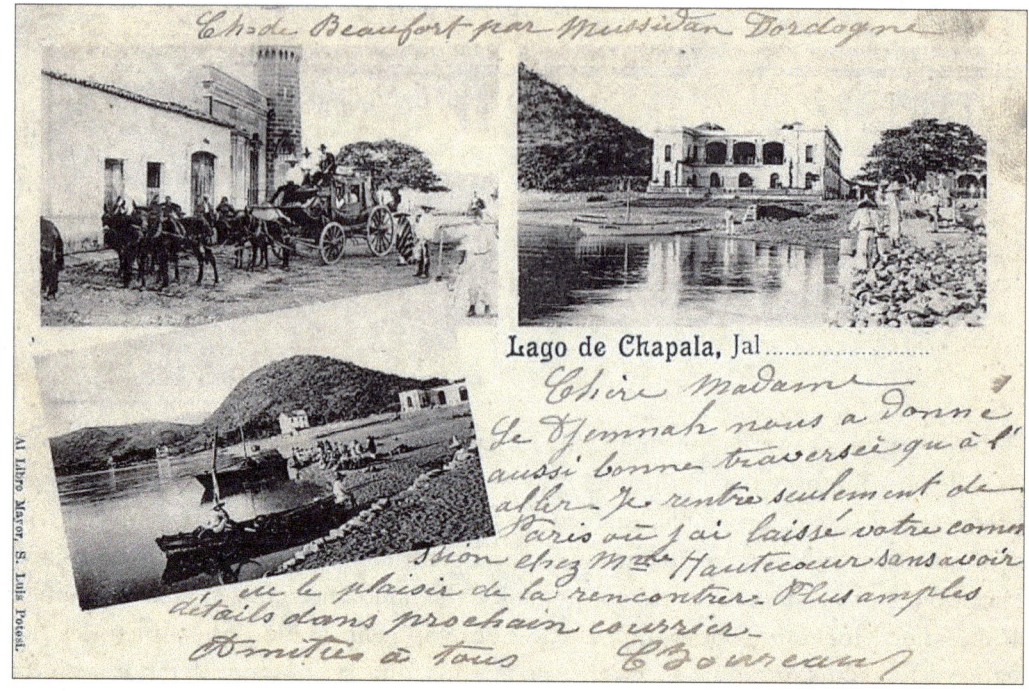

1.2. *Multiview of Chapala, c. 1901. W Scott & C B Waite (rt); J Kaiser.*
This triple view postcard published by Kaiser (photographs on left by Winfield Scott) was mailed in 1902. The top left photograph was first published in US magazine Harper's Bazar *in 1900. The turreted building behind the stagecoach is Villa Ana Victoria. On the extreme right, a water carrier is walking towards the camera. The Hotel Arzapalo, which opened in 1898, appears in both the bottom left image (still under construction) and—with its second story complete—in the top right.*

bookstore called Al Libro Mayor in the silver mining boom town of San Luis Potosí. Together with his brother Arnoldo, he moved most of his business to Guadalajara in 1899, where he opened a similar store named Al Libro de Caja.

Among the most distinctive early postcards of Chapala are several triple-view cards, published by Kaiser and printed in Germany, which feature three small images and lots of white space. Known images on these cards include fishing boats on the beach (identical to figure 1.1), the Hotel Arzapalo, the church, a stagecoach, Villa Tlalocan and Villa Josefina (formerly Casa Albión). Clearly, in some cases, the same photograph was used by more than one publisher.

There was a dramatic increase in the number of companies producing and marketing postcards in Mexico after 1902, when Kodak introduced a paper that could be printed on directly from a negative. Most early Mexican postcards were printed in Europe (the quality of printing in Austria and Germany was unsurpassed), and a small number of early cards were produced in the US. But Mexican printers caught up quickly and soon became competitive in terms of quality.

The apogee of Mexican postcards was from 1902 to 1910. Successive advances in film and camera technology led to much higher quality photographs. Capturing suitable images at the start of the century required ample time and a steady tripod to hold the large cameras then in use. The height of the tripod governed the composition, with the foreground very prominent in photographs taken from eye height or below.[3] When Kodak introduced smaller, lighter, more portable cameras, and more sensitive film, photographers could finally capture high-quality images from, for example, a small boat bobbing about on the ripples of the lake. Such developments created a huge range of new possibilities in terms of techniques, subjects and effects. At the same time, improvements in printing gave publishers more control over the definition, clarity and contrast of the final images.

This period coincided with the final years of Porfirio Díaz's dictatorship, a period when adopting both European ideas and US technological innovations was encouraged. European and US capital flowed into Mexico to finance factories, railroads and tourism. As the railroad network expanded, a trickle of international tourists became a torrent. Aided by intense overseas promotional campaigns (by the government and the railroads), Mexico opened itself up to the world. A growing number of hotels and Mexican curio shops catered to discerning tourists. Wealthy Mexicans also began to travel, and some very prominent families purchased second homes at Lake Chapala.

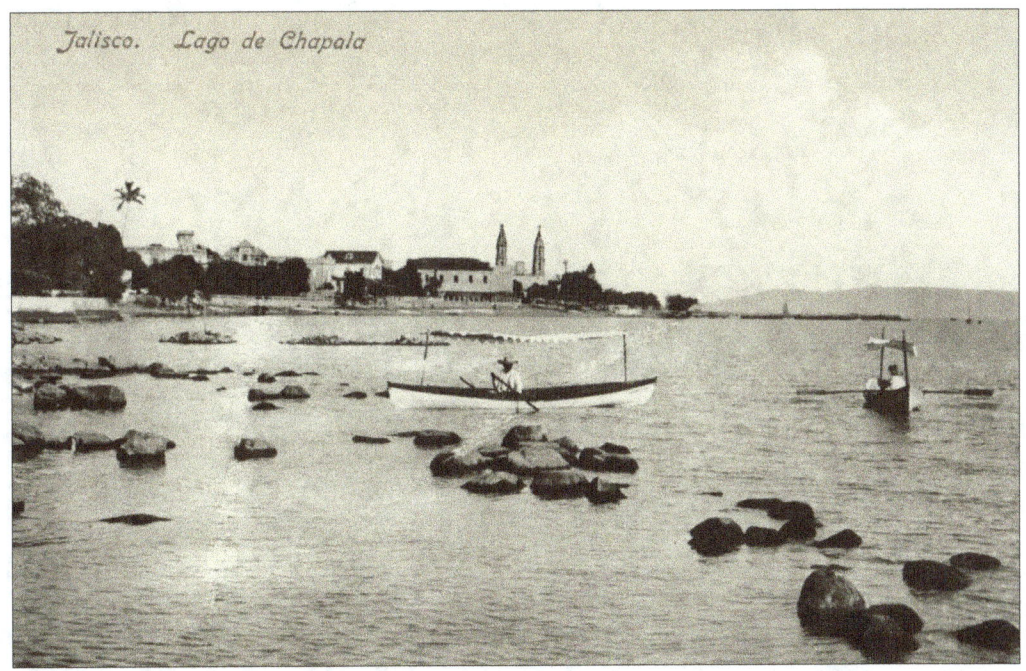

1.3. *Lake Chapala, c. 1908? Latapi & Bert.*
This classic early postcard conveys a suggestive combination of beautiful landscape, fine buildings, quiet beaches, calm lake and rowing boats for leisure. Chapala seduced tourists.

By 1910 more than 150 different publishers, including several US firms, were producing postcards for use in Mexico. Postcard sales fell during the following decade (the Mexican Revolution) and never fully recovered. In terms of international tourism, Mexico's postcards had already projected its identity and appeal overseas. The choice of subject matter for postcards had gradually molded and massaged foreigners' perspectives of Mexico.

In addition to commercial publishers, a number of skilled amateur photographers portrayed the Chapala area and deserve a mention. Hotelier Antonio Mólgora presumably gave away or sold his postcards to guests staying at the various hotels he managed; his son was also a fine photographer and produced numerous postcards. José Edmundo Sánchez, who owned a lakefront bar in Chapala, commercialized many of his own outstanding images of the town of Chapala as postcards in the 1920s and early 1930s. Equally good, and even more prolific, was photographer Jesús González, who began taking, printing and selling postcards of Chapala in about 1938.

Many of the picture postcards publicizing Lake Chapala were carefully crafted visual messages about the area's appeal and attractions. The public relations function of postcards is readily apparent in the cards published by the Mexican consulate in Milan, Italy, in about 1900. The first of two views of Chapala looks from the lower

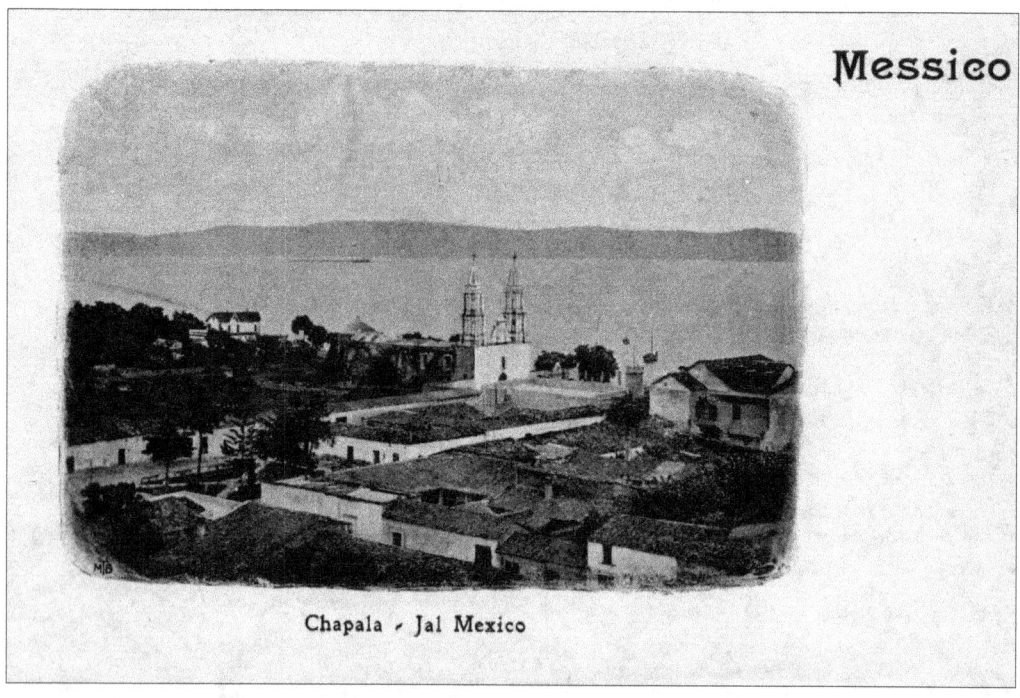

1.4. *View over Chapala, c. 1900. Mexican Consulate, Milan, Italy.*
The prominent building left of the twin-spired parish church of San Francisco is Villa Carmen. Immediately right of the church is Villa Ana Victoria. Both buildings were demolished prior to 1950.

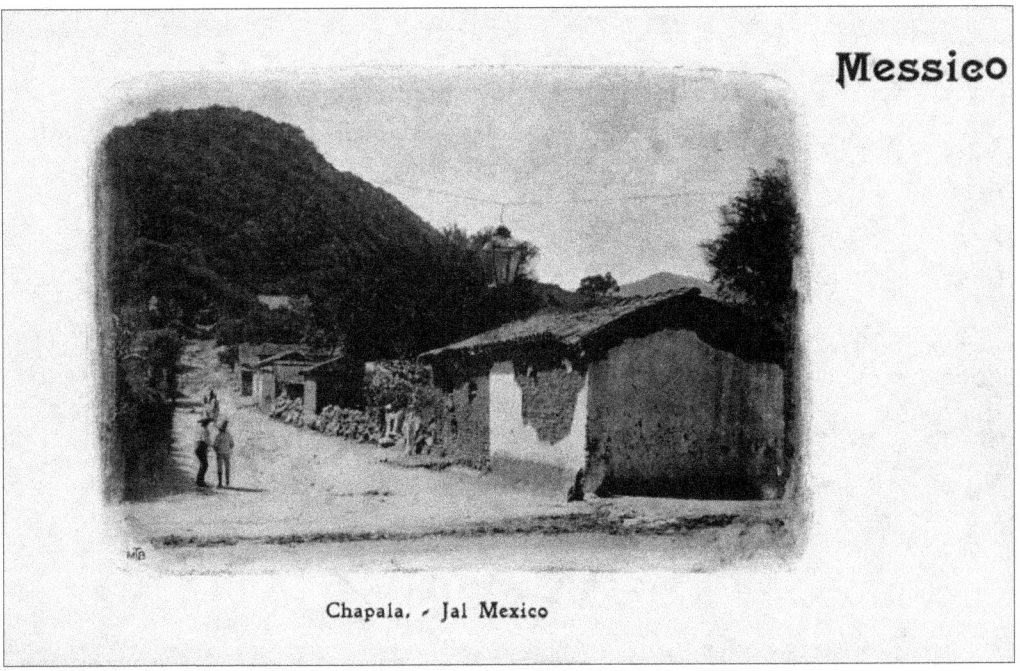

1.5. Calle San Miguel, c. 1900. Mexican Consulate, Milan, Italy.
Apart from the picturesque hill, it is hard to see why this image would appeal to Italians unless it was on account of the similarities in building style and landscape to parts of the Mezzogiorno.

slopes of Cerro San Miguel over the tiled roofs of the town towards the church, with Scorpion Island and the southern shoreline visible in the distance. The buildings date this picture to between 1898, when the Hotel Arzapalo opened, and 1904, when construction began of Casa Braniff.

It is easy to see why this image was chosen to promote Lake Chapala as an alternative tourist destination to the many beautiful lakes in Italy. As Anglo-American writer William Carson commented about Chapala at that time:

> The little village, with its big white church and mountainous background, bears a wonderful resemblance to some of the lake villages in northern Italy, and makes a most beautiful picture. This little bit of lake might be taken for a scene on Como; but the waters of Chapala are slightly yellowish instead of blue.[4]

The second consulate postcard is a much more unusual choice of subject. It shows humble, single-story, tiled roof, adobe dwellings extending up Calle San Miguel (now Calle López Cotilla) to the base of Cerro San Miguel. This is the earliest postcard of Chapala to show a decidedly non-tourist scene.

As an aside, there are many other Italian links to the story of tourism in Chapala. No fewer than five managers of the Hotel Arzapalo were Italian: Alberto Anzino, Francisco Mantice, Francisco Olivero, Antonio Seimandi and Antonio Mólgora. Prominent Italians who visited Chapala included Adolfo Dollero, who penned a detailed

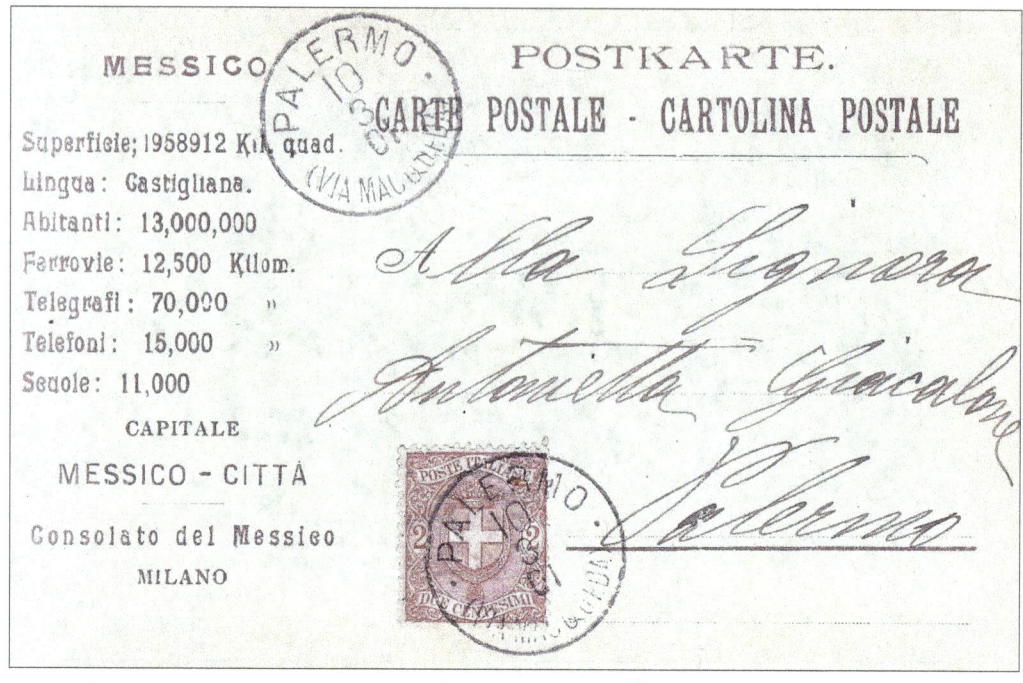

1.6. *Reverse of Mexican Consulate in Milan card, c. 1900.*
The statistics on the reverse (address side) of these cards pre-date the 1900 census, when Mexico's population was recorded as 13.6 million. The railroad figure was even more out of date: Mexico had 12,000 kilometers of railroad tracks in 1884 and an estimated 24,000 kilometers by 1898.

description of the village in *México al día (Mexico Today)*, and Guadalajara architect Angelo Corsi, who built or remodeled several fine residences.

The collecting and study of picture postcards (deltiology) became one of the most popular and widespread collectible hobbies the world had ever seen, a way of vicariously experiencing foreign countries at a time when long-distance travel was time-consuming and expensive. Collecting postcards became a craze for thousands of people across Mexico, and senders often asked to initiate an exchange of postcards. In 1908, at the peak of collecting fever, Mexican primary school teachers were urged to participate:

> Now that the illustrated postcard has become so common, collections can be formed of cards related to Geography in all its different manifestations; the teachers of some places can establish an exchange of postcards with those of other places to the benefit of everyone, especially the children.[5]

The rapid adoption of postcards as an alternative to letters had profound social consequences. Letters were private and allowed writers to describe actions, thoughts and feelings at length. The romantically inclined could write on perfumed pages and enclose some token of their love. While postcards saved senders both time and money, they were clearly not private,[6] far better suited for brief, non-contentious comments like "Wish you were here."

Mailing cards with pictures of a beautiful vacation villa, exotic scenery or luxury hotel, such as the Hotel Arzapalo in Chapala, was a way of hinting at social one-upmanship—announcing, "Look at me. I am wealthy enough to unwind for a week at Lake Chapala."

The shift from letters to postcards (echoed in some respects by the much more recent trend away from print to online communication) was lamented by many. A social commentary page for women in *El Tiempo Ilustrado*, a popular Mexico City weekly, called the popularity of illustrated postcards "a true epidemic" and advised readers in 1909 that:

> Postcards, illustrated or not, should be used only sparingly. They are not the correct medium for correspondence and many people feel that… they should only be used with merchants and subordinates.[7]

Nicaraguan poet Rubén Darío disagreed. He argued that the illustrated postcard was ideal for loving, sentimental correspondence. Sending a lovingly selected picture postcard meant "I send you both my soul and the soul of the landscape."[8] Darío was writing during the Revolution, which heralded a renewed focus on nationalism and a growing awareness and acknowledgment of the rich cultural heritage—art, dress, folk art and customs—of Mexico's indigenous groups. In the context of Lake Chapala,

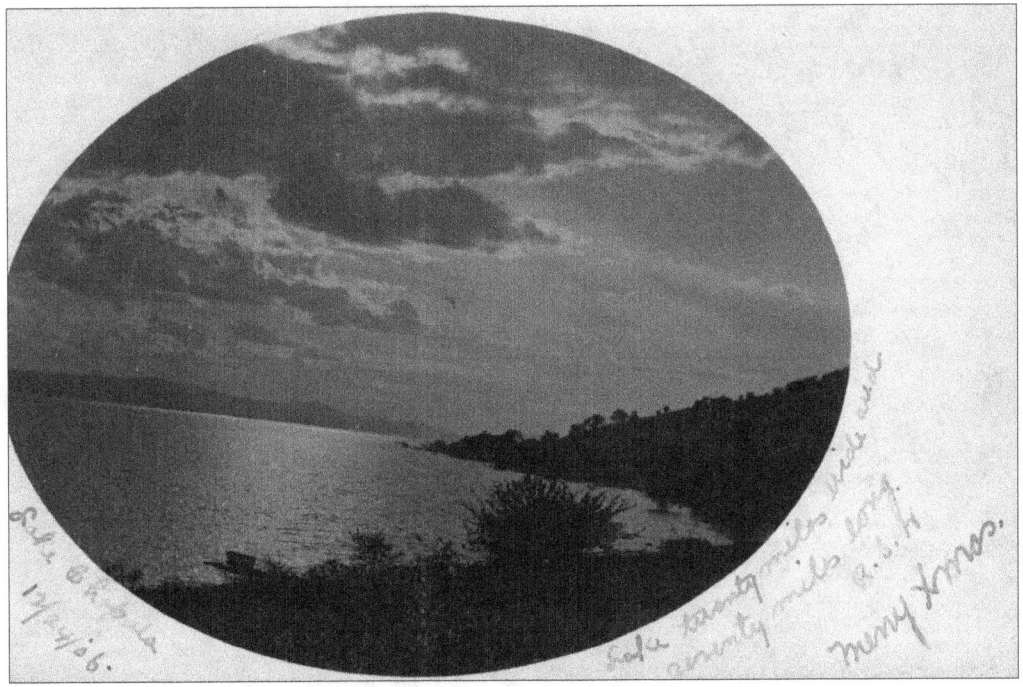

1.7. *Clouds over Lake Chapala, c. 1906.*
Multiple copies are known of this image by an unknown photographer. This particular example was written and mailed with Christmas greetings in 1906.

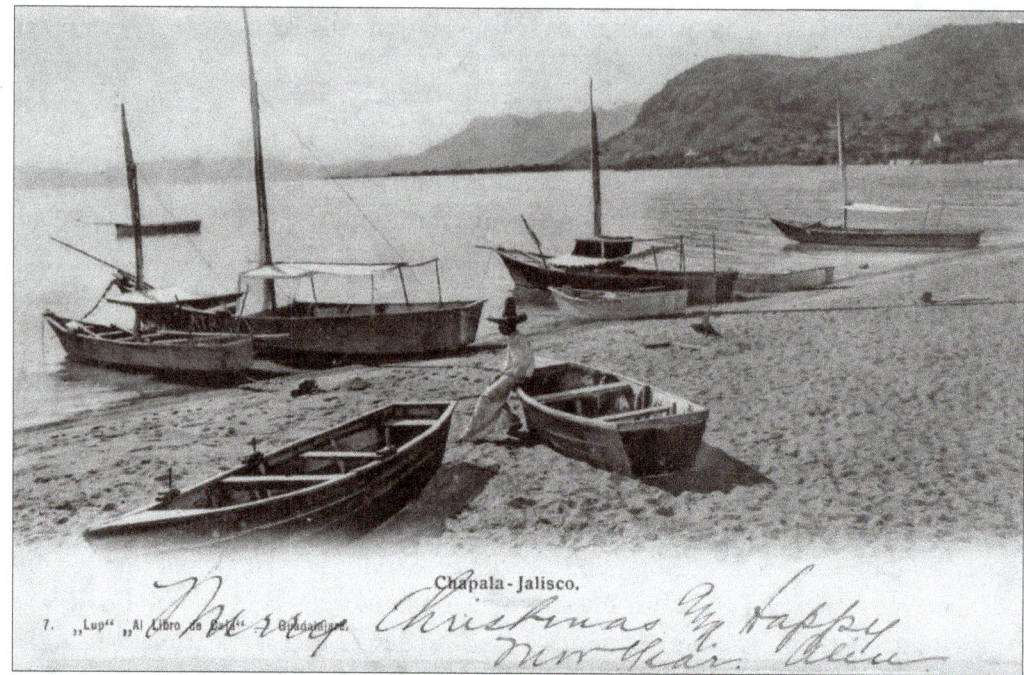

1.8. Boats on the beach, Chapala, photo ≤1902, postcard c. 1906. J M Lupercio; J Kaiser. This card, published by Juan Kaiser, was a well-composed scene by Guadalajara photographer José María Lupercio.

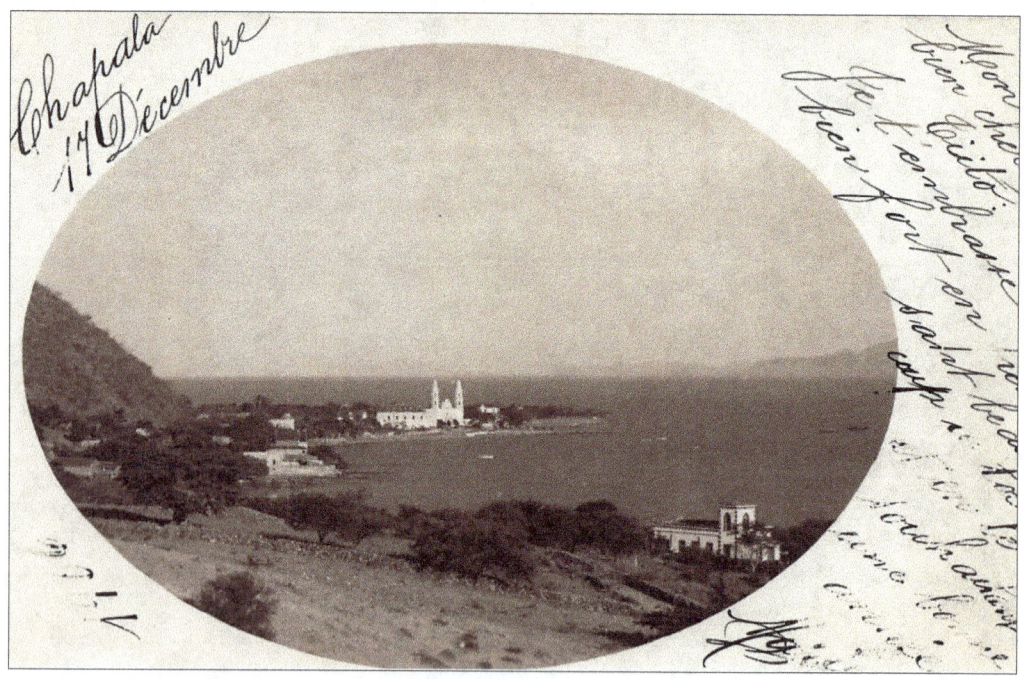

1.9. View from the hillside above Villa Montecarlo, c. 1900. W Scott.
Mailed to France in 1906, this oval image is from a rectangular photograph first published in a 1902 book. A greatly cropped version was published as a postcard in about 1906.

subjects such as fishermen and their nets, rarely photographed prior to 1920, finally found their way into the portfolios of postcard companies.

The popularity of commercial picture postcards declined after the 1930s as cameras became even simpler, more portable, more reliable and, above all, more affordable. Though the craze for postcards was on the wane, some local and regional companies—such as Laboratorios Julio in Guadalajara—and enterprising individuals—such as Jesús González in Chapala—continued to commercialize postcards of Lake Chapala into the 1940s and beyond.

Early illustrated cards had an undivided back, reserved exclusively for the name and address of the intended recipient; any correspondence had to be written on the front. Designers of these cards often left sufficient white space around the image to encourage senders to add brief messages. Several cards of the Hotel Arzapalo in Chapala have "My room" written alongside an arrow pointing to the relevant upper-story window.

Another strategy, used by those who wanted to write far more than the available space allowed, was to write first in one direction and then rotate the card through 90 degrees and write at right angles over the top of their previous writing.

By 1907 postal regulations worldwide allowed the mailing of postcards with a divided back, where a vertical line separated a space for correspondence from a space reserved for the recipient's details and a postage stamp. This change was first enacted in the UK (1902), then mainland Europe and Mexico (1905) and the US (1907).

The spaces allocated to correspondence and address respectively were not always equal. Cards published shortly after the introduction of divided backs often reserved significantly more than half for the address.

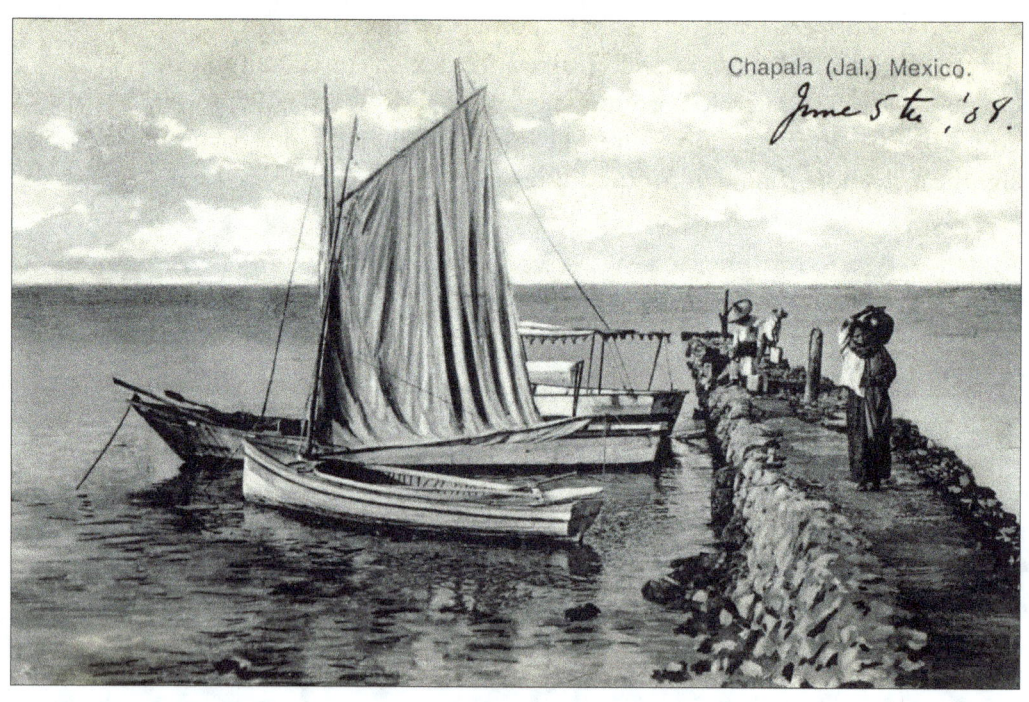

2.1. *Boats at a rustic pier, c. 1906. J M Lupercio?; T Schwidernoch.*
Printed in Austria, this postcard, looking as much like a painting as a photograph, was mailed in June 1908 with a short message saying there was "nothing as pretty as this charming resort on the lake." The woman walking toward the camera past the gaff-rigged sailboat is shouldering a pitcher of water from the lake.

2

By boat, stagecoach and train

This chapter considers how improvements in transport during the nineteenth and early twentieth centuries caused the focus of economic activity at Lake Chapala to shift away from the southern shore (chapter 4) towards the town of Chapala (chapters 3 and 5) and the area further east near Ocotlán (chapter 6).

Boats, ships and piers

Lake Chapala has long played an important role for transport, enabling farmers, fishermen and merchants in any of the lakeside villages to move animals, produce and goods relatively easily (by boat) to places that otherwise required difficult, hazardous and slow overland journeys. In the case of relatively isolated villages, such as Ajijic, this remained true until the 1940s.

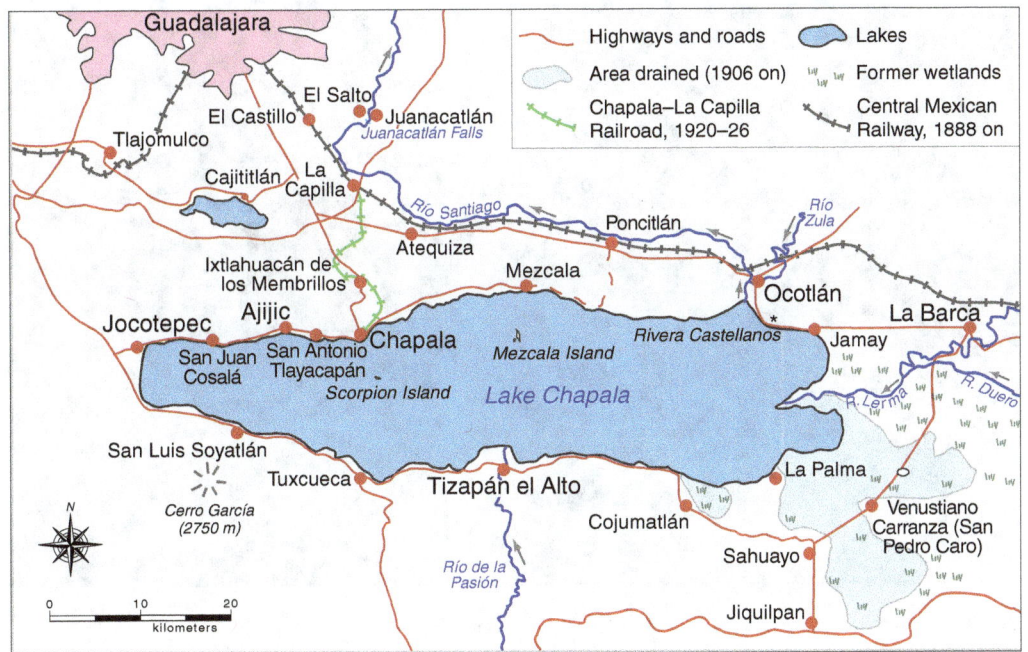

Map 1. The Lake Chapala region

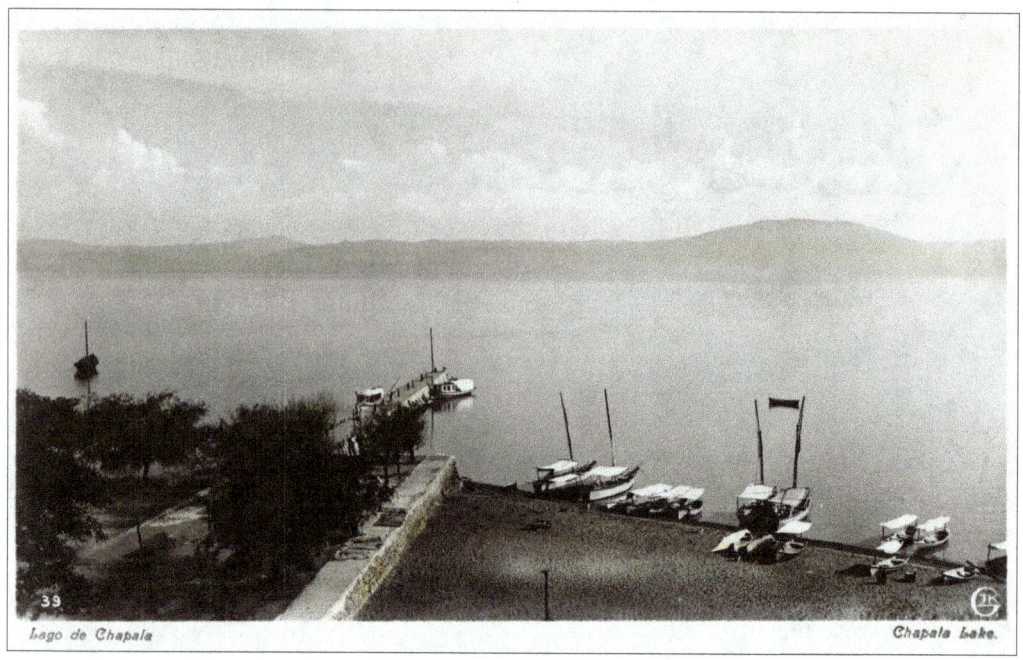

2.2. Chapala pier and waterfront, c. 1903. J Kaiser.
In April 1898 the state government had given Chapala $100.00 towards completing a new pier, with numerous benches and trees for shade.

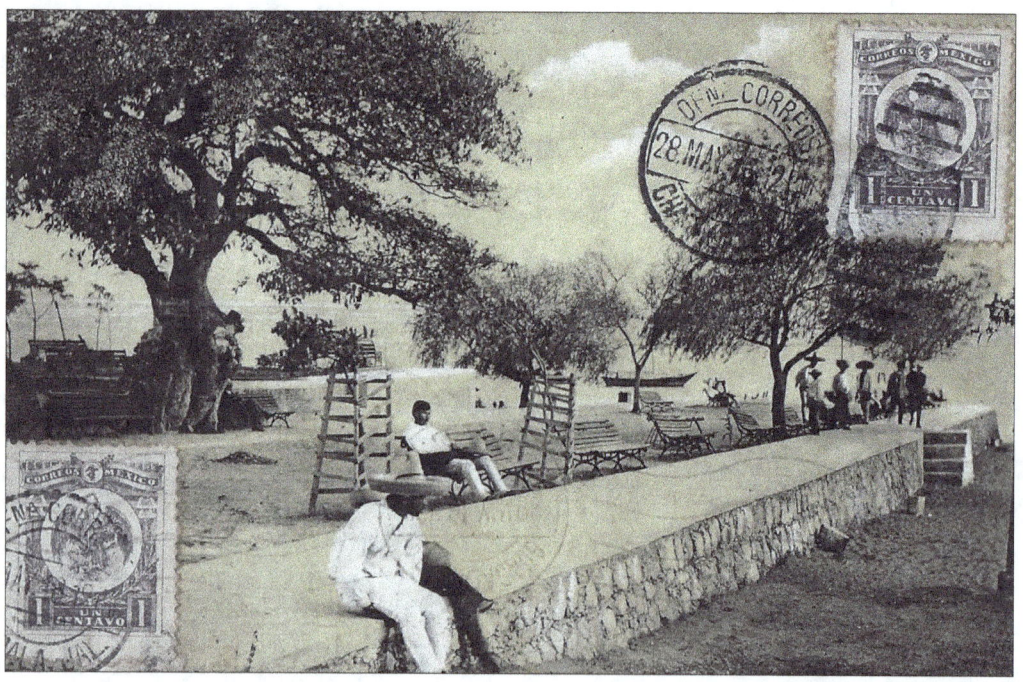

2.3. Chapala pier and waterfront, c. 1910. J Kaiser.
The approach to the pier in Chapala, with its trees and benches, was the perfect place to relax, people watch, and enjoy a beautiful sunset.

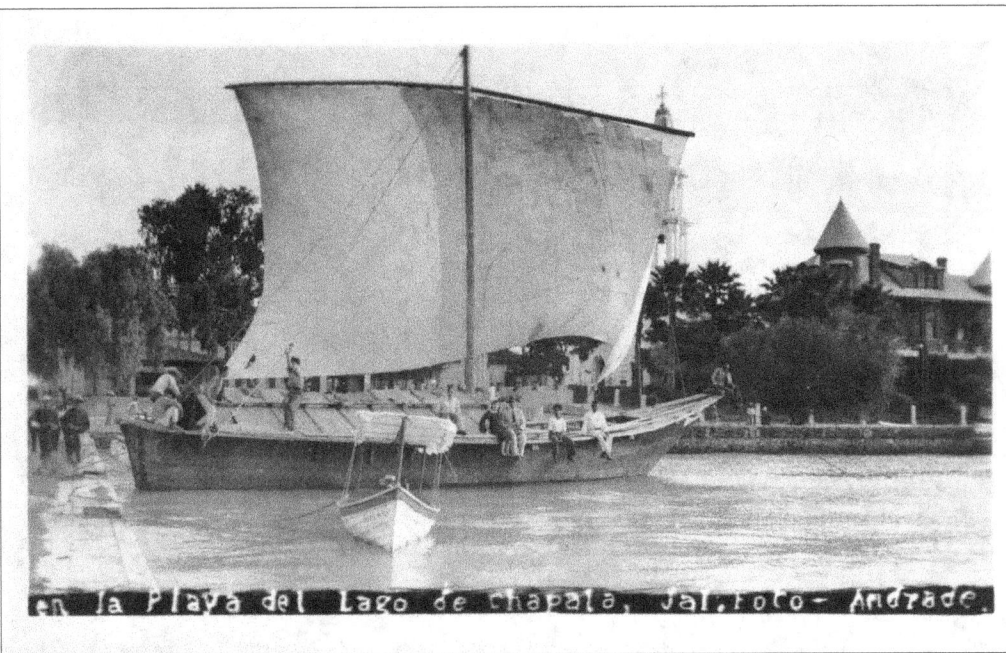

2.4. Sail canoe moored at the main pier in Chapala, c. 1935? Andrade.
The largest piers offered sufficient depth of water that even large cargo-carrying vessels could tie up to load and unload.

The lake was a vital link in the regional transportation network connecting central Mexico to Guadalajara. In the nineteenth century the south shore of the lake was at least as important in economic terms as the northern shore. Local craft criss-crossed the lake every day ferrying all manner of goods and provisions from one small port to the next.

Several different kinds of vessels were in use, including fishing skiffs, flat-bottomed launches (*canoas*), large sail canoes (*canoas de vela*) and, from the 1860s, paddlesteamers, which were faster and could carry more cargo than their competitors.

Almost every village, however small, had its own pier or jetty. Larger places like Chapala had several small piers, some for public use, others built privately by local property owners. The smallest piers were rudimentary constructions, made by piling rocks at right angles to the beach. But they served their purpose:

> A rude pier of rough stones extends into the water, and here one can embark in a rowing or sailing boat or a naphtha launch and take trips up and down the lake. There are one or two old-fashioned steamers on it, but they do not make regular runs and have to be chartered for special trips… [and] a number of small fishing schooners.[1]

Such rustic piers remained important well into the second half of the twentieth century, especially for the transport of wood and fresh produce. Larger towns, with more resources, built docks of wood, baked bricks, quarry-cut stone blocks, iron and cement, which were much stronger and more permanent structures.

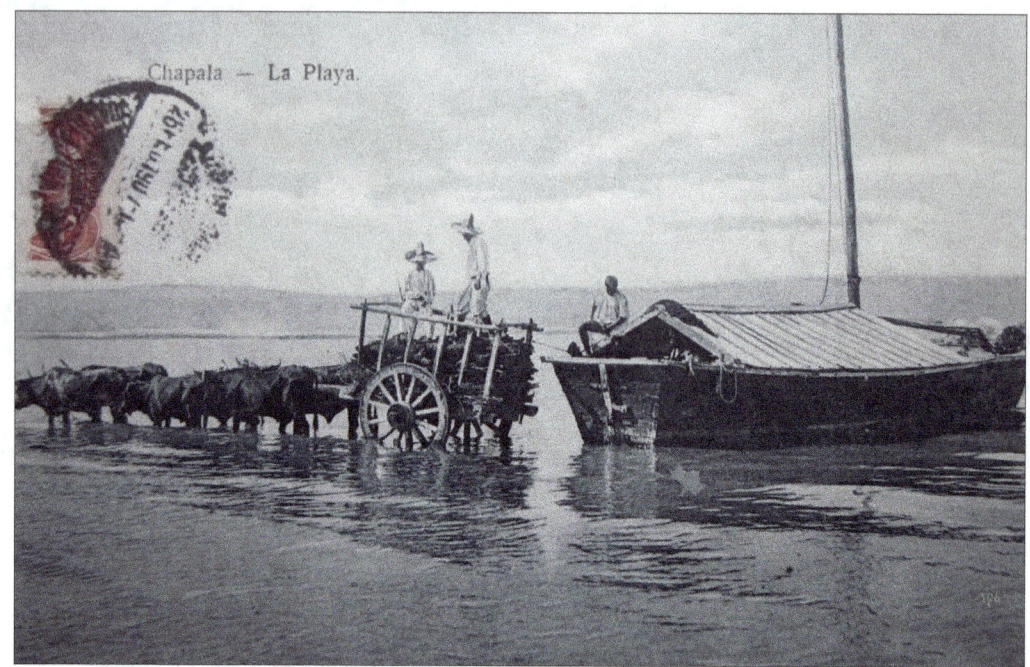

2.5. *Transferring cargo from sail canoe to cart, c. 1903. J M Lupercio; M Hernández.*
*A team of oxen waits patiently for a heavy cargo (perhaps wood) to be unloaded from a large, covered sail canoe (*canoa*). A cart this size could carry about one cord of wood (128 cubic feet).*

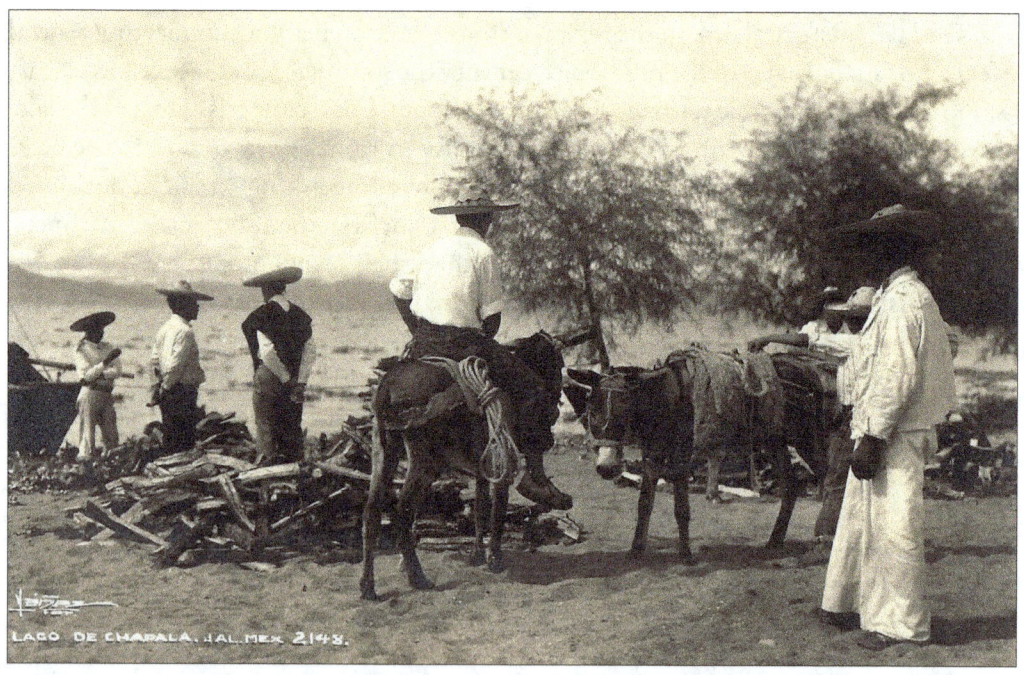

2.6. *Trade or transfer of wood from burro to boat, c. 1935. M Yañez.*
Trade in wood remained important even after the last steamship had been taken out of service. Villagers still needed firewood, both for lime kilns and for household kitchens.

The utility of piers depended on the lake level. In times of drought they were left high and dry, of no use to traders and fishermen. On the much rarer occasions when the lake rose so high that it washed over them, their use became hazardous.

The pier in Chapala provided a popular focal point for the village. Construction of a new pier—12 meters (40 feet) wide and 72 meters (240 feet) in length—in 1898 was completed in time for the Independence Day celebrations that September.[2] Leafy trees and comfortable benches enhanced the appeal of sitting here for a lazy afternoon, to watch the world go by. The Chapala Yacht Club opened a second, much longer pier, using wooden pilings, in 1911. It was abandoned within a few years, because of the Revolution, and burned down in an unfortunate accident on 18 November 1916, when a jilted lover set fire to his sweetheart's letters and threw them over his shoulder.

Sail canoes had names such as *Tapatía*, *La Sirena*, *La Virgen*, *La Tempestad*, *Eloisa*, *Lupita*, *La Universal*, *La Juanita*, *Amada Alicia* and *La Patria*. Among the larger vessels was the motorized sail canoe *La Palma*, which carried up to 300 sacks of grain and fifty passengers on its regular run from Ocotlán to the village of Mezcala.[3]

Some cargo vessels preferred not to use the local pier. For example, it was easier to offload firewood onto the stockpiles maintained on beaches to supply steamships if this was done as close as possible to the woodpile. Wood was the fuel for the boilers which powered the large paddles at the stern of the ship. Piles of wood were stacked at strategic points so that there was always a readily available supply along the routes

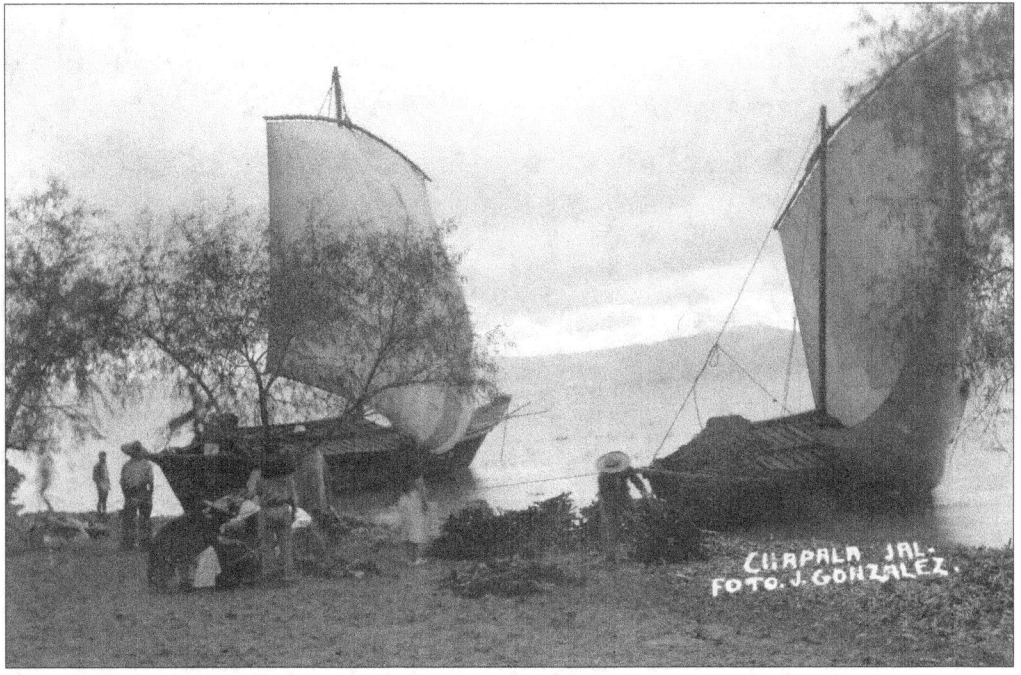

2.7. *Sail canoes unloading wood, c. 1944. J González.*
The provision of wood to lakeside villages, for both domestic and industrial use, continued to be important well into the 1940s.

that they traveled. On average, the sternwheelers burned about two cords of wood an hour while traversing the lake.

Large quantities of firewood were also required to fuel the lime kilns working in many villages, and for domestic use, primarily in kitchens, while fashioned timbers were needed by the local mining industry and in some forms of construction.[4]

Woodsellers (*leñeros*) were respected members of the community who played a role in preserving social cohesion. The most important ties between families came through marriage. The elaborate support system required for marriage extended from *pedidores de novia*—respected third parties of confidence who would help smooth the path for a formal proposal—all the way to the much more modest *leñeros* who supplied the firewood needed for the improvised kitchens where the wedding meal would be prepared.[5]

The first steamship on the lake was commissioned in 1866 by the Compañía de Navegación del Lago de Chapala y Río Grande (Company for Navigation on Lake Chapala and the Río Grande), a group of Guadalajara investors.[6] The *Libertad* (Freedom) was built in San Francisco, disassembled, brought to San Blas, and then carried over the mountains by donkey-power to Chapala for reassembly. This steamship, the first iron steamship ever built in California, was a sternwheeler, 23 meters (75 feet) in

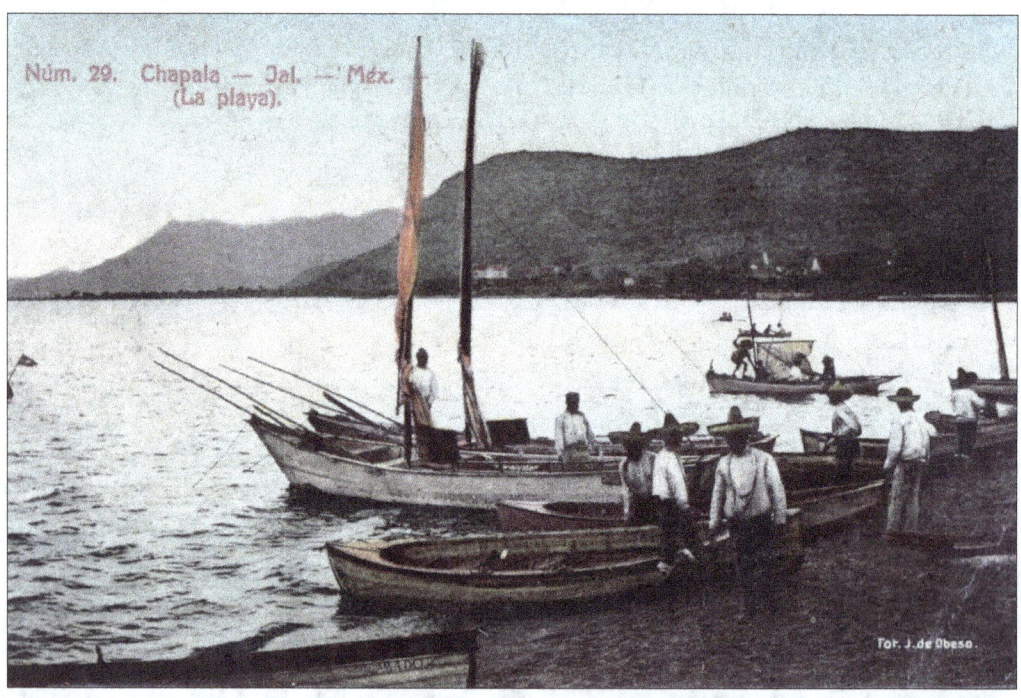

2.8. *Fishing boats on Chapala beach, c. 1907. J de Obeso; Alba y Fernández.*
Fishing boats were anchored in the shallows or pulled high up the beach for much of the day, ready for use early the following morning. The typical single-masted canoas were very versatile, used for both passengers and cargo. Fishermen also used smaller rowing boats; the one nearest the camera is named Cazador *(Hunter)*.

length and powered by two wood-burning 75-horsepower engines; it could carry 100 passengers. The contractor for the ship's construction, Scotsman Duncan Cameron (1827–1903), subsequently moved to Mexico to oversee the ship's reassembly and its operations. The *Libertad* was launched on the lake in early June 1868 at a ceremony presided over by General Ramón Corona, who later became Jalisco state governor.[7]

For most of its life, the *Libertad* offered regular sailings from Chapala to La Barca, Ocotlán and Jamay every Saturday, returning the following Monday, and to Tuxcueca, Tizapán and La Palma on Wednesdays, returning the next day. Several other steamships were launched on the lake in the latter years of the century, competing for cargo and passengers. They included the *Chapala*, which was launched in 1881 by Manuel Capetillo and his wife, Josefa.[8]

Steamships were not without their risks. The worst tragedy was on 24 March 1889 when the *Libertad* capsized while approaching Ocotlán at the eastern end of the lake; 28 passengers lost their lives. The ship tipped over, it is said, because merrymaking passengers all rushed simultaneously to the same side of the vessel as it approached the shore. The *Libertad* was refloated within a couple of months, and continued in service, under a new name, for several more years.

In an entirely different kind of accident, the steamship *Chapala* cost British consul Lionel Carden an entire household of furniture. Carden's furniture was in a *canoa* being towed across the lake by *Chapala* in 1896 towards his newly completed residence, Villa Tlalocan, when a stray spark set the *canoa* on fire. It sank to the lake bed, taking all Carden's possessions with it. Fortunately, Carden managed to obtain replacement furnishings before President Díaz visited him in Chapala later that year.

Steamships continued to play an important role in moving goods and people across Lake Chapala well into the twentieth century. Despite their early success, by the 1930s the days of steamers were numbered, superseded first by the train from La Capilla to Chapala and then by the automobile. As road vehicles became safer, more convenient and faster, the heyday of Lake Chapala shipping drew to a close.

Stagecoaches

Before the advent of trains and motor vehicles, people from Guadalajara (*Tapatíos*) who wanted to visit the lake had to walk, ride or take a stagecoach (*diligencia*) to Chapala. The first regular Guadalajara–Chapala stagecoach service began in 1866; the trip could be done in ten hours, but usually took twelve or more.

The excitement of riding the stagecoach was aptly summarized by English author Mrs Alec Tweedie, who visited Chapala in about 1900:

> The heavy old coach hanging on thick leather straps swung from side to side; boulders on the road, rivers across the path and suchlike trifles sent us flying from our seats ever and again; but nothing really happened, it was all in the day's work, and nerves are not permitted in Mexico.[9]

Travel writer J Phillip Terry, the driving force behind *Terry's Mexico Handbook for Travellers*, thought night-time rides were equally exciting.

> A night ride on a diligencia is generally very picturesque. A lackey accompanies the driver and holds aloft flaring pine torches which cast a weird light over the landscape and the speeding animals.[10]

Trains

Getting to the lake became easier as Mexico began to lay its extensive railroad network, which eventually connected almost all parts of the country. Inter-city travel over long distances by horseback or stagecoach through rugged terrain and bandit country made trips slow, uncertain and hazardous. The railroads enabled anyone who could afford to travel to reach more distant destinations in relative comfort and safety.

The Mexican Central Railway opened its railroad from Mexico City to Ciudad Juárez via Irapuato in 1884. Almost immediately, the Empresa de Navigación por Vapor en el Lago de Chapala y Río Lerma, owned by the Loweree brothers, began advertising that the fastest (though it still required about four days each way) and most comfortable way to travel between Mexico City and Guadalajara was by combining the Mexican Central Railway with two stagecoaches and its steamship *Chapala*. Passengers boarded the train in Mexico City for Irapuato, then took a stagecoach to La Barca, on the River Lerma, where they caught the steamer to Chapala. They then

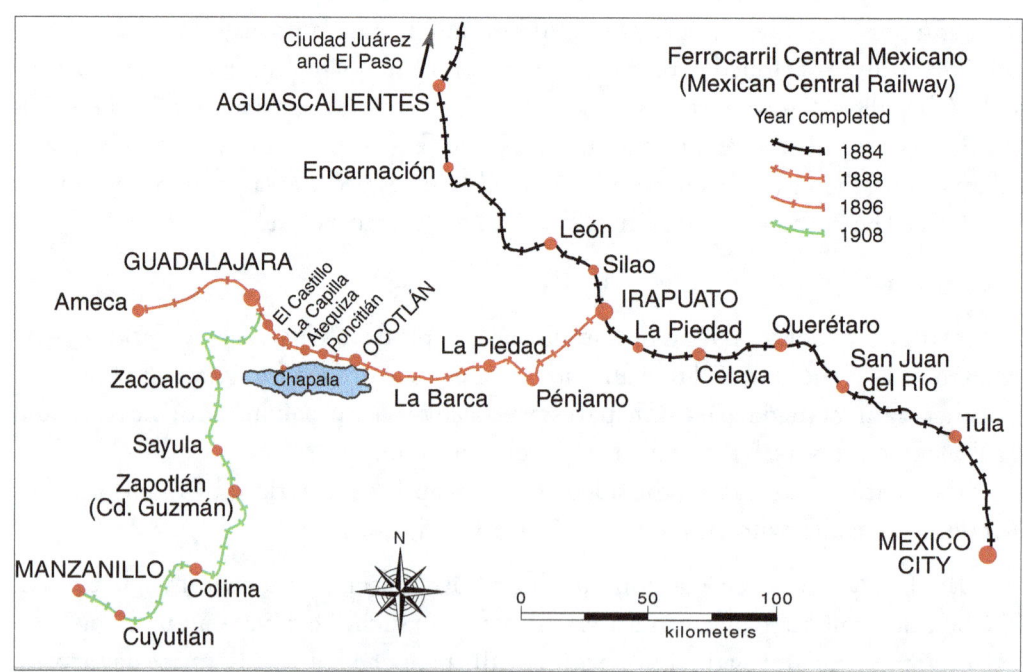

Map 2. The Mexican Central Railway

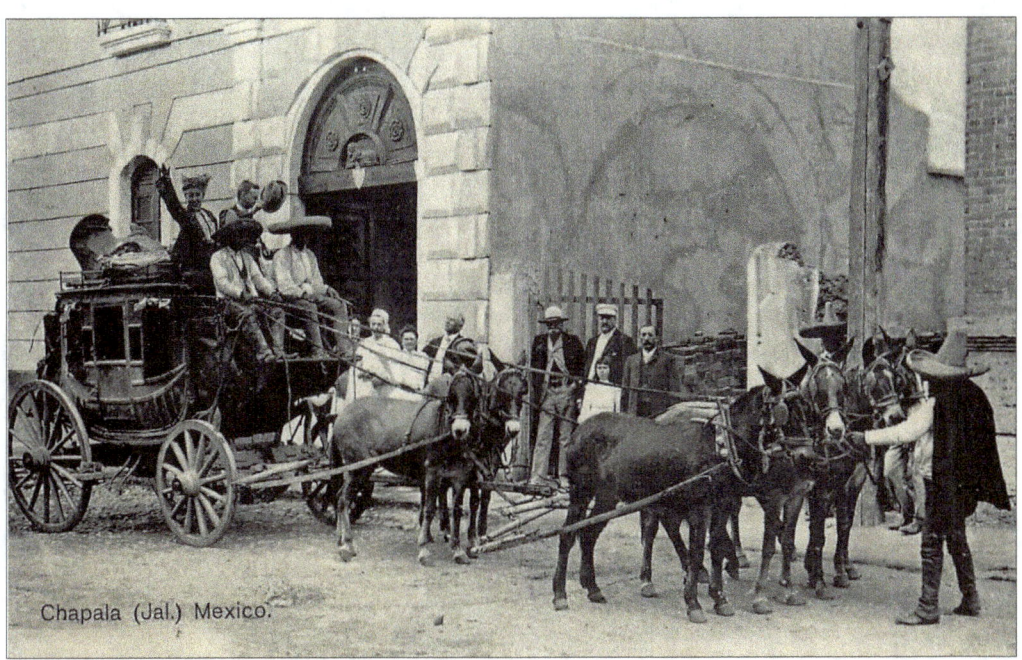

2.9. Stagecoach outside Hotel Arzapalo, Chapala, c. 1906. J M Lupercio?; T Schwidernoch. A similar card, mailed by guests at the Hotel Ribera Castellanos near Ocotlán, took only five days to reach Virginia. The message explained why they had opted to stay near Ocotlán in preference to Chapala: "Would you like a souvenir of Mex? This is the coach they use to go from the R.R. [railroad] to the hotel on Lake Chapala fourteen miles. We are staying at a place on the same lake but only three miles from the R.R."

completed their trip to Guadalajara riding on a second stagecoach, all for the bargain price of $18.00 first class, $16.00 second.[11]

Getting to the lake became even more straightforward after the Mexican Central Railway added a branch line from Irapuato to Guadalajara via Ocotlán, Atequiza and El Castillo in 1888. This branch line reduced the travel time between Mexico City and Guadalajara to less than a single day. Passengers could finally travel between Mexico's two largest cities in relative comfort and, usually, with only a single change of train.

Ocotlán was the nearest station to Lake Chapala on this branch line, and Atequiza was the nearest station to the town of Chapala. As a result, from this moment on, Chapala-bound travelers had a choice of routes. The first option was to take a train to Atequiza and then complete the final twenty kilometers of the journey either on horseback or via the daily Atequiza–Chapala stagecoach. Alternatively, travelers could leave the train at Ocotlán and board the steamer that left Ocotlán for Chapala at about 9.00am and returned in the afternoon.

Traveling by stagecoach was uncomfortable; it was also unreliable. Stagecoach service was often impossible during the rainy season, owing to the poor and deteriorating state of the wagon roads. In July 1904, Chapala hotel owners Victor Huber and

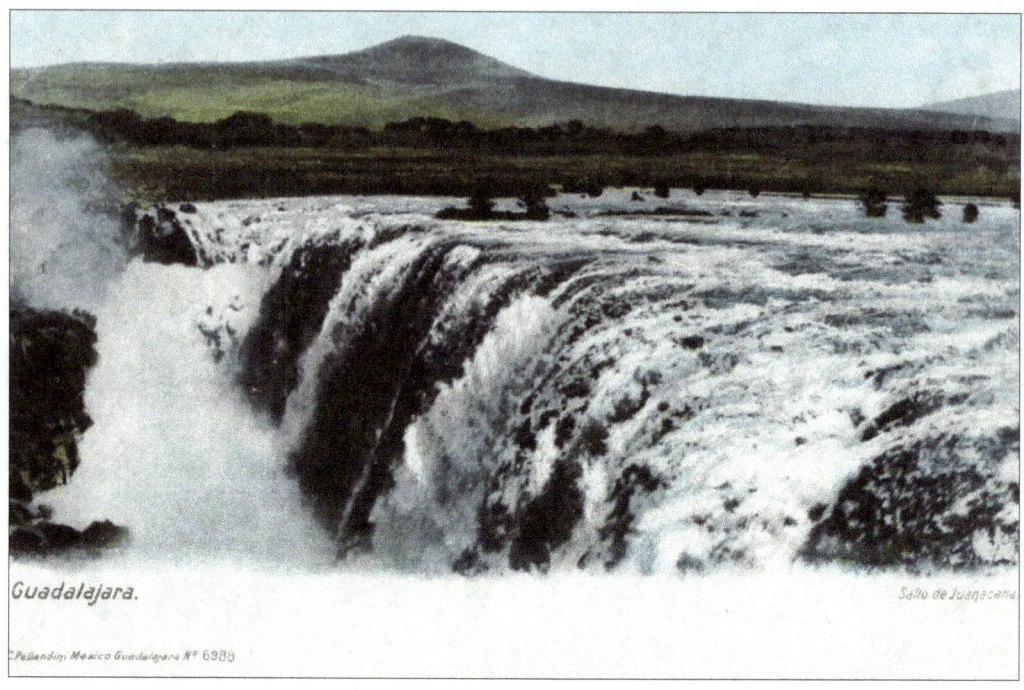

2.10. Juanacatlán Falls, c. 1905. C Pellandini.
The magnificent waterfalls of Juanacatlán, where the River Santiago tumbles over a 35-meter-high cliff. The nearest station to the falls was El Castillo, from where a tramway ran to the falls, dubbed the "Niagara of Mexico" in early travel guides.

Ignacio Arzapalo joined forces to finance repairs and reopen the road before October. Passengers paid one peso ($0.50) each way for the Hotel Victor Huber stagecoach between Chapala and Atequiza.[12]

There were other reasons for delays, too, which could cause travelers to miss their train. Vitold de Szyszlo, writing in 1913, described how he and fellow passengers left Chapala in plenty of time one morning, but were still well shy of Atequiza when the stagecoach driver's "drunken habits and inordinate taste for tequila" suddenly sent the stage hurtling towards a ravine. De Szyszlo, sitting next to the driver, was barely able to control the mules and send the coach into a tree instead. The passengers survived but, needless to say, they missed their intended train.[13]

The completion of the Irapuato–Guadalajara branch line of the Mexican Central Railway in 1888 brought many more tourists to the region. The station of El Castillo, about 20 kilometers southeast of Guadalajara, was conveniently close to the Juanacatlán Falls, one of Mexico's most famous waterfalls. Regardless of their direction of travel, rail passengers could disembark at El Castillo and visit the falls for a few hours before continuing their journey.

When British journalist James Charlton visited in 1890, he described leaving Irapuato—"the strawberry station, from which fresh strawberries are shipped every day in the year"—for the El Castillo station, from where he and his fellow travelers were taken in open tramcars, drawn by mules, to the waterfalls, "The Niagara of Mexico."[14] The mules were later replaced by an electric tramline.

A hydroelectric power power plant was installed at Juanacatlán in 1893. The Río Grande yarn and textile factory was opened alongside it five years later. Its owners imported textile machinery from England and modeled their entire operation on a British factory. An imposing entryway led to an internal plaza separating two large buildings, one for yarn and the other for fabric. In 1907 the Río Grande factory employed 1650 workers and produced 760,000 kilograms of textiles and yarns, making it by far the most important textile mill in Jalisco in terms of both employment and output.[15] This mill marked the start of the massively important industrial corridor centered on El Salto which emerged during the latter years of the twentieth century.

Towards the eastern end of the lake, the railroad went through Ocotlán, very close to where the River Santiago leaves Lake Chapala. Not surprisingly, Ocotlán became an important staging point for travelers wanting to see the lake or take a steamer trip to stay in one of the lakeside villages. Passengers could disembark from their train at Ocotlán, walk or take a short tram ride to the wharves on the banks of the River Zula, near its confluence with the Santiago, and then board a boat to take them to Lake Chapala. Various tourist-related services, including a fine hotel, were soon operating in or near Ocotlán. (chapter 6)

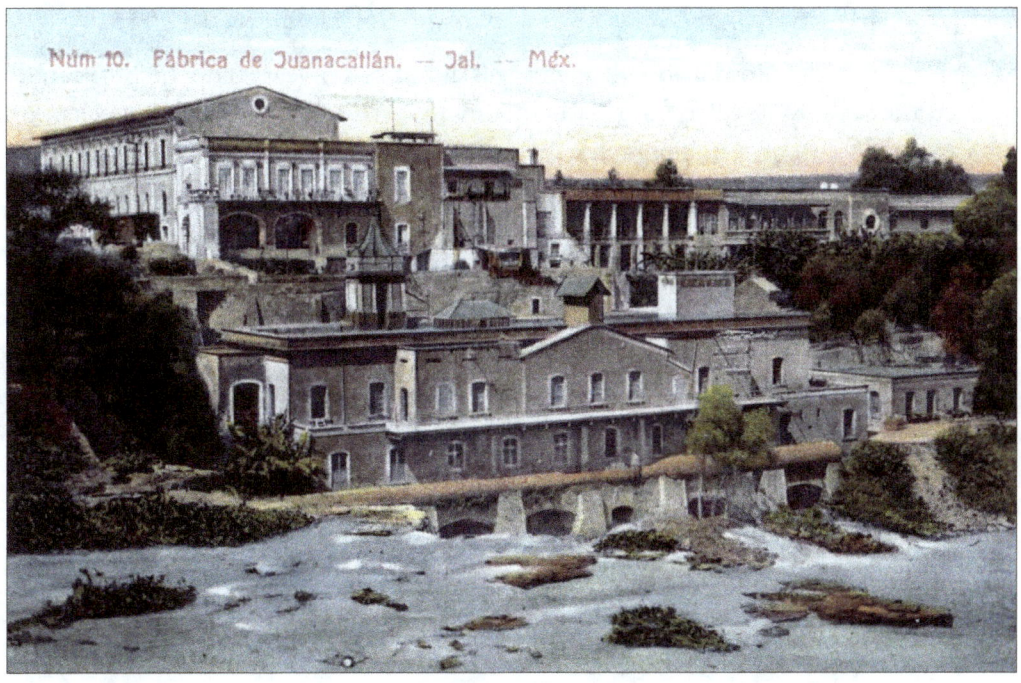

2.11. *Textile mill and power plant at Juanacatlán Falls, c. 1908. Alba y Fernández. Mailed to France, 1909. The best view of the Juanacatlan Falls was from the roof of the power station, the building directly below the textile mill, which opened in 1898. In 1899 the falls became the first ever landscape to be depicted on a Mexican postage stamp.*

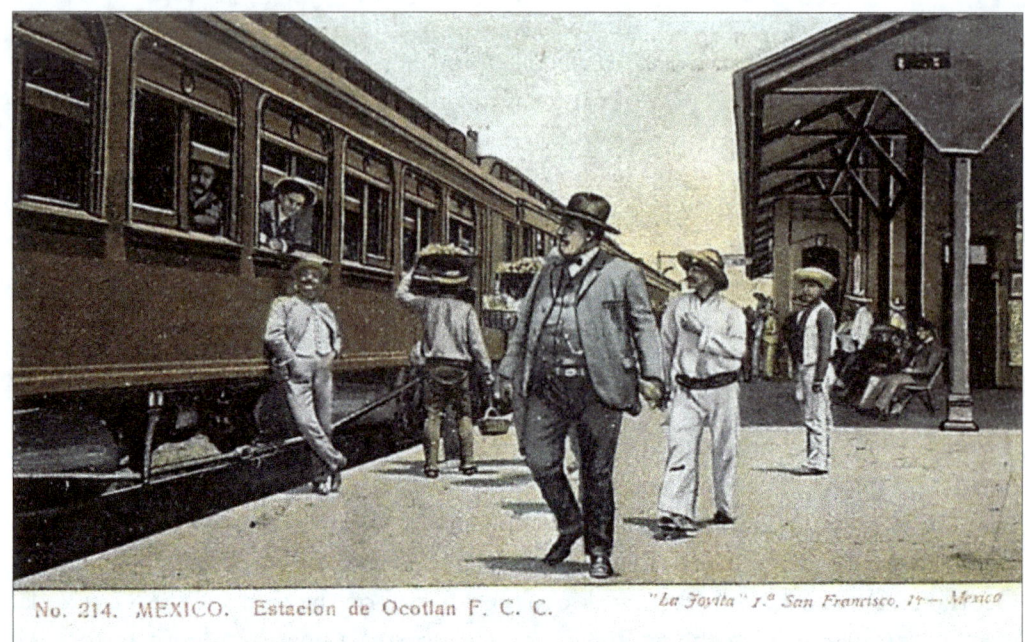

2.12. Ocotlán Railroad Station, c. 1905. W Scott?; La Joyita.
This image may have been taken by Winfield Scott, a professional photographer who lived locally and undertook commissions for the Mexican Central Railway.

Mexican author José Ruben Romero was about seven years old when his family crossed the lake by steamer from La Palma in 1897 to take the train from Ocotlán to Mexico City. In an autobiographical novel, Romero painted a vivid portrait of the station and the train:

> The train that I thought was a precious toy turned out to be something heavy and ugly, full of smoke, with an intolerable odor.... I had no alternative but to entertain myself with the movement about the station: well-dressed travelers from Guadalajara who strolled in the sun; others buying jugs of plum wine, fresh cheeses, or fruits. Groups of farmers arrived, the men with valises of striped chintz on their shoulders and full baskets in their hands; the women dressed in brightly colored percales, with squeaky new shoes that caused them to walk as if on thorns.[16]

The story of the more direct railroad which operated between 1920 and 1926 linking Chapala to El Castillo on the Mexican Central Railway begins in chapter 5.

3

Chapala at the end of the nineteenth century

The expansion of Mexico's railroad network played a decisive role in Lake Chapala becoming an important tourism destination in the final years of the nineteenth century. The Mexican Central Railway, having opened its branch line from Irapuato to Guadalajara in 1888 (map 2), was well aware of the potential income to be derived from tourism, and immediately began touting the appeal of both the journey and the lake.

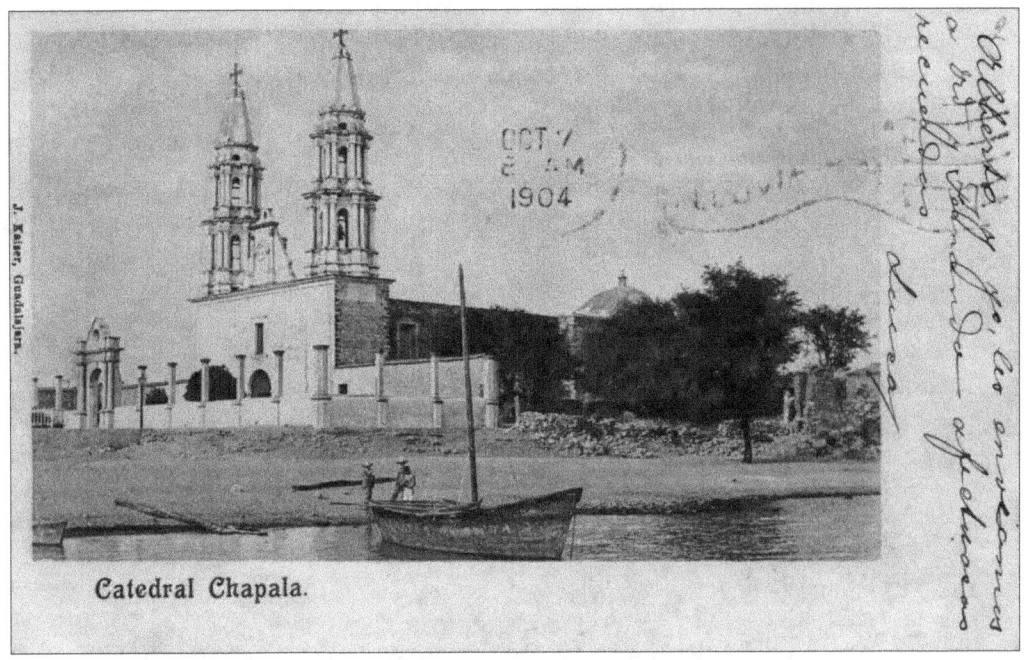

3.1. *San Francisco Church, Chapala, c. 1902. C B Waite?; J Kaiser.*
The lake was originally much closer to the church than today. This photograph dates from between 1897 (when the church clock was installed and the atrium fenced) and 1904 (when construction began of Casa Braniff, conspicuously absent from this image). The caption on the card is mistaken: the main church in Chapala has never been a cathedral, only a regular parish church.

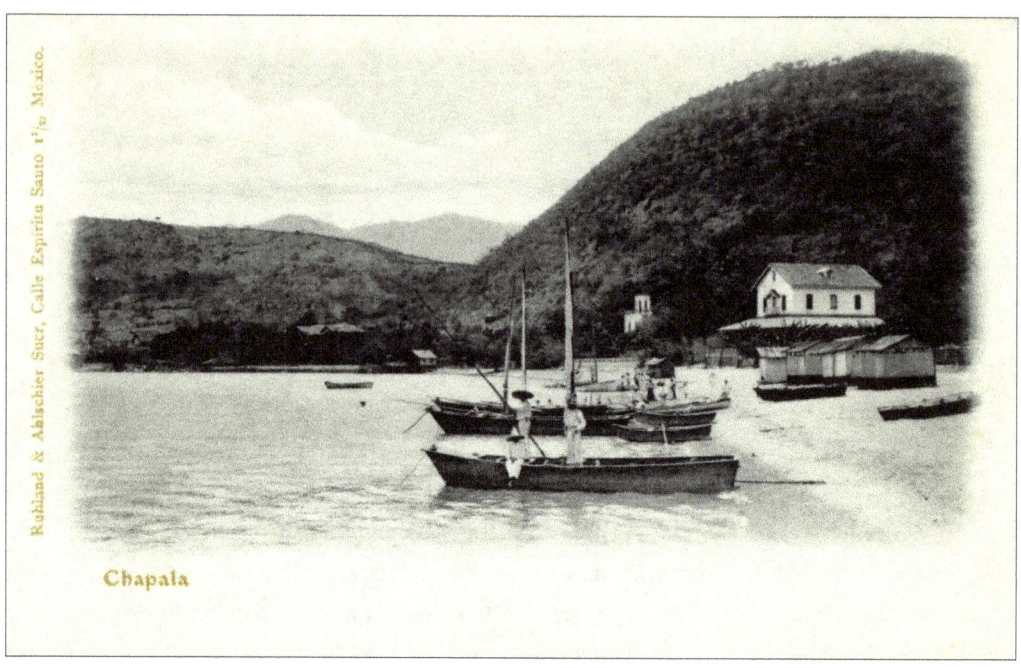

3.2. *The waterfront, Lake Chapala, c. 1901. W Scott; Ruhland & Ahlschier.*
Winfield Scott took this photograph shortly after the turreted Villa Paz (right of center) was built. Casa Albión is at the extreme left. The white house with sloping roof is Casa Capetillo.

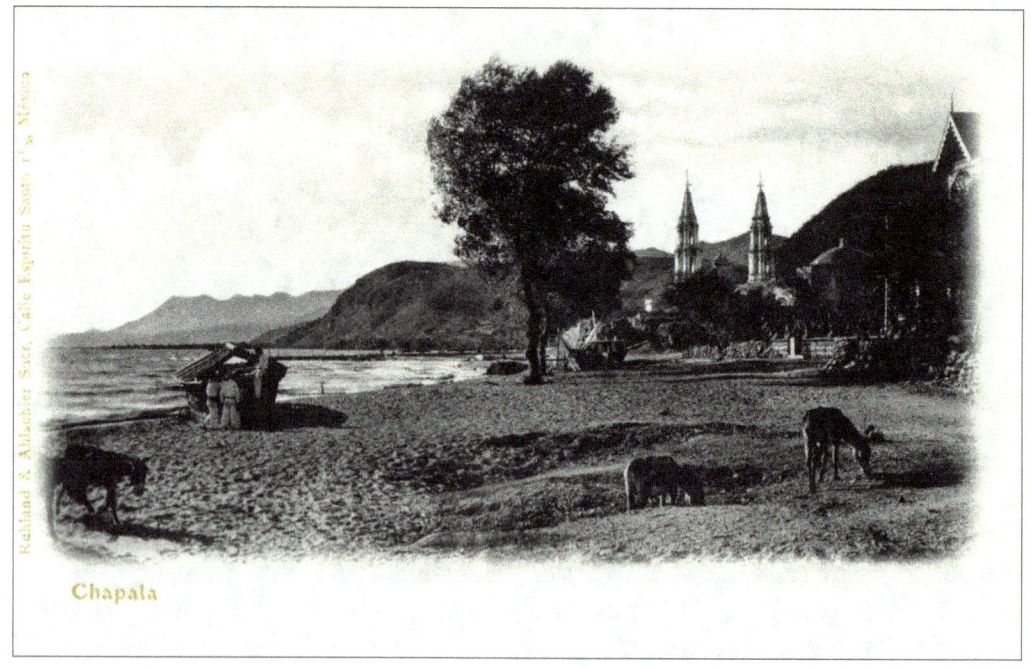

3.3. *Chacaltita beach, c. 1901. J M Lupercio; Ruhland & Ahlschier.*
Boatmen and burros on Playa Chacaltita. The peaked roof at the extreme right belongs to Villa Carmen, completed in 1898.

It commissioned American writer Thomas Rogers in 1892 to write about all the places which its ever-expanding network was opening up for travelers. Rogers predicted a bright future:

> Chapala is sure to become more and more a favorite watering place. Already there are some fine summer 'seaside-cottages' there, and in the offing you can see a yacht! With a combination of delightful climate and hot springs, with mountain climbing, boating, bathing, and fishing as recreations for visitors, why shouldn't charming Chapala become the finest health and pleasure resort in Mexico?[1]

What was Chapala like in the 1890s? The most prominent building in the village was its principal church, La Parroquia de San Francisco de Asís. The original church on this site, founded in 1548 by Franciscan friar Juan de Almolón, was rebuilt several times before being replaced with the current building in the mid-eighteenth century. The bell towers were a slightly later addition: an inscription in the southern tower offers a date of 1878. The clock above the church's main entrance was installed in about 1897, at roughly the same time as a fence was added to delimit the boundaries of the atrium.

The original friary (*convento*), which had but a single cleric, was constructed immediately south of the church. By the end of the nineteenth century the friary was

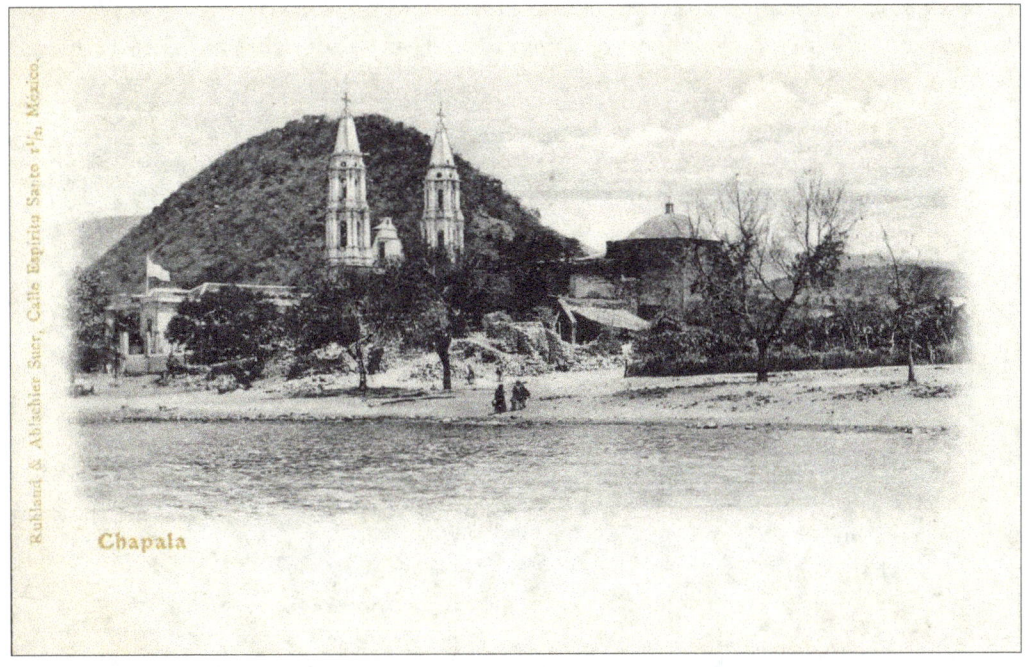

3.4. *Church and Cerro San Miguel, c. 1901. Ruhland & Ahlschier.*
The San Francisco church, silhouetted against Cerro San Miguel. Left (west) of the church, the flagpole identifies Villa Ana Victoria. The two figures on the beach (Playa Chacaltita) appear to be women fetching water from the lake. Immediately behind them are the heaps of friary rubble that had to be cleared away before Casa Braniff could be built.

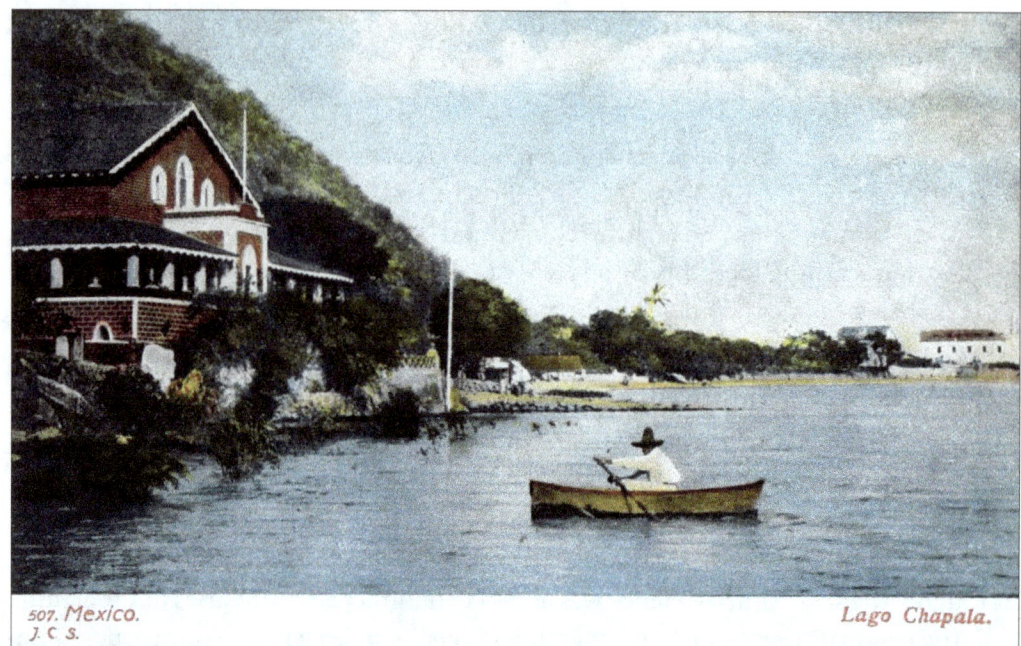

3.5. *Villa Josefina (formerly Casa Albión), c. 1901. C B Waite; Iturbide Curio Store.*
Casa Albión, the picture-perfect Swiss-style chalet built by Septimus Crowe in 1896, cost less than $8000. It had garden terraces, a private harbor for his smart yacht, and a flower-bedecked piazza with flagstaff.

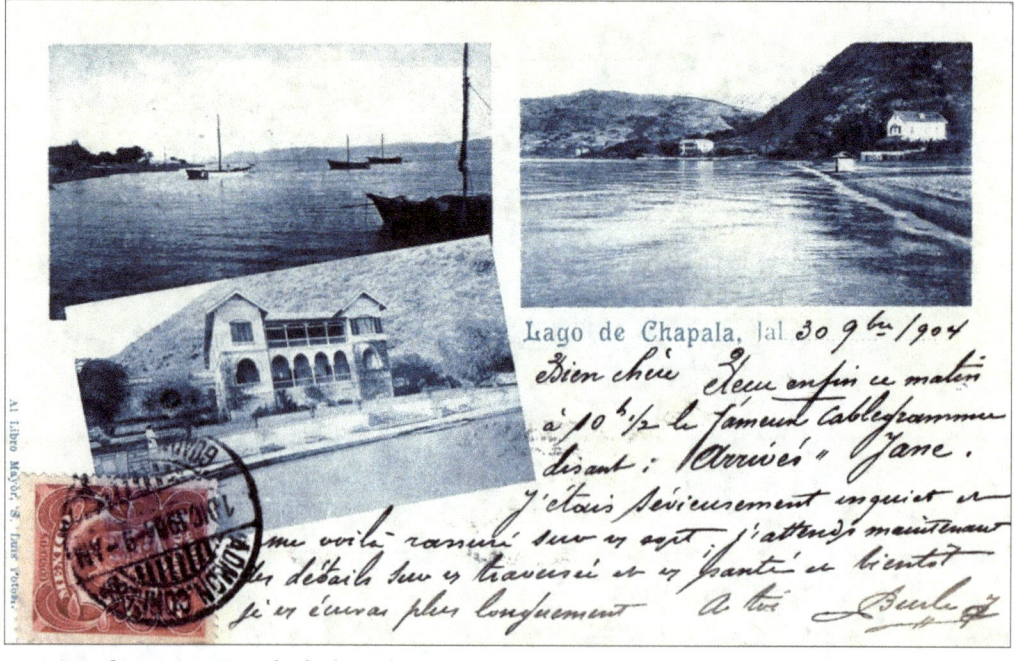

3.6. *Triple view postcard of Chapala, c. 1900. C B Waite; J Kaiser.*
The photograph of Villa Tlalocan (lower left) is the work of Charles Betts Waite. British consul Lionel Carden spent about $10,000 to complete the beautiful modern villa.

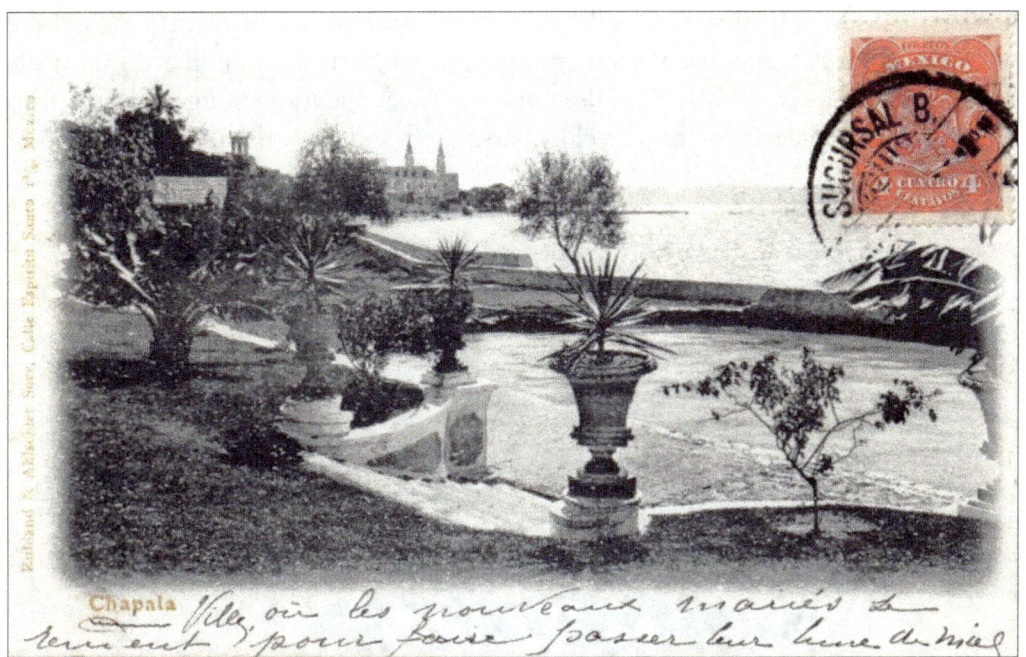

3.7. View from the garden of Villa Tlalocan, c. 1905. J M Lupercio; Ruhland & Ahlschier. Ornamental flower pots beautified the lakefront garden of Villa Tlalocan. It was common for high society couples to honeymoon in Chapala. This card was mailed to France; the message translates to "Town where newlyweds often choose to spend their honeymoon."

already in ruins, used only for stabling horses. It was also the site of lime kilns producing the quicklime for the plaster and mortar required by local builders, and used for the church steeples.[2] Construction of the iconic Casa Pérez Verdía (later Casa Braniff) on this site began in 1904.

The beach that extended from the church towards the east was known as Playa Chacaltita. In 1900 only a small number of residences fronted onto this beach. The most luxurious was the two-story Villa Carmen, whose peaked roof makes it easy to identify on early images. Built by Roberto and Manuela de la Mora, it was first occupied in December 1898. Slightly further to the east, Villa Ochoa, a stately two-story building belonging to Carlos Ochoa Arroniz, was completed a few months later.

Along the beach west of the church by 1900 were several imposing lakefront mansions and villas, the earliest of them almost certainly dating from the 1880s. Closest to the church was Villa Ana Victoria, built by Prussian émigré Eduard Collignon and his wife, Ana Victoria Stephenson, and completed by the mid-1890s. Heading westwards from the pier, the other early residences in this direction included Casa Capetillo, Chalet Paulsen, Villa Tlalocan, Casa Albión (later Villa Josefina) and Villa Montecarlo.[3]

Casa Capetillo and Chalet Paulsen (later Villa Paz) were built, respectively, by Manuel Capetillo Quevedo (1848–1922), owner of Hacienda Buenavista near Ixtlahuacán de los Membrillos, and wealthy German-born businessman Ernesto Paulsen, who owned La Palma, Guadalajara's most prestigious furniture and hardware store. The original architect of Chalet Paulsen may have been Charles Strange, an American architect in Guadalajara who was a close personal friend of Paulsen.

The British Connection

As for the other three villas already named, an eccentric Englishman, Septimus Crowe (1842–1903), was directly responsible for both Villa Montecarlo and Casa Albión, and indirectly responsible for Villa Tlalocan. Villa Montecarlo, Crowe's first home at Lake Chapala, was one of the 'cottages' referred to by Thomas Rogers in 1892.

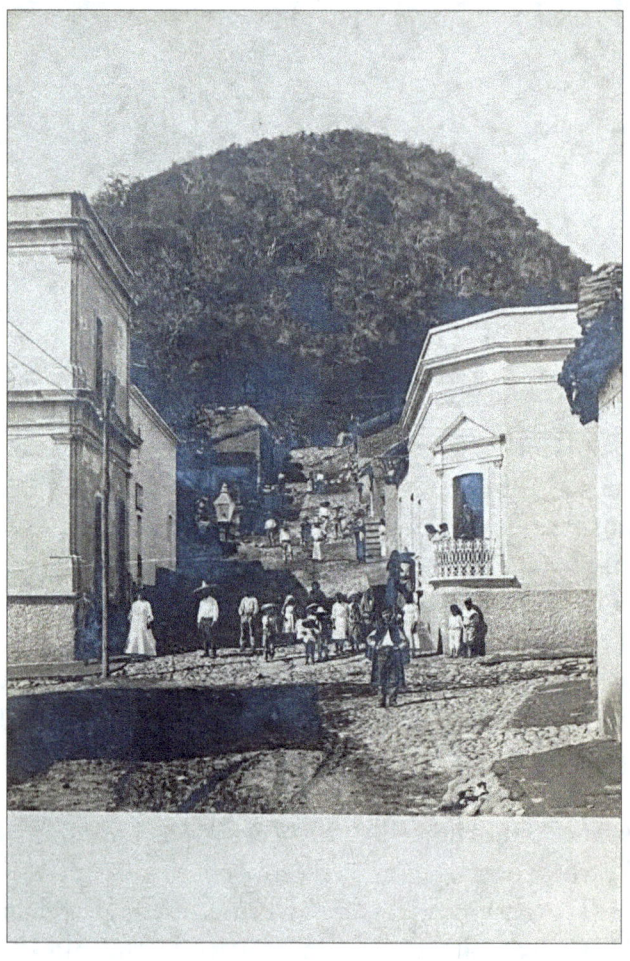

3.8. *Calle de San Miguel, c. 1904?*
View looking west up Calle de San Miguel (now López Cotilla) to the base of Cerro San Miguel, the small volcanic hill, where there was once a Franciscan hermitage. This is the setting for the opening scene of A Dream of a Throne, *the first ever novel (English or Spanish) entirely set at Lake Chapala.*

It is unclear when Crowe first saw Lake Chapala, but it was probably love at first sight. As a keen yachtsman, he must have been thrilled at the prospect of exploring the lake by boat. Crowe, who had a stake in a Mexican mining company, built a chalet named Monte Carlo (now spelled locally as a single word) overlooking the lake. As more foreigners looked to settle in Chapala (some at his invitation), in 1895 Crowe decided to sell Villa Montecarlo to Cora Alice Townsend and build himself another home, named Casa Albión, right on the lake, with a small private harbor for his imported yacht. Townsend, the widow of wealthy hacienda owner and diplomat José Martín Rascón, gave it as a Christmas gift to her parents: Mary Ashley Townsend, a well-known New Orleans poet, and her husband, Gideon.[4]

In about 1901, Crowe built a third house, Villa Bela, and sold Casa Albión to US-born Guadalajara beer magnate Joseph Maximilian Schnaider (1858–1922), known in Mexico as José María Schnaider. The new owner renamed it Villa Josefina, after his wife, and it still bears her name to this day.

Crowe was also instrumental in persuading Lionel Carden, the British consul to Mexico, to build a home in Chapala. With money no object, Carden and his wife, Anne Eliza Lefferts, commissioned noted British architect George King, who had offices in Mexico City and Guadalajara, to build them a stately vacation home. In 1897, a year after the house was completed, the Cardens played host to President Díaz's wife, Carmen Romero Rubio, over Easter.[5] In 1899, on being appointed British consul in Cuba, Carden sold Villa Tlalocan to German-born copper magnate Carlos Eisenmann, who had made his fortune in Mexico from mining and land speculation.

Septimus Crowe's important role in promoting Chapala was fully acknowledged by "Arabella, Countess O'Loughnan" in her fulsome tribute of him after his untimely death in 1903. She and Crowe had, she wrote,

> met at Chapala where he was greatly loved and esteemed and will be much missed by the small and great, for he was the pioneer in making Lake Chapala an attractive summer resort for the foreigners of the republic. Of this the people of Guadalajara and the residents of the lake have often assured me.[6]

The positive contribution of Septimus Crowe was formally recognized by the municipality of Chapala in 1912 when a short street was named in his honor.

Given all these illustrious home owners, Marie Robinson Wright was able to report in 1897 that "Lake Chapala is a summer resort of the highest grade, and is frequented by the most prominent residents of Guadalajara and other large towns."[7]

By then, the construction of Chapala's first modern hotel, the Hotel Arzapalo, was well underway. Guadalajara businessman Ignacio Arzapalo Palacios (1837–1909) had foreseen the growing demand for tourist accommodation in Chapala and began building his eponymous 36-room hotel right on the waterfront, immediately west of the pier, in 1896. When the emblematic building opened in 1898, it transformed the village virtually overnight, and propelled it full-speed into the twentieth century. For

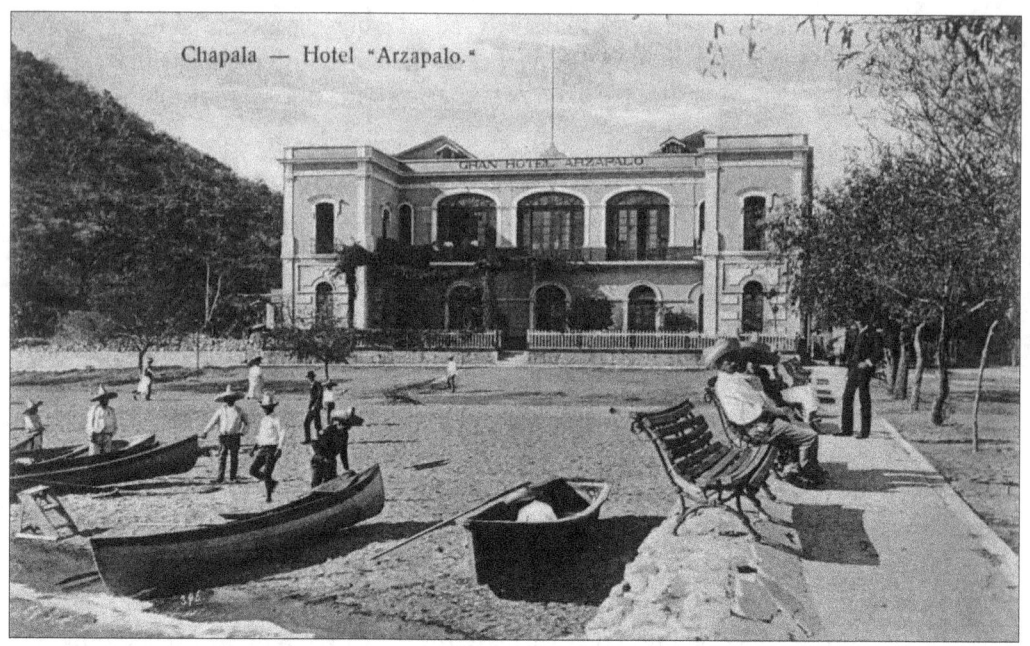

3.9. Hotel Arzapalo, c. 1906. J M Lupercio?; M Hernández.
A girl named Adriana mailed this card back home: "My dear mother, I'm enchanted in Chapala, I have never in my life seen a place so enchanting or more picturesque. This postcard will show you the hotel where we are staying; the balcony of our room is right over the beach and looks directly onto the lake. The scenery we have in view is delicioso." A later version of this image, published by T. Schwidernoch in Austria, removed the boats and figures from the lower left, presumably either because of damage to the original plates or because someone decided that it made for a cleaner, more powerful image.

its time, the hotel was a remarkable project: the first substantial purpose-built hotel in any small community in Mexico. What's more, it was financed entirely by domestic (Mexican) capital and not by foreign investment.

There were rival hostelries, but none so well appointed as the Arzapalo. Across the street, a small guesthouse, Posada Doña Trini, had long welcomed visitors; it was subsequently upgraded and transformed into the Hotel Victor Huber.

Advertisements for the Hotel Arzapalo extolled the virtues of the climate, the rooms, the location, the medicinal waters, and the "pleasure boats and baths on the lake, owned by the hotel." They called Lake Chapala "The Switzerland of America," and boasted that the Hotel Arzapalo was "The only inland Bathing Resort in the Republic." When it opened in 1898, room rates at the Arzapalo varied from $2.50 to $4.00 a day, more than twice the then going rate at Posada Doña Trini.[8]

The Italian Connection

The Hotel Arzapalo's first manager, Italian-born Alberto Anzino, absconded the following January with more than $500 in gold, silver and bank notes.[9] Despite his bad luck with Anzino, Arzapalo clearly liked the idea of having his hotel under European management, and subsequently hired several other Italians to ensure the comfort of the hotel guests!

The opening of the Hotel Arzapalo in 1898 marked the start of international tourism in Chapala. Over the next decade all manner of rich and famous individuals stayed there.

The buzz created by the presence of so many well-heeled Mexicans and foreigners attracted the attention of itinerant artists, such as Canadian William Townsley Benson and German Paul Fischer, as well as writers like American author Charles Embree, who, while honeymooning in Chapala, wrote *A Dream of a Throne* (published in 1900), the first novel in English set entirely at Lake Chapala. They were the forerunners of the area's vibrant artistic and literary community today.

During the 1890s the improved accessibility of Lake Chapala, combined with its moderate elevation, benevolent climate, thermal waters and attractive scenery, had made it the choice locale for discerning tourists, whether they sought a place to rest and relax, or somewhere to swim, fish and hunt.

One 1899 advertisement, for instance, beneath the memorable slogan "Sunshine and Strawberries Every Day in the Year," pointed out that the railroad traversed the "tableland of Mexico," with its "most desirable resorts for the summer (as well as for

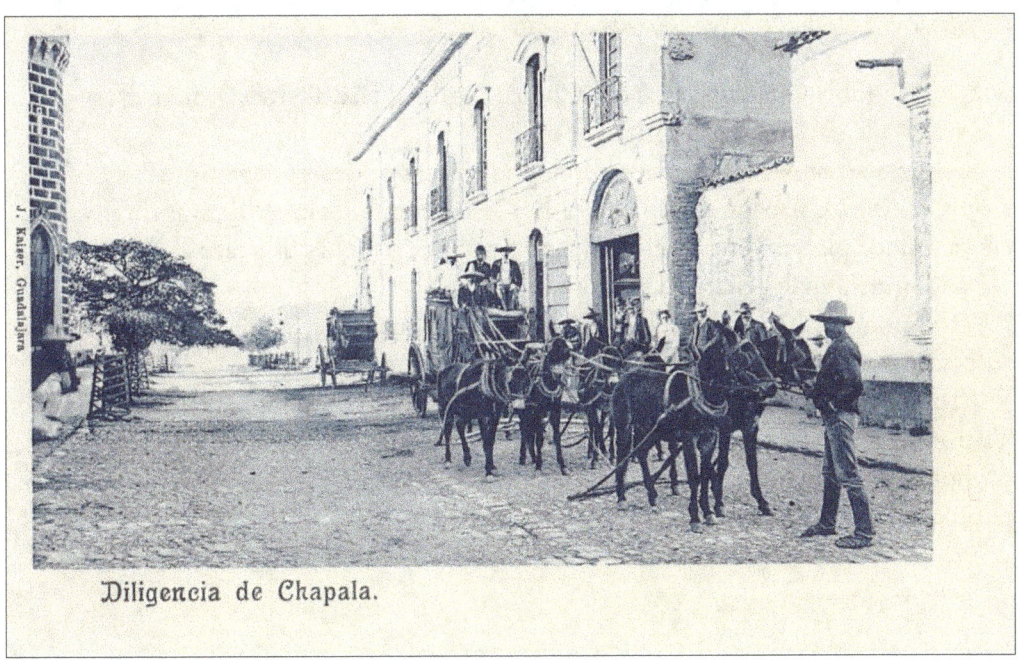

3.10. Hotel Arzapalo stagecoach (diligencia), c. 1903. J M Lupercio?; J Kaiser.
This hotel on Calle del Muelle, the road leading down to the pier, owned two stagecoaches for daily service to and from Atequiza railroad station, as well as several carriages (guayines) for special trips. On the extreme left is the side wall of Villa Ana Victoria.

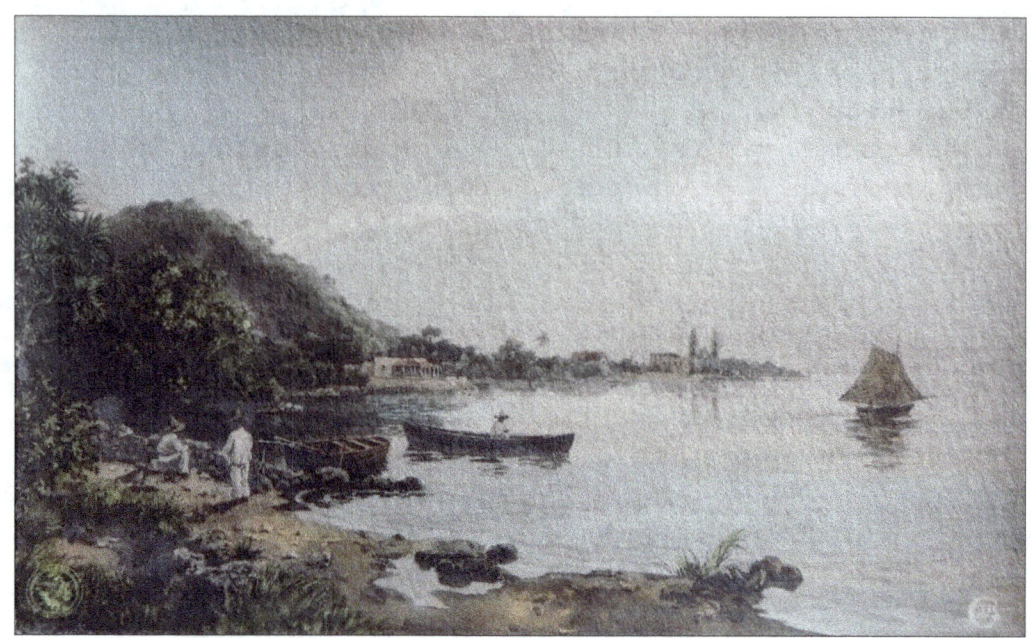

3.11. Chapala landscape, a painting by Paul Fischer, c. 1899. P Fischer; J Kaiser. German-born painter Paul (Pablo) Fischer (1864–1932) lived most of his life in Mexico and painted several watercolors of Lake Chapala. The Hotel Arzapalo is shown as having two stories, so this painting was completed after 1898.

winter)," notably Guadalajara, Lake Chapala and Aguascalientes, "where every day in the year is pleasant and every night cool."[10]

Almost all of Mexico's other hotels and tourist options at the time were in large towns or cities. Chapala, which had only 1753 inhabitants in 1900, was totally different: a unique place to escape city life and savor the delights of peace and quiet, clean air, and health-giving thermal springs.

The groundwork had been laid. Chapala was about to enjoy a decade of unparalleled success as a tourist destination.

The village of Chapala was not the only location on the lake to benefit from tourism. Taking advantage of its proximity to Ocotlán, the Hotel Ribera Castellanos (chapter 6), built on farmland overlooking the lake, also enjoyed considerable international popularity in the early decades of the twentieth century.

4

South shore: Tizapán el Alto and La Palma

Until the late nineteenth century, economic activity around Lake Chapala was divided almost equally between its southern and northern shores. The most important settlement on the southern shore was (and is) Tizapán el Alto.

Tizapán el Alto

According to Franciscan chronicler Nicolás Antonio de Ornelas Mendoza y Valdivia, writing in about 1690:

> This village is close to Lake Chapala, and, in addition, the river called 'of the passion' flows close by; they call it that because—in the middle of some rocky crags that box in the river—paintings of all the insignia of the passion of Christ our Lord can be divined, very clearly and very well done.[1]

Tizapán el Alto was at least as important a settlement as Chapala, on the opposite shore, at the end of the nineteenth century. In 1885, for instance, its population of 6919 was significantly greater than the 5197 reported for Chapala, while both Ocotlán (7022) and Jocotepec (10,913) were larger than either of them.[2] All these figures were for the entire municipality. Fifteen years later, the formal census in 1900 allows us to compare the figures for the principal settlement in each municipality: the village of Tizapán had 2020 inhabitants, Chapala 1753, Ocotlán 4014 and Jocotepec 4074.

Tizapán el Alto's economy was centered on agriculture and the Hacienda San Francisco Javier. The hacienda, now in ruins, was part of a large swathe of land awarded to Alonso de Ávalos, a cousin of conquistador Hernán Cortés, for services rendered in the early sixteenth century. In the 1620s the hacienda was acquired by a wealthy Spaniard, Joaquín Fermín de Echauri; the hacienda remained in the Echauri family, which raised cattle, mules and horses there, for more than two hundred years.

The hacienda acquired its own boats to transport produce to market, including a cargo *canoa* named *La America* which took sugar, *piloncillo* (unrefined cane sugar) and alcohol to Ocotlán.[3]

According to an 1888 account of the region, "The rich, fertile soil around Tizapán el Alto produced corn, beans, wheat, barley, potatoes, camote, jícama, chiles, watermelons, cantaloupes, sugarcane, vegetables, coffee and a long list of fruit trees."[4] During the latter part of the nineteenth century, the Hacienda San Francisco proved profitable for several different owners, producing sugar, alcohol, soap, flour, and tanned leather in its mills and workshops.

The varied agricultural activity at Tizapán el Alto was noted in a 1902 Report on the Trade of Mexico, issued by the UK Foreign Office:

> Mexico… offers almost every conceivable climate, and consequently every form of agriculture is possible. I have seen this on one single estate at Tizapán el Alto…. Side by side, fields of sugar cane, barley and wheat are growing; in the orchard bananas, pomegranates and apples, coffee and potatoes, the whole range of vegetable produce of the temperate and sub-tropical zones.[5]

Produce from the south shore of the lake, "including tomatoes from Tizapán el Alto and onions from Cojumatlán," was shipped across the lake to Chapala for onward transportation to Guadalajara by mule train. Of the dozen or so inns (*mesones*) used by merchants for overnight stays in Guadalajara, almost all the traffic from Lake Chapala went to El Comercio in the city center, conveniently close to the Mercado Corona, the city's major market.

The strategic significance of Tizapán el Alto during the nineteenth century was recognized by novelist Charles Fleming Embree, who used it as one of the locales for

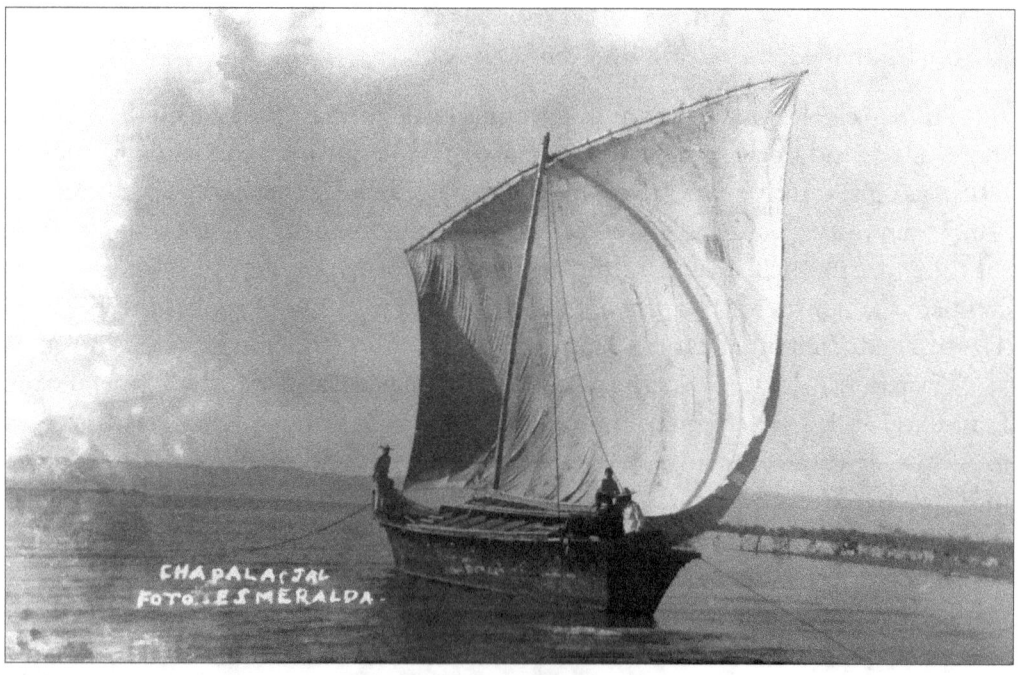

4.1. *Lake Chapala sail canoe, c. 1945. Foto Esmeralda.*
Produce from the south shore was shipped across the lake on large sail canoes, with their massive trapezoidal sails, for onward transportation to Guadalajara and other cities.

his novel *A Dream of a Throne*, published in 1900. Embree's descriptions of the lakeside villages are almost unparalleled in their geographic accuracy. In regards to Tizapán, Embree wrote:

> The town of Tizapan lies at a short distance from the lake.... Between water and land there is a stretch of marsh for several hundred yards, watery, pierced by the spears of a million reeds that rise thick and green to a height of some feet. Here flock ducks in great numbers. The marsh is flat, bewildering, and dreary. Through its middle a stream, called the Tizapan River, cuts out more than one course, having formed a delta. The town itself is like the greater part of Mexican towns, narrow and crooked streets with the low houses (joined together) shutting those streets in and making them seem even narrower.... The mountains rise only a little way behind the town, jagged and huge. Before them is a stretch of rolling green fields. The river, coming from the peaks, dashes down through this pastoral scene with a vivacity that has laid bare a rough and rocky bed whereon the water boils till it passes through the town.[6]

The low, joined-together houses and narrow streets led to a terrible tragedy in Tizapán el Alto in 1902, when a massive fire engulfed forty-three houses, leaving many families homeless.[7]

A short distance from the center, the Tizapán el Alto pier was always busy with the comings and goings of the dozens of *canoas* and boats that ferried its agricultural produce across the lake, mainly to La Barca and Ocotlán, and brought in people and supplies. Not far from the pier was an underwater seepage of petroleum, where the lake was always oily, and unsuitable for bathing. Local boatmen collected the tar that gushed up at this point to paint their boats and make them totally watertight.[8]

In 1895 the scheduled steamship service on Lake Chapala left Ocotlán at 2.00pm every Tuesday and called in at La Palma before mooring overnight at Tizapán el Alto. On Fridays the steamer left Ocotlán at 7.00am and visited La Palma and Tizapán el Alto before overnighting in Tuxcueca. Its return trip to Ocotlán the following day arrived in plenty of time for passengers to catch the evening trains from Ocotlán to Mexico City and Guadalajara.[9]

Lake transport was never without its risks. Sailors needed to read the winds carefully and were at the mercy of unexpected squalls and storms. In 1905 the ever-present dangers were brought home to villagers when a terrible storm swept over the lake one February night and wrecked a number of sailing vessels. Three cargo-carrying boats en route from Tizapán to La Barca capsized in the middle of the lake, and twelve people drowned.[10]

Three years later, in September 1908, a violent rainstorm led to massive flooding. The normally quiescent Río de la Pasión rose four meters (thirteen feet) in a matter of hours, severely flooding parts of the town and "causing many adobe houses to crumble and fall." Several residents were missing, presumed drowned, and property losses were estimated at about $100,000. Dozens of families lost their homes and all their possessions.[11] The rampage of the river also resulted in considerable damage to the Hacienda San Francisco.

A similarly sudden storm in October 1930 cost the lives of fifteen persons who had crossed the lake to Tizapán for a lunchtime picnic. Their boat floundered on the return trip and only six of the party survived.[12]

Tizapán el Alto remained an important source of agricultural products and staging point for all manner of goods being transported from Michoacán to Chapala and Guadalajara into the early decades of the twentieth century.

Following the Mexican Revolution, a series of land reforms between 1919 and 1937 confiscated almost all the land formerly belonging to the Hacienda San Francisco Javier for redistribution. Ironically, this led to a decrease in total agricultural output and a reduction in the total number of jobs available locally, causing many of the town's younger inhabitants to emigrate and seek work elsewhere.

Cojumatlán Bay (Bahía de Cojumatlán)

Transporting goods across the lake in the nineteenth century was at the mercy of other risks besides storms. Vessels laden with valuable cargo were sometimes attacked by pirates.[13] Their center of operations, according to most reports, was Cojumatlán Bay (Bahía de Cojumatlán) near the south-east corner of the lake, and conveniently close to the Jalisco-Michoacán state border. Cojumatlán Bay was shallow and relatively isolated. When overland communications eventually improved, the pirates' criminal activity diminished. After Cojumatlán Bay dried up completely in the early years of the twentieth century, this former pirate lair became fertile farmland.

La Palma

Visitors to the small village of La Palma de Jesús, located at the south-east corner of Lake Chapala, will see few signs today that this humble-looking settlement was once the largest port in the state of Michoacán, responsible for far more trade than any of the state's seacoast towns.[14]

Before the advent of trains and motor vehicles, water-borne transport was the fastest and most efficient means of moving goods and people between villages. La Palma was strategically important during Mexico's War of Independence as the main port supplying the arms and provisions needed by the insurgent group occupying Mezcala Island. In one of the most glorious episodes in Mexican history, a determined band of 'rebels' occupied the island for four years (1812–1816), and defied repeated attempts by determined Spanish Royalists to dislodge them. The insurgent leaders included La Palma-born priest Marcos Castellanos, and Luis Macías, who owned Hacienda La Palma, which the Royalists razed to the ground in retaliation.

Many of the items that passed through La Palma in the nineteenth century originated from as far away as Mexico City, as British author Rose Georgina Kingsley

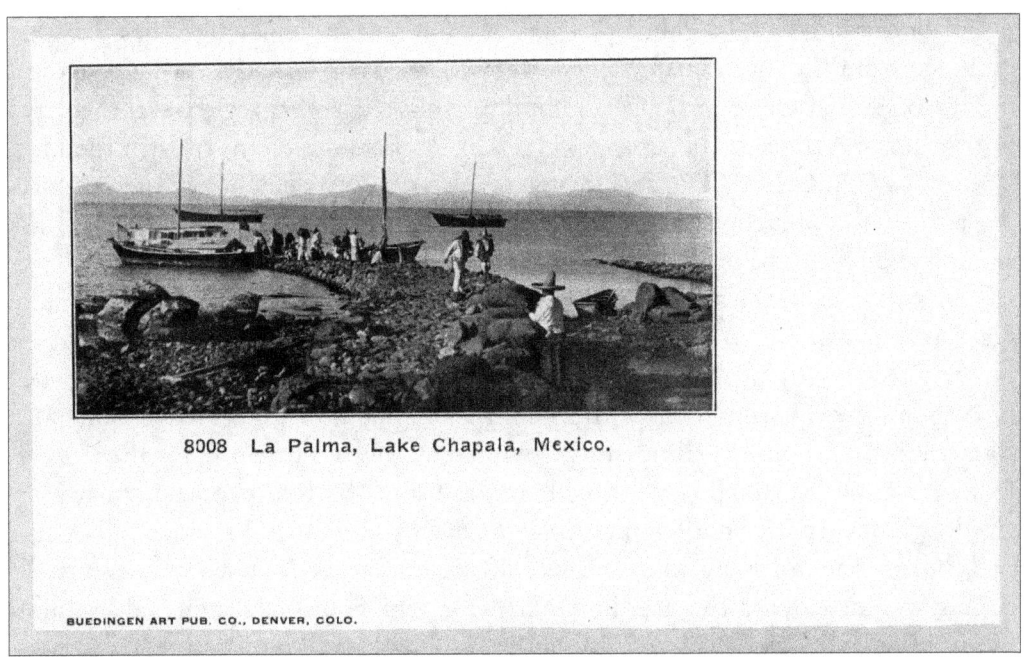

4.2. Pier at La Palma, c. 1901. Buedingen Art Publishing Co.
Because the back of this early card, published in Colorado, was reserved for the address and stamp, the front incorporated ample white space for a handwritten message.

recognized. Kingsley, the oldest child of the Rev. Charles Kingsley, the celebrated English clergyman and novelist, visited Lake Chapala in 1872 in a party led by railroad entrepreneur (and founder of Colorado Springs) General William Jackson. Kingsley refers briefly to the steamboat (*Libertad*) belonging to "Mr. C." (Duncan Cameron) before highlighting the role played by La Palma in regional trade:

> Just across the lake at this point is La Palma or Tequiqui, a place to which great part of the goods for the Western States are brought by a mule route from the city of Mexico via Morelia.[15]

In the 1890s prolific American author Frances Christine Fisher explained why she thought La Palma was the most scenically appealing of all the lakeside towns:

> Nothing could be imagined more picturesque than the scene. Over the rocks that lined the shore the water was splashing and breaking in sparkling waves, immense trees with great gnarled roots that in themselves would have made a picture spread their green canopy of shade over rocks and water, while a little higher, under the clusters of feather-palms which gave a name to the place, was the Indian village—low houses thatched with palm-leaves grouped around a tiny chapel. Behind, in close proximity, rose the hills, which here receded a small space from the water's edge, and a wealth of luxuriant vegetation made this the greenest, shadiest, most sylvan nook conceivable.[16]

Prior to the 1920s, La Palma was part of an important regional trading axis that extended from the interior of Michoacán northwards to Ocotlán and other points in Jalisco. All manner of produce and building materials were regularly transported across the lake between La Palma and Ocotlán. According to some reports, the small steamships plying that route were unable to keep up with demand for their services and a small fleet of independently owned open *canoas* was anchored beside the wharf, waiting to pick up and transport the slack.

At least two steamships floundered part-way across the lake from La Palma to Ocotlán: the *Michoacán* in 1937 and the *Manzanillo* in 1941. The *Michoacán* was carrying a Swiss passenger, Mr Ottiger, manager of the Nestlé plant, which had opened in 1935 in Ocotlán, back home with 27 churns of milk after a short inspection of his company's milk cooling facilities near Cojumatlán. Twenty-five minutes after leaving La Palma a sudden squall or whirlpool sank the ship. All four people on board survived, two of them by holding onto milk churns for five hours. Providentially, those two churns were (for some unknown reason) only half-full. The men were eventually rescued by a fisherman who heard their cries for help. Four years later, and at almost the same location, the *Manzanillo* caught fire after an explosion. Four people jumped ship, despite not being able to swim, and drowned; the others climbed onto the roof of the vessel and were rescued by passing boats. The ship's captain was detained but eventually cleared of any responsibility.[17]

The only known postcard of La Palma (figure 4.2) shows activity on its rustic pier shortly before the time when the small village of about 700 inhabitants enjoyed its heyday for the transport of people and cargo to and from Michoacán and beyond.[18] In later years the demise of lake transport and the village's relative isolation from the highway left La Palma struggling to find a way to thrive.

Complementing its function as a port, La Palma also developed a sizable fishing industry, which sustained many local families. That was just as well since, prior to the Revolution, all the agricultural land in the area was held in large estates (haciendas) by rich *hacendados*,[19] leaving the local populace with insufficient land of their own. By the time villagers gained control of more land—following land disbursements in 1923—the port was already struggling to compete with the speed and flexibility of land-based transport. The village, ignored by highway planners, and with its fishing industry threatened by fluctuating lake levels and higher levels of pollution, fell into near-terminal decline.

5

Chapala 1900–1920: the golden age of tourism

What would it have been like to spend a few days in Chapala in 1908, when the village's reputation as a vacation destination was at its peak?

The easiest way to get to the lake from Guadalajara was via the 7.00am Mexican Central Railway train to Ocotlán. This arrived in Ocotlán in good time to board the Lake Chapala Navigation Company steamer *Rápido*, which was scheduled to leave for Chapala at 10.00am and arrive there in time for a leisurely lunch and siesta. This did not always go smoothly. In April 1908, for instance, the *Carmelita*, owned by the same company, overturned throwing fourteen passengers into the lake; fortunately no lives were lost.[1] For the return trip, the steamer left Chapala at 6.30am in order to

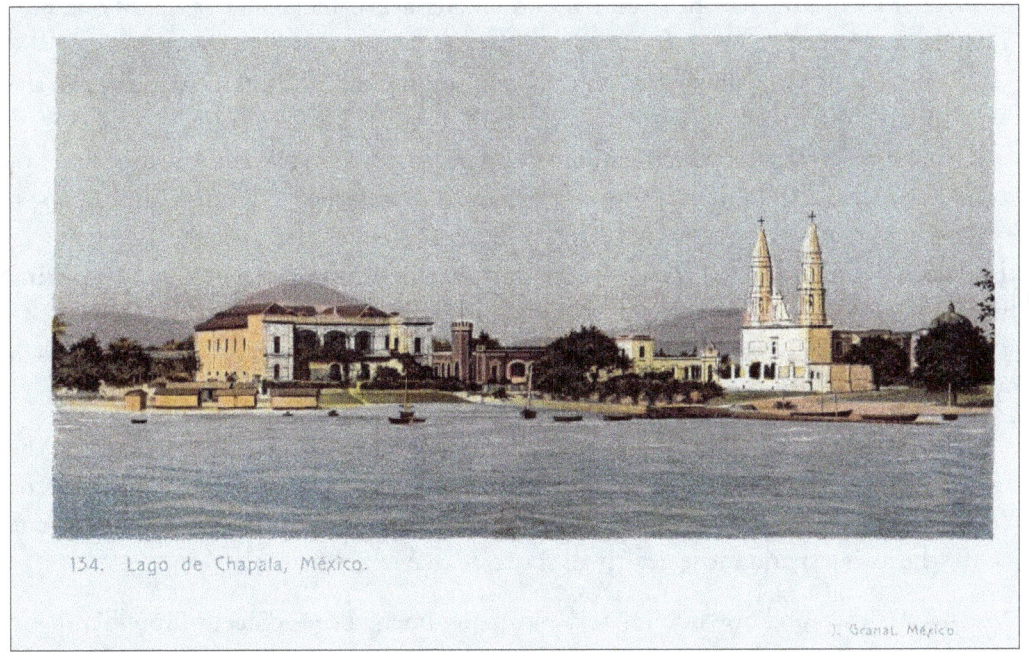

5.1. *Chapala waterfront, c. 1904. W Scott; J Granat.*
From left to right, the most prominent buildings on the waterfront are the Arzapalo Hotel (opened in 1898), the turreted Villa Ana Victoria and the San Francisco parish church.

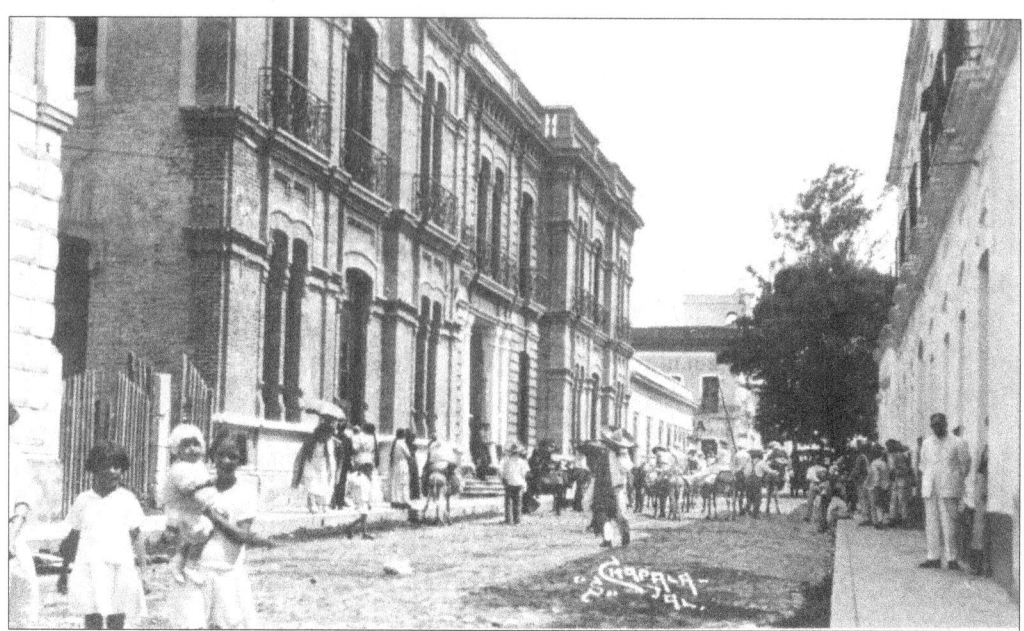

5.2. *Hotel Palmera, c. 1920. J E Sánchez.*
Opposite the Hotel Victor Huber (right), the attractive 60-room Hotel Palmera (left), designed by Guillermo de Alba, first opened in 1908.

connect at Ocotlán with the train back to Guadalajara. Tickets were $3.00 one way, $5.00 return.[2]

Approaching Chapala by steamship, two prominent buildings hove into view: the twin-spired church and a grand two-story building, the Hotel Arzapalo.

The Hotel Arzapalo, which had opened a decade earlier, was one of three fine hotels in Chapala in 1908. It was the only one overlooking the beach, and also the most expensive, though its prices remained the same as when it first opened. According to the leading guidebook for travelers, the daily rate—even for the best rooms during high season—was only $4.00, and this included three meals.[3]

The hotel was always known for its high standards. When it first opened, Owen Wallace Gillpatrick, a correspondent for *The Mexican Herald*, enthused that:

> The Arzapalo has some fifty rooms, a large sala and diningroom overlooking the lake, and is provided with a bar and billiard table. The cooking is excellent and the bread is all made in the house. The hotel is situated in what is, beyond doubt, one of the loveliest and most healthful spots in all Mexico.[4]

In 1907 the hotel's owner, Ignacio Arzapalo, opened the adjacent Hotel Palmera, where, despite its elegance, rooms and food were significantly less expensive: between $2.00 and $2.50 a day. His decision to build a second hotel was a response to the growing popularity of the village, particularly during Easter week and major holidays when rooms were often at a premium. Arzapalo commissioned local architect Guillermo de

Alba to design him a larger and even better appointed hotel than the Arzapalo. The brick, iron and cement building with superb interior woodwork cost $100,000 to complete. Arzapalo was proved right: the hotel, which derived its name from the tall palm tree growing in its central patio, was filled to capacity when it opened in 1908, even though the rooms had yet to be painted![5] Many of its rooms offered views of the village jardín on the other side of Calle del Muelle.

Across the street from the Palmera was the similarly priced Gran Hotel Victor Huber, which had originally been the Posada Doña Trini, the only decent place to stay in the 1880s. Guadalajara businessman Victor Huber, who owned a grocery store selling imported products and fine wines, bought the Posada for $12,000 in April 1904, undertook renovations, and rebranded it in 1907 as the Gran Hotel Victor Huber.[6]

All three hotels were on the same block of Calle del Muelle, the narrow main street which ended at the pier. The regular stagecoaches serving the busy hotels had to compete for space with the occasional private automobile. Traffic congestion was eased somewhat when a new street was made in 1907 parallel to the beach, connecting Calle del Muelle to Calle del Templo, the road in front of the church.

Guests at any of the hotels usually took a siesta after lunch—the local specialties were caldo michi (fish soup) and whitefish—before perhaps strolling to the beach for an afternoon swim. Bathing huts on the beach could be rented to preserve public decency while visitors changed into swimwear. The huts, first erected in 1897, had to

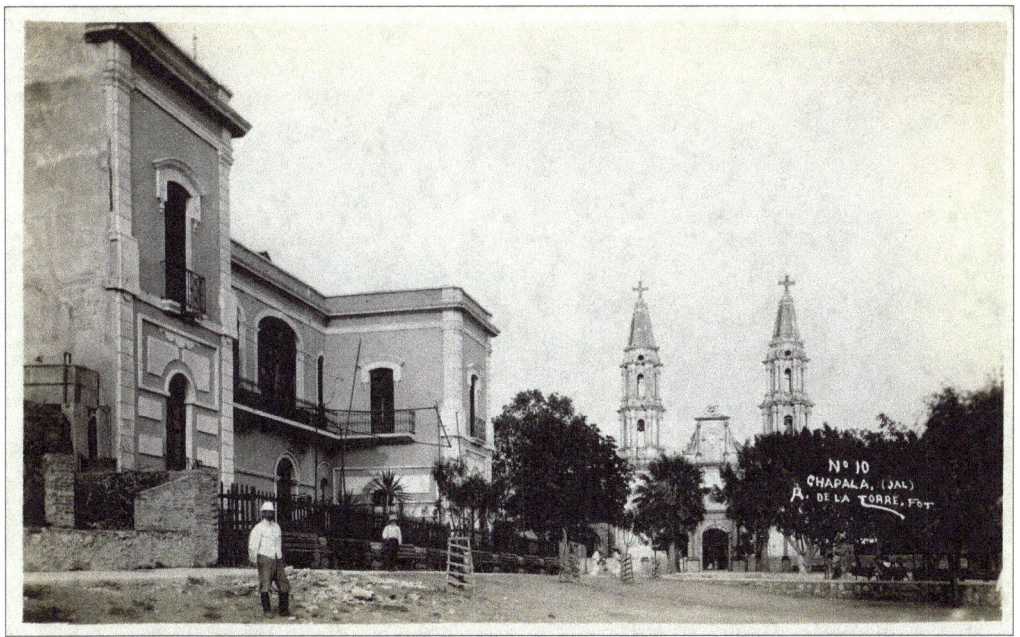

5.3 *The Hotel Arzapalo and San Francisco church, c. 1908. A de la Torre.*
This hotel was the only one in Chapala that was situated right on the beach.

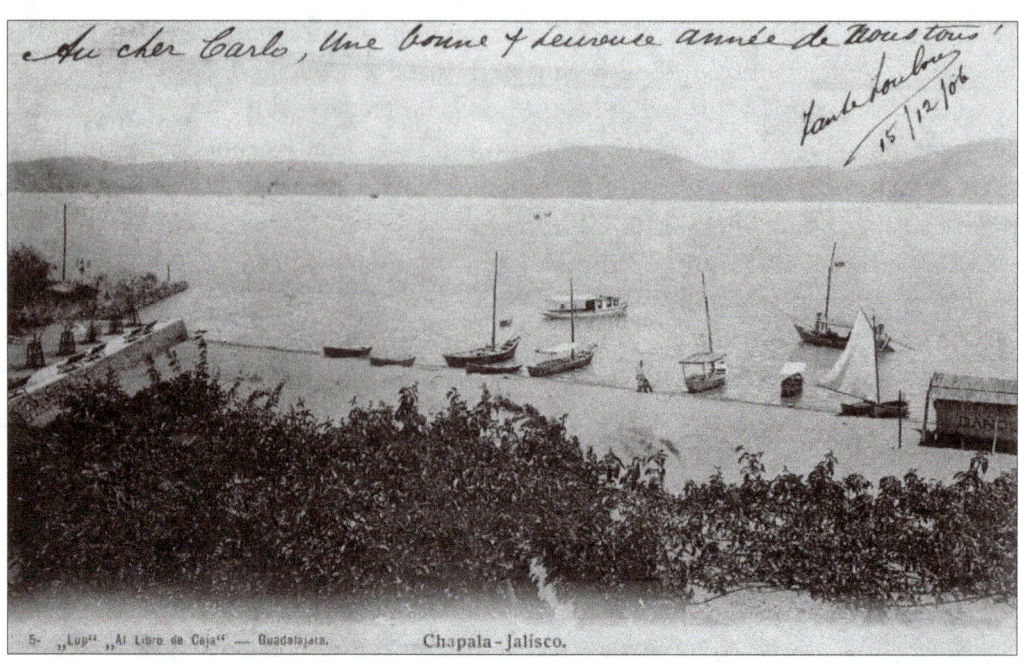

5.4. *View from Hotel Arzapalo, c. 1905. J M Lupercio; J Kaiser.*
The best rooms were on the upper floor of the hotel at the front, from where guests enjoyed this view of the pier and beach, with their daily rhythm of activities, to the lake and the mountains beyond.

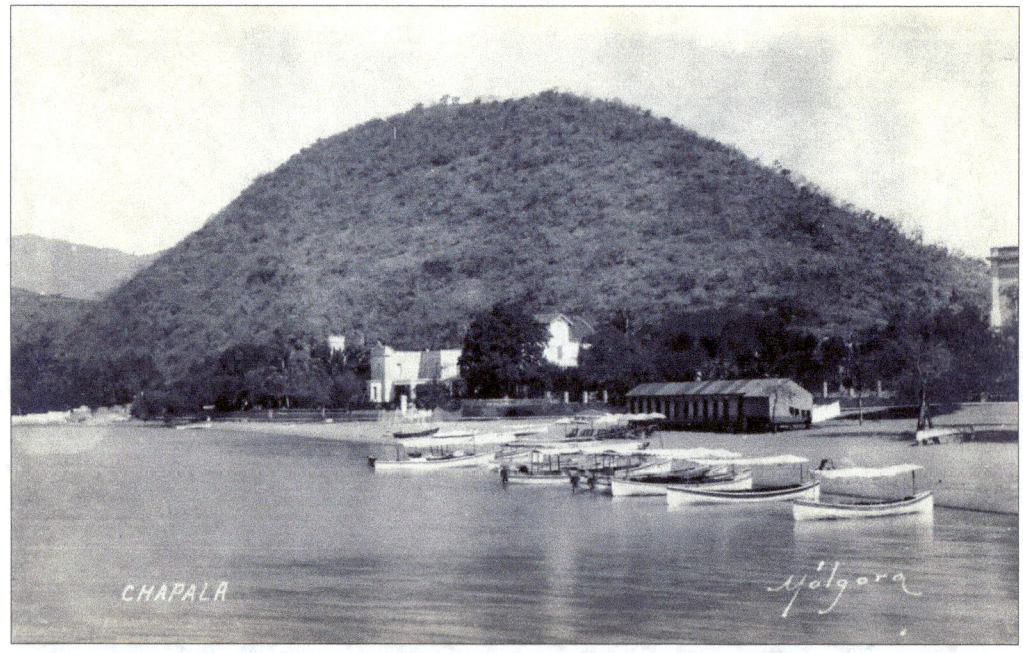

5.5 *Bathing huts on the beach, c. 1920. Mólgora (Antonio Mólgora Espinosa?).*
Ignacio Arzapalo, Manuel Capetillo and Manuel Enríquez erected bathing huts on the beach in 1897, even before the Hotel Arzapalo had opened.

be "similar in style... [and] sufficiently elegant to beautify the town." Arzapalo and Capetillo paid 25 centavos a month for a permit, because their huts were for private use only; entrepreneur Manuel Enríquez paid three times as much, because he rented his huts to the public.[7]

Then, as now, visitors to Chapala commented favorably on the quality of the light and the beautiful sunrises and sunsets. At night, moonlight reflected off the lake and cast a perfectly charming glimmer over the village. As Gillpatrick recognized:

> While the lake is often perfectly still during the afternoon, a breeze comes after sunset and soon little waves are running up on the beach. The moon makes a silver track across the water; you hear a soft lapping along the shore, and the scent of flowers pervades the shaded balcony of the hotel.[8]

US naturalist Edward Nelson, aboard a boat, waxed even more lyrically about the evening light on Lake Chapala:

> The sun had gone behind the distant mountains in a golden glory, and as the rich afterglow slowly faded the mellow sound of vesper bells came floating across the water. Then a brilliant array of stars came out and the black shore line twinkled cheerfully with village lights.[9]

The pier saw peaks and troughs in activity through the day, as boats of all kinds arrived and left. The numerous benches nearby made this an ideal place to people watch.

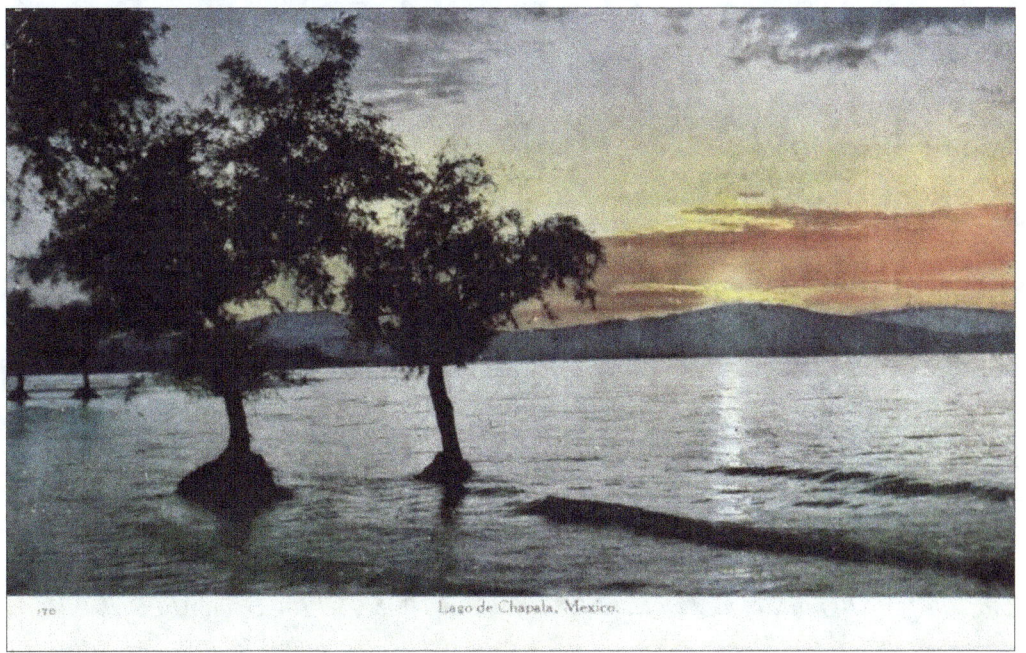

5.6. Sunset, c. 1908. Calpini y Cia.
Spectacular sunrises and sunsets have always been the norm at Lake Chapala.

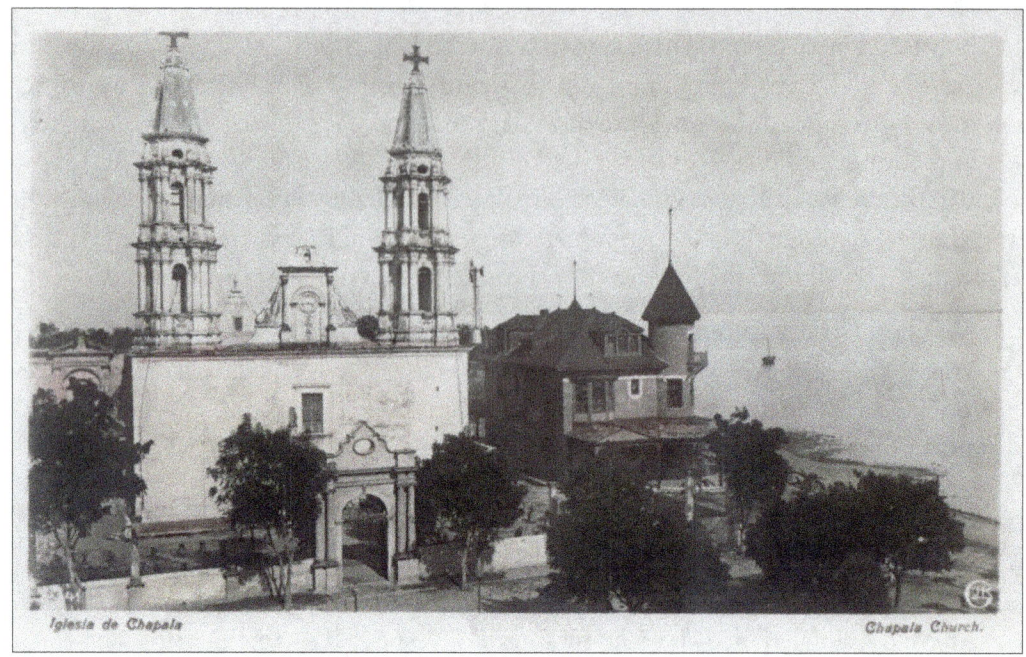

5.7 San Francisco Church, Chapala, c. 1908. J Kaiser.
The church clock was donated in about 1897 by Eduard Collignon, at the same time the atrium was fenced. Right of the church is Casa Braniff, dating from 1904.

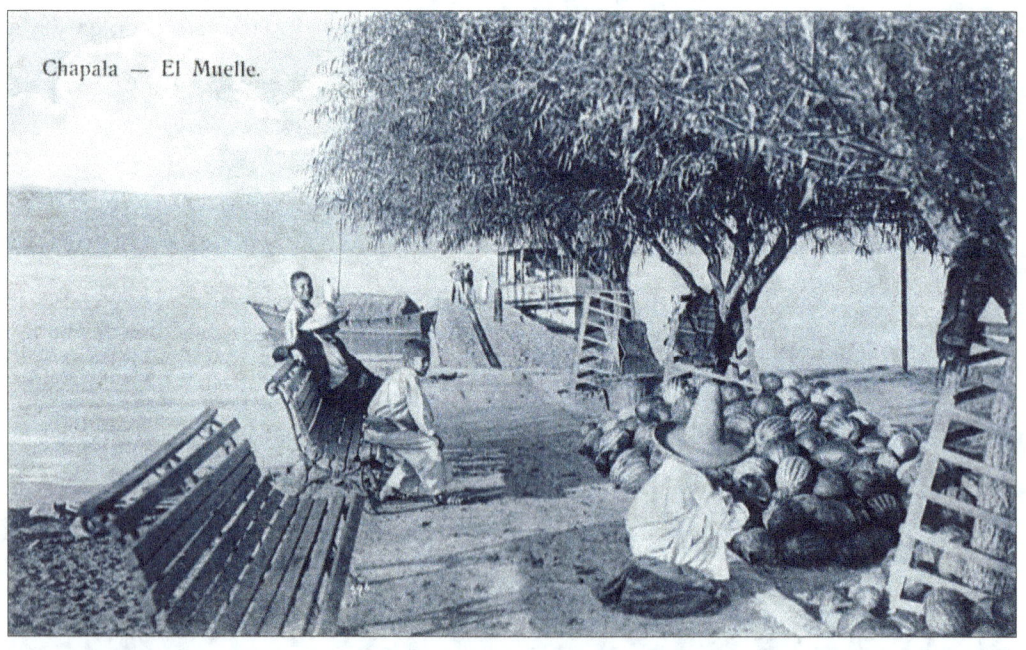

5.8. The pier (El muelle) and watermelon vendor, c. 1906. J M Lupercio; M Hernández.
Taken by José María Lupercio, one of the greatest Mexican photographers of his time, the original, larger photograph reveals that the vessel moored at the end of the pier was the Ramón Corona, named for the Jalisco state governor assassinated in 1889.

The pier was shaded from the afternoon sun by trees, planted when the Hotel Arzapalo opened; wooden cages protected their trunks from accidental damage.

Between the Hotel Arzapalo and the church was Villa Ana Victoria, one of Chapala's most distinctive early buildings (figure 5.1), built in the 1890s by Prussian émigré Eduard Collignon and named for his wife, Ana Victoria Stephenson. Tragically, Ana Victoria died suddenly shortly after the building was completed.[10]

For a few years in the early 1900s, house boats were popular, and no doubt served as a status symbol. In April 1900, for instance, Mexico City residents Tomás Braniff and his wife held a party at Chapala on board their new house boat; the guest list included Mr and Mrs Lorenzo Elizaga, Septimus Crowe, Eliza Paulsen, Alvaro Fernández del Valle, and Manuel Cuesta Gallardo.[11]

A few years later, Tomás' brother Alberto bought the iconic residence that locals still call Casa Braniff to this day. Located in close proximity to the church, on the site of the first friary in Chapala, the magnificent $40,000-house was begun in 1904 and completed the following year. Commissioned by influential Guadalajara lawyer and historian Luis Pérez Verdía, it was designed by British architect George Edward King, who had previously built Villa Tlalocan for British consul Lionel Carden.[12] Alberto Braniff, a wealthy Mexico City businessman and godson of President Díaz, purchased the house and all its furnishings in 1907 as a gift for his recently widowed mother.[13] Braniff, an aviator, rose to fame in 1910 when he made the first successful aircraft flight in Latin America.

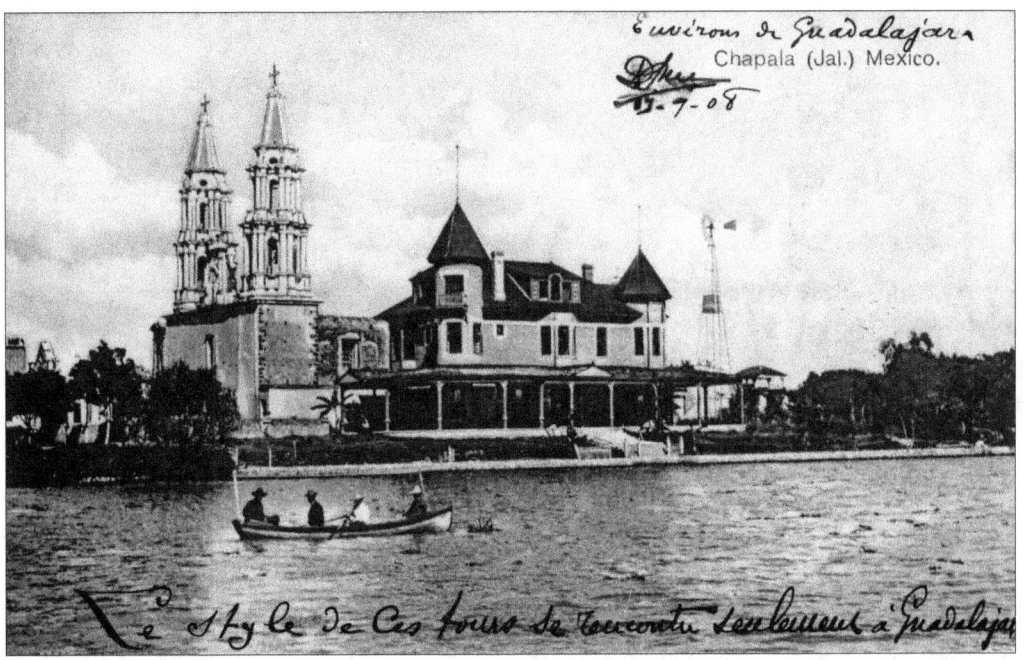

5.9 *Casa Braniff (formerly Casa Pérez Verdía), c. 1906. J M Lupercio; T Schwidernoch. The ornate Porfirian-era Casa Braniff was built as the vacation home of Luis Pérez Verdía.*

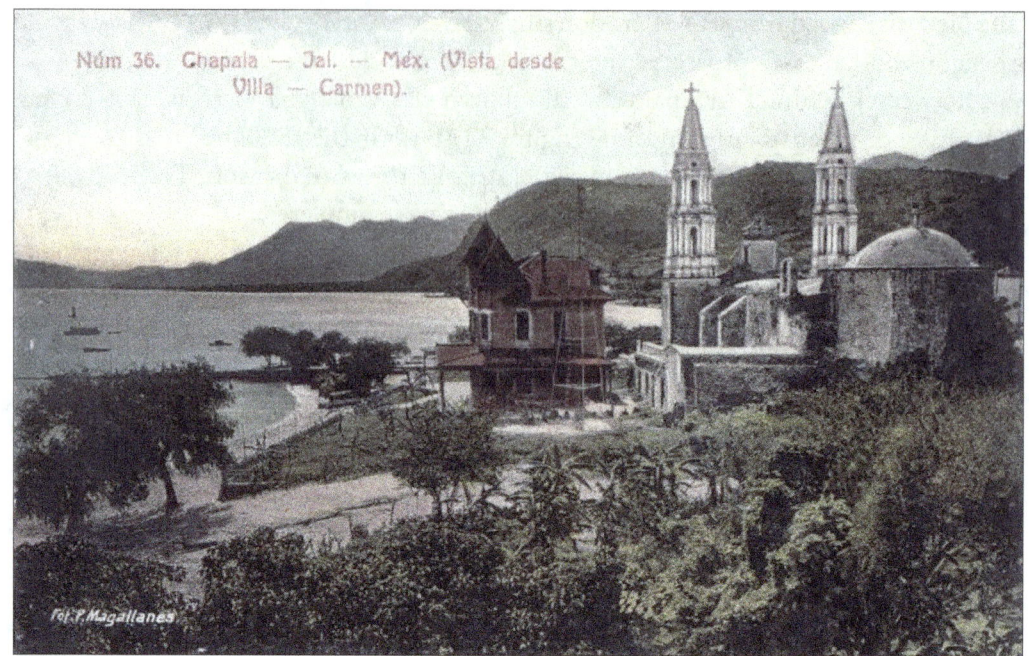

5.10. *View of Casa Braniff from Villa Carmen, c. 1908. P Magallanes; Alba y Fernández.*
This unusual angle of the Casa Braniff and the church was taken from the roof of Villa Carmen.
The laneway between the two residences eventually became Calle Juárez.

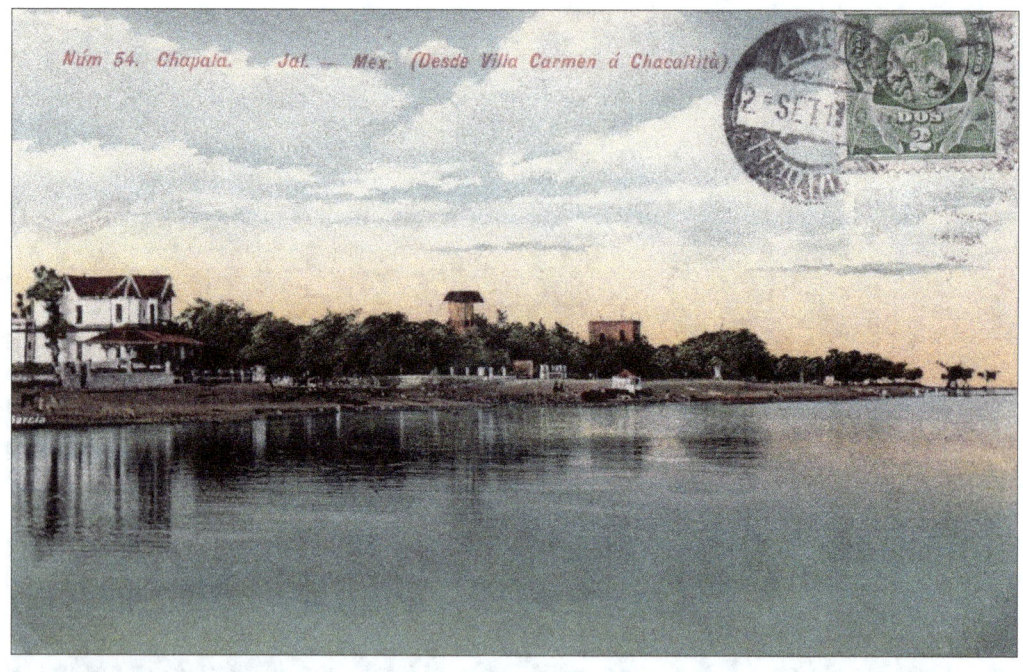

5.11. *View from Villa Carmen to Chacaltita, c. 1908. J V García; Alba y Fernández.*
Villa Carmen is at the extreme left of this view of the shoreline east of the pier. This beach,
Chacaltita, extended as far as where the yacht club and Acapulquito restaurants are today.

East of Casa Braniff, older and almost as photogenic, was Villa Carmen. The two images of Villa Carmen below (figures 5.11 and 5.12), apparently taken only a year or two apart, show how much the level of the lake varied both seasonally and from one year to the next. The lowest level of the lake in the first thirty years of the twentieth century occurred in 1916. Between 1914 and early 1916, the lake level fell by three meters, before making a full recovery in the second half of 1916.

The lake has helped meet local needs for centuries, and it was common in 1908 to see animals on the beach or in the shallows. In the sixteenth and seventeenth centuries herdsmen used the grassy marshlands at the eastern end of the lake as summer pastures for vast flocks of sheep from as far away as Querétaro.[14] In the twentieth century farmers introduced pumps—initially hand-operated, later electric—to move lake water onto their fields and irrigate their crops. As the city of Guadalajara grew in size, so did its demands for lake water, precipitating a series of crises in lake level since the 1950s.

West of the pier in 1908, the first large residence was Casa Capetillo (chapter 3). Its owner, Manuel Capetillo, received $25.00 in 1899 for land to construct the short, narrow street (formerly named Porfirio Díaz, now Aquiles Serdán), between his residence and Casa Galván.[15] Famous local architect Guillermo de Alba completed his own family home, Mi Pullman (now lovingly restored), just up the street in 1906.

Casa Galván (figure 5.13) was built in 1904 by forty-year-old widow Gabriela Galván. When María Pacheco (the widow of Ignacio Arzapalo) bought it in April

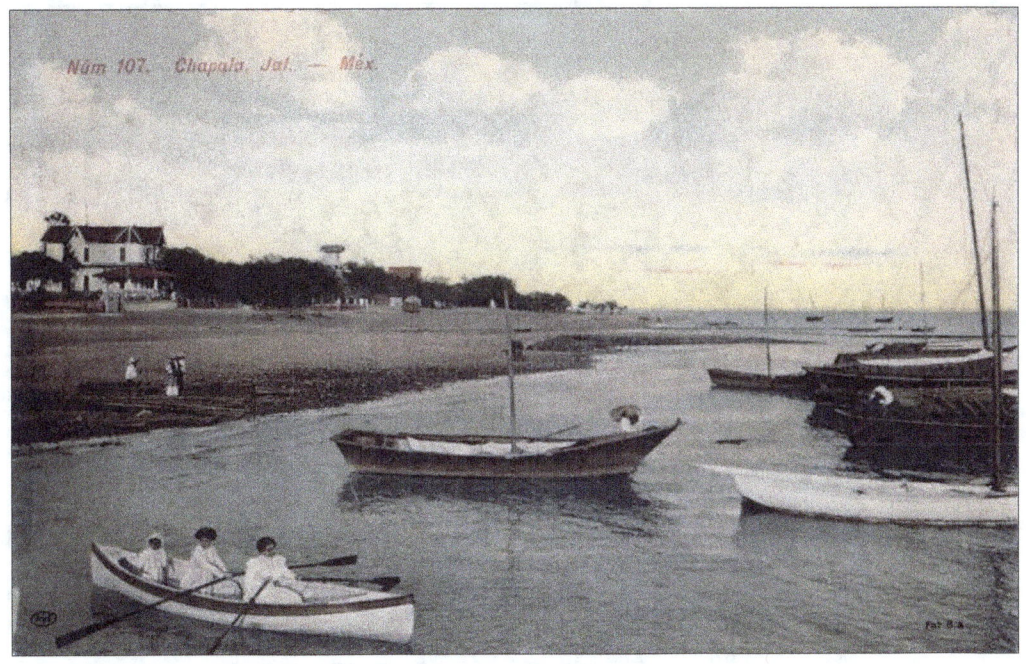

5.12. *Rowboat on the lake, c. 1910? Fot B A; Alba y Fernández.*
In this charming familial scene, two young women, accompanied by a child, are rowing towards the shore. Renting a rowboat cost $0.75 an hour in 1908.

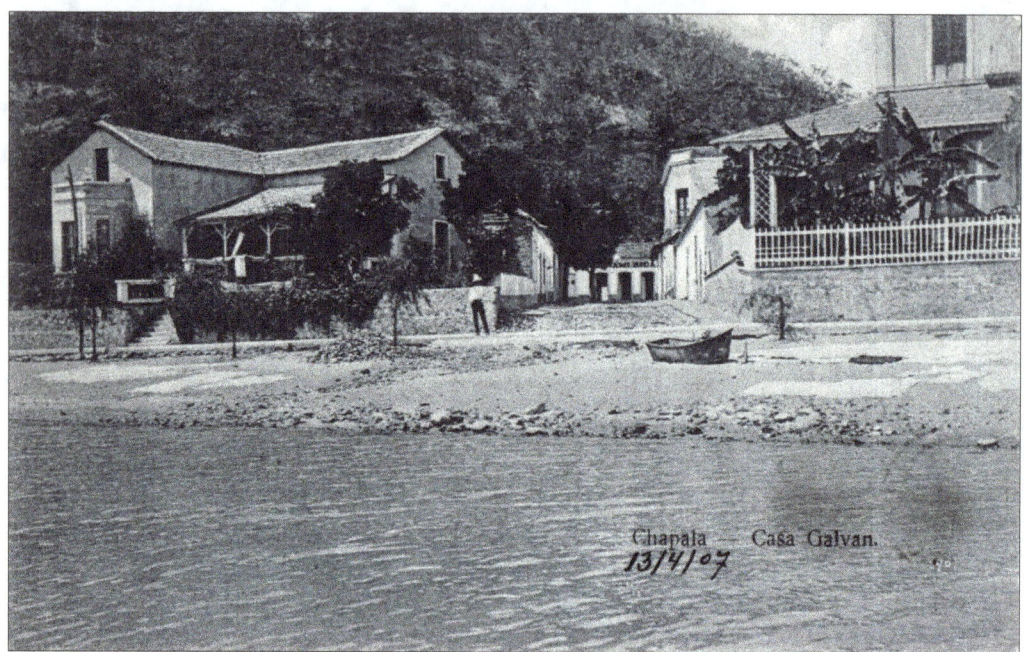

5.13. *Casa Galván and Casa Capetillo, c. 1906. J M Lupercio; M Hernández.*
Casa Capetillo (right) was one of the earliest vacation cottages in Chapala. Casa Galván (later Villa Aurora) cost $12,000 when it was built in 1904.

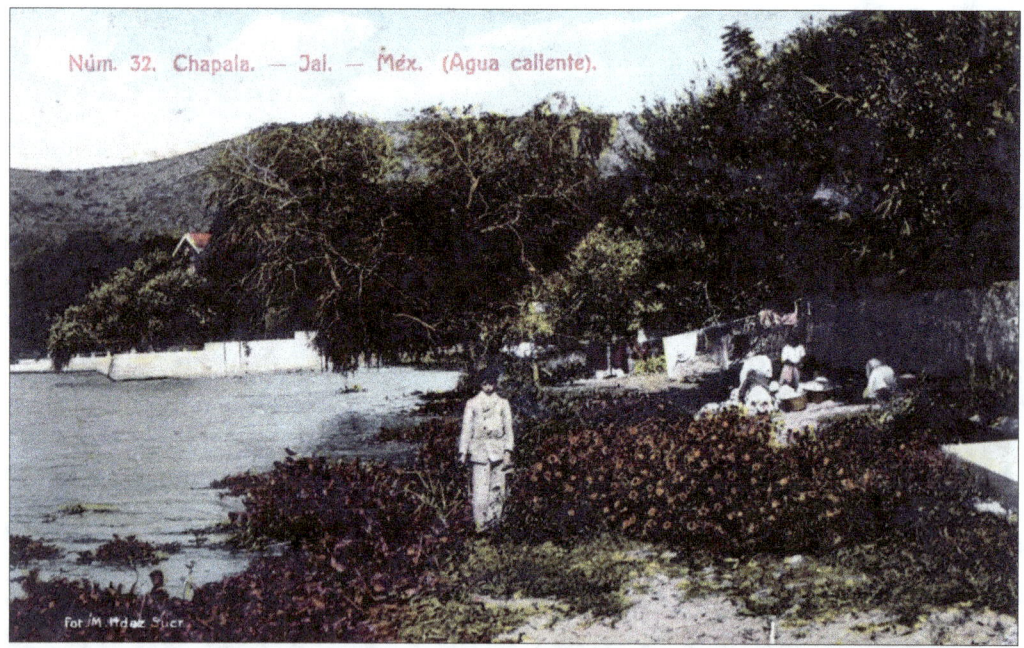

5.14. *Agua Caliente, c. 1907. M Hernández Sucr; Alba y Fernández.*
Near the site of Las Delicias, women are hand-washing laundry in the warm water before drying garments on a line stretched between trees. The mass of water hyacinth (left) was inaccurately colored when tinted. The weed was already recognized as a serious problem.

1916, she renamed it Villa Aurora.[16] Its most notable later occupant was Norwegian entrepreneur Christian Schjetnan, the visionary early promoter of Chapala who eventually succeeded, against all the odds, in completing the branch railroad to the town from La Capilla on the Mexican Central mainline.

A few steps further along the lakefront is Chalet Paulsen (later Villa Paz), with its unusual turreted tower. In addition to business interests in Guadalajara, its owner, Ernesto Paulsen, held a majority stake in the Lake Chapala Navigation Company, which ran steamship services on Lake Chapala. Along with other prominent Guadalajara businessmen, including Ignacio Arzapalo, Paulsen formed the Jalisco Development Company, which planned several massive projects for Chapala: the provision of electricity, irrigation and a public water system, an electric railroad linking the village to Guadalajara, and the construction of a serviceable road to Guadalajara.[17] The company's only success was in getting electricity installed. As for the road, it was to be several decades before driving from Guadalajara to Chapala was commonplace, and several more before it became easy.

Immediately west of Chalet Paulsen, at the foot of Cerro San Miguel, was Chapala's first public thermal water baths, known as Las Delicias. The therapeutic qualities of the warm water springs of Chapala had attracted many well-known

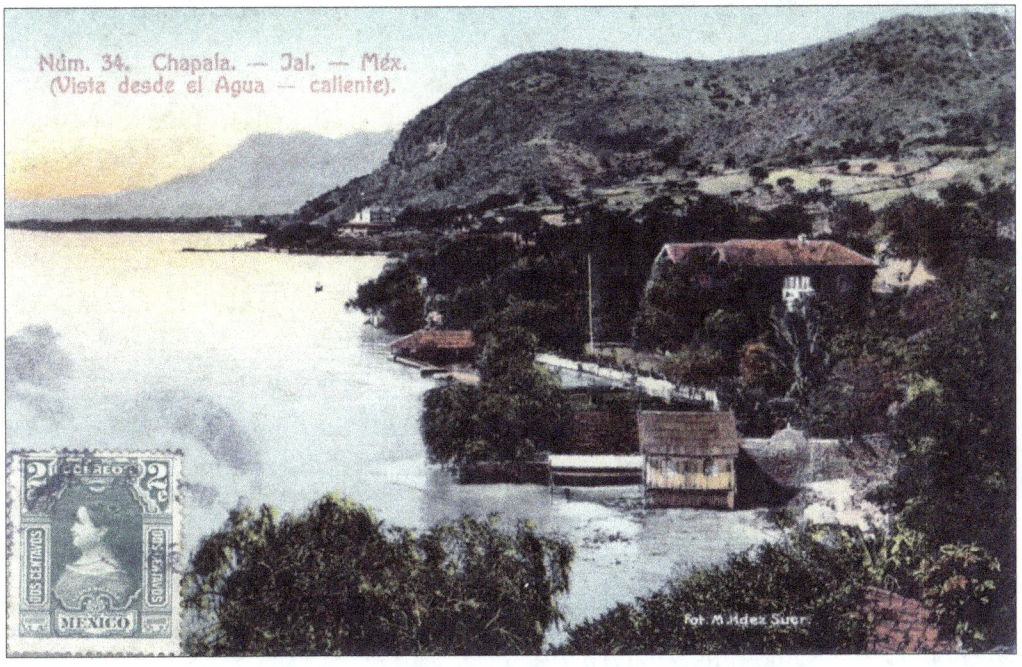

5.15. *View west from Agua Caliente, Chapala, c. 1907. J M Lupercio; M Hernández Sucr; Alba y Fernández. The red-roof to the right of center is Villa Tlalocan, with its small private harbor and boathouse. The white building in the distance is Villa Montecarlo, then owned by Aurelio González Hermosillo. The magnificent scenery that surrounds Lake Chapala is evident in this image; sadly, unbridled development has changed this bucolic landscape for ever.*

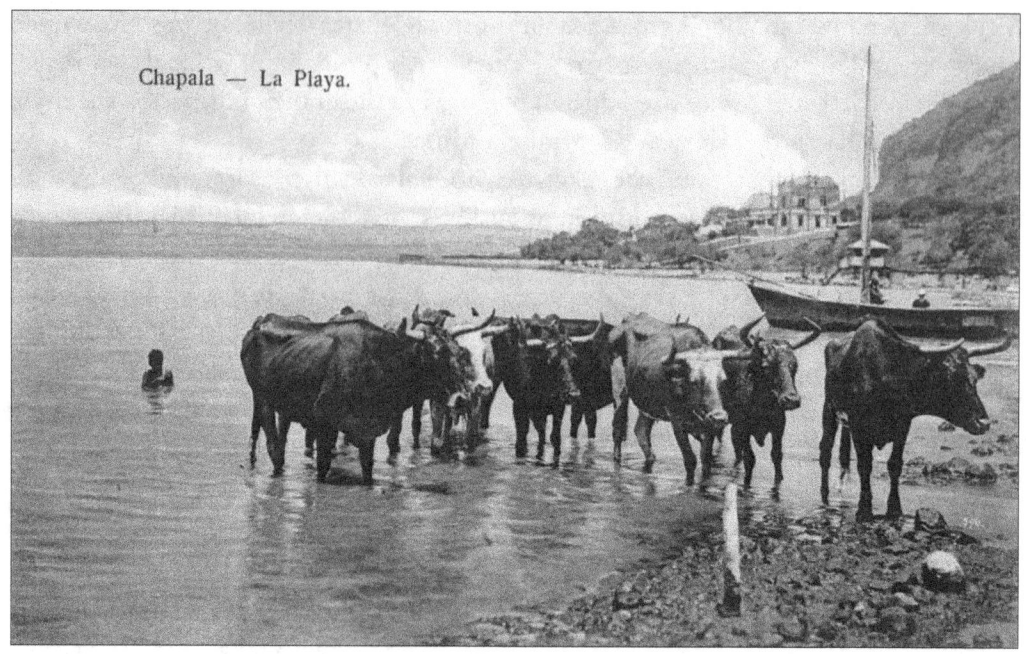

5.16. Cattle on the beach, c. 1906. J M Lupercio; M Hernández.
The scaffolding on the large building in the background (Villa Montecarlo) dates the photograph to 1905-6, when the villa was undergoing renovations.

visitors over the years. By 1902, two cement tanks had been installed, one of them the size of a swimming pool.[18] When President Díaz visited Chapala in 1908 to stay with his wife's inlaws, he enjoyed a daily bath each morning in these health-giving pools.[19] On account of these waters, the street running west from the center of Chapala was named Agua Caliente; after being extended in 1910 to reach San Antonio Tlayacapan and Ajijic, the street was renamed Avenida Hidalgo.

Nearby, also at the foot of Cerro San Miguel, another thermal spring was bottled as mineral water in the early decades of the twentieth century. Salvador Pérez Arce, who owned the spring, sought permission in 1907 to sell flavored drinks and potable spring water to the public. He and his son installed a bottling machine and began marketing the iron-rich mineral water using the somewhat unimaginative brand name "Chapala."[20]

The original plaza in the village center was immediately north of the Hotel Victor Huber. The plaza was relocated at the end of the 1940s when the entire town center was redeveloped. This 'modernization' required the demolition of the block shared by the hotel and the adjoining Villa Ana Victoria.

In 1910, in an effort to improve decorum, the town council announced that it was no longer permitted for anyone to walk onto this plaza wearing a straw sombrero (the kind worn by the local *campesinos* in figure 5.17). At the same time, authorities were tightening up on public health and prostitution. Police were ordered to enforce the requirement that prostitutes had a current permit; permits cost 50 centavos (25 cents) each time, and required proof of a medical check every two weeks. Rafael Madrid was the medical practitioner appointed by the council to perform these checks, in addition to his duties overseeing vaccinations, responding to accidents and looking after the medical needs of prisoners.[21]

A journalist visiting in 1909 described how next to the "tiny plaza adorned with orange trees and other tropical vegetation" was a street market or tianguis, where every Sunday "picturesque natives from the surrounding country pour into the little town and gather."[22] Another foreign visitor, writing at the same time, explained what was on sale:

> Under multicolored awnings are mounted pyramids of fruit and vegetables, bananas, oranges, lemons, watermelons, melons, papayas, mameyes, lettuces, sweet potatoes, red and hot peppers. Elsewhere, zealous merchants offer fresh tortillas and tamales of golden cooked corn, and pulque, the smell of which fills one with intense repulsion. On the other side of the square, cluttered stalls display sombreros, wool sarapes and leather huaraches.[23]

Overlooking the plaza was Cerro San Miguel. Owned by the municipality of Chapala, it was sold for $25,000 in 1908 in order to fund Chapala's first Palacio Municipal, which opened two years later. The purchasers, three men from Guadalajara, planned to terrace the hill, build a cog railroad, and sell building plots. From the top of Cerro San Miguel the wonderful view over the village took in distant islands and

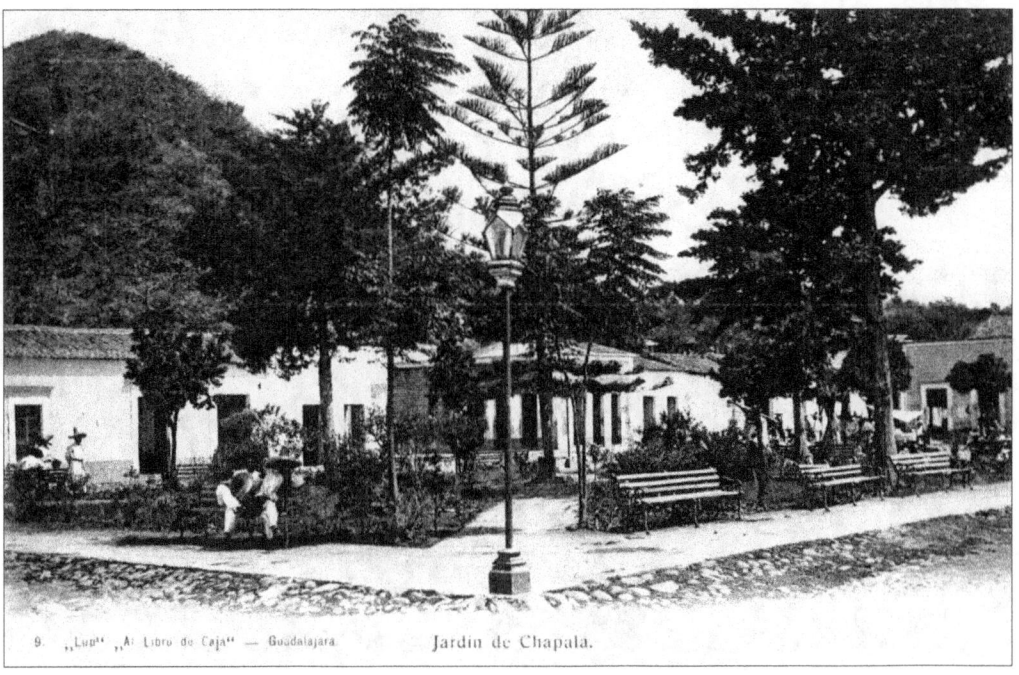

5.17. *Plaza (jardín) of Chapala, c. 1903. J M Lupercio; J Kaiser.*
Large trees shaded the many benches in this communal space, from where the low height of surrounding residences at the time allowed an uninterrupted view of Cerro San Miguel.

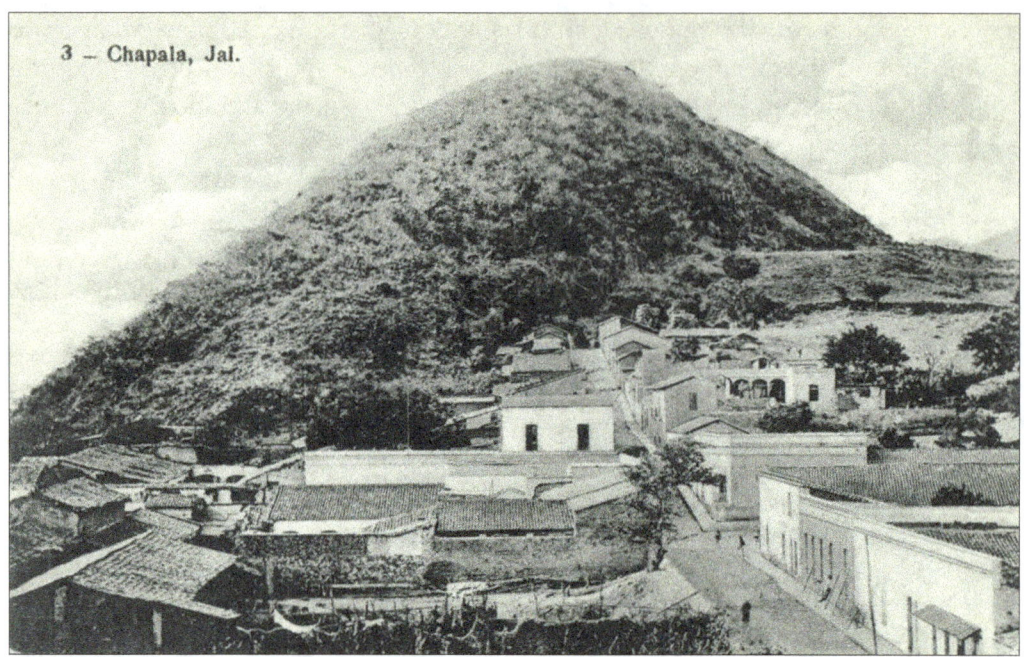

5.18. *Cerro San Miguel, c. 1910. B de Alba.*
For day-trippers and tourists alike, the short hike up Cerro San Miguel for the view over Chapala and across the lake was a popular activity.

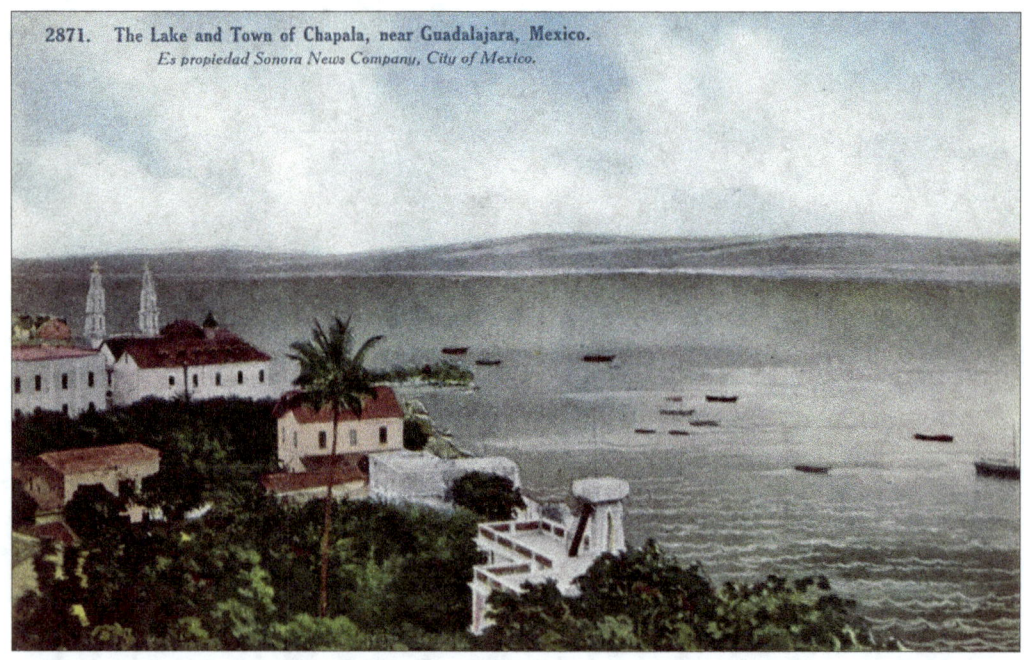

5.19. *View over Chapala, c. 1906. W Scott?; Sonora News Company.*
The prominent shoreline buildings (left to right) are the San Francisco church, the Hotel Arzapalo, Casa Capetillo (steep red roof) and Villa Paz (white turret).

the far shore of the lake.[24] Like many other grandiose plans of the time, the project to develop Cerro San Miguel never got off the ground. A decade later residents living in cottages close to the hill became alarmed at reports that "a large tiger" had made his lair there and was carrying off poultry and roosters. The mountain cat was surprised and killed before it could claim too many more victims.[25]

By 1908 the view from Cerro San Miguel to the west revealed a succession of villas and estates that already stretched almost as far as the eye could see. The only practical way at that time to reach some of the more distant properties was by boat.

Boats for up to ten passengers could be hired in 1908 for $5.00 an hour.[26] A boat ride west afforded the best views of Villa Tlalocan and Villa Josefina, and was the easiest way to reach the two largest estates in the area: Villa Montecarlo and Villa El Manglar.

A short sail past the stately Villa Tlalocan (chapter 3), built by Lionel Carden, was Villa Josefina, the former Casa Albión of Septimus Crowe, which had been bought in 1901 by US-born Guadalajara beer magnate Joseph Maximilian Schnaider. Schnaider had partnered with Ignacio Arzapalo and Ernesto Paulsen to establish the Jalisco Development Company, with its grandiose plans. In 1916, he placed Quinta Josefina at the disposal of General Venustiano Carranza, one of the main leaders of the Revolution, who became the 37th President of Mexico the following year.[27]

Further west was the small pier serving Villa Montecarlo, Septimus Crowe's first home at Lake Chapala, situated on a bluff overlooking the lake. Crowe had sold it

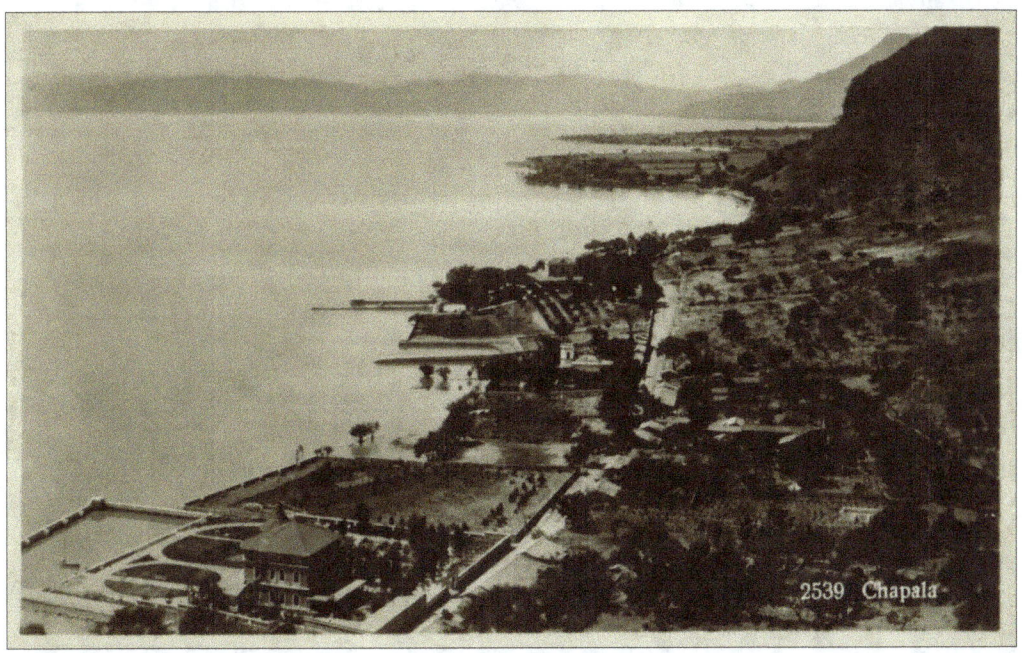

5.20. *Chapala panorama looking west, c. 1916? H Brehme.*
The building at the bottom left is Villa Reynera. Hugo Brehme took this photo prior to the 1918 remodeling of Villa Montecarlo (on the promontory in the center of the image).

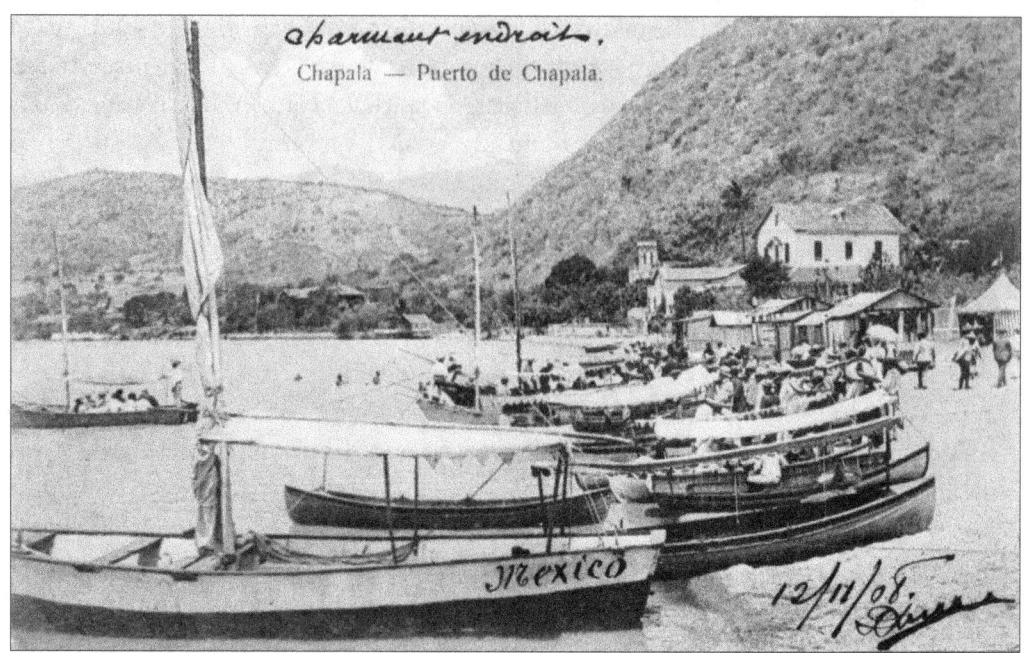

5.21. *Boats on the beach west of the pier, c. 1906. J M Lupercio; M Hernández.*
The multiple tourist boats and crowds of people on the beach show precisely how busy Chapala could be on weekends and holidays even as early as 1906. The most prominent building, with the steep roof, is Casa Capetillo. To its left is the turret of Chalet Paulsen (Villa Paz).

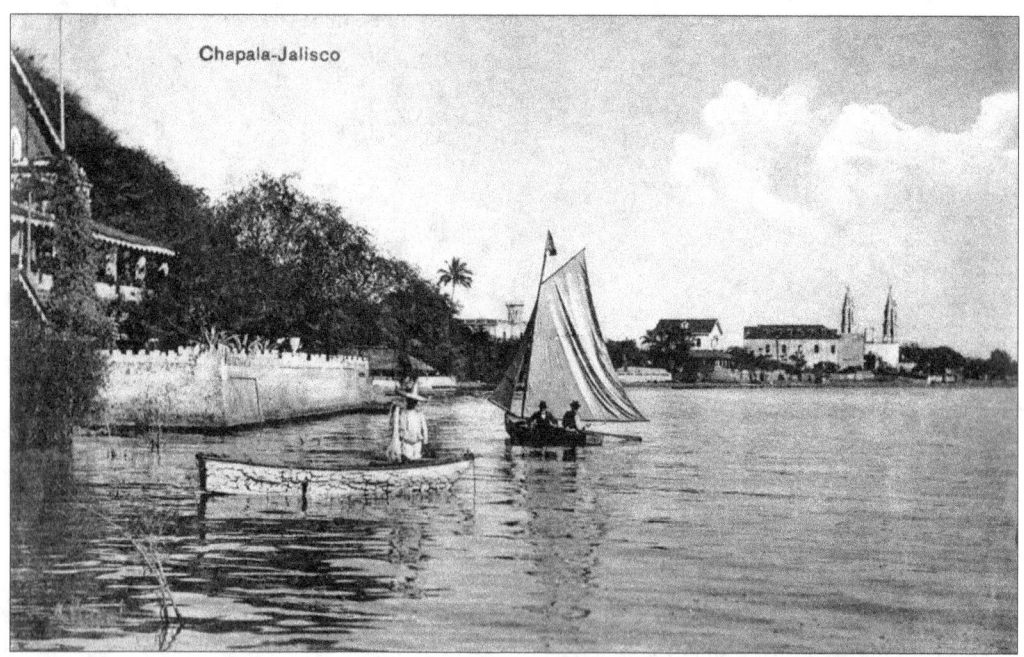

5.22. *Villa Josefina (formerly Casa Albión), c. 1908. J M Lupercio; J Kaiser.*
Seen from the lake, Villa Josefina (aka Casa Schnaider) was especially photogenic.

to Cora Alice Townsend in 1895. Even though Villa Montecarlo, with its beautifully landscaped grounds sloping down to the shore, is only a few hundred meters from the center of Chapala, it was much easier—prior to the late 1930s—to access it by boat than by road. The same was true for many of the grander lakeside properties in Chapala, which led to a proliferation of small private piers and jetties along the shoreline.

After Cora and her parents died, the villa and several contiguous parcels of land were acquired (in about 1904) by Aurelio González Hermosillo, who later decided to replace the existing building with a much more elaborate residence. He commissioned Angelo Corsi in 1918 to oversee this grand remodeling.

Yet further west is the narrow strip of land jutting out into the lake occupied by the historically significant Villa El Manglar, originally owned by inlaws of President Porfirio Díaz. Lorenzo Elizaga, a prominent and well-connected Mexico City lawyer, and his wife, Sofía Romero Rubio y Castelló (President Díaz's sister-in-law), built El Manglar at the start of the twentieth century.

Even so, when the president visited Chapala for a weekend in January 1904, he chose to stay with Eduard Collignon at Villa Ana Victoria, and did not sleep at El Manglar, perhaps because his mother-in-law was staying there at the time! When Díaz returned to Chapala for Easter the following year, he stayed at El Manglar. His next documented visit to Chapala was for Holy Week in 1908, when the presidential party arrived from Ocotlán in motor boats owned by Manuel Cuesta Gallardo and Arturo Braniff. During their week at El Manglar, President Díaz and his wife watched a regatta

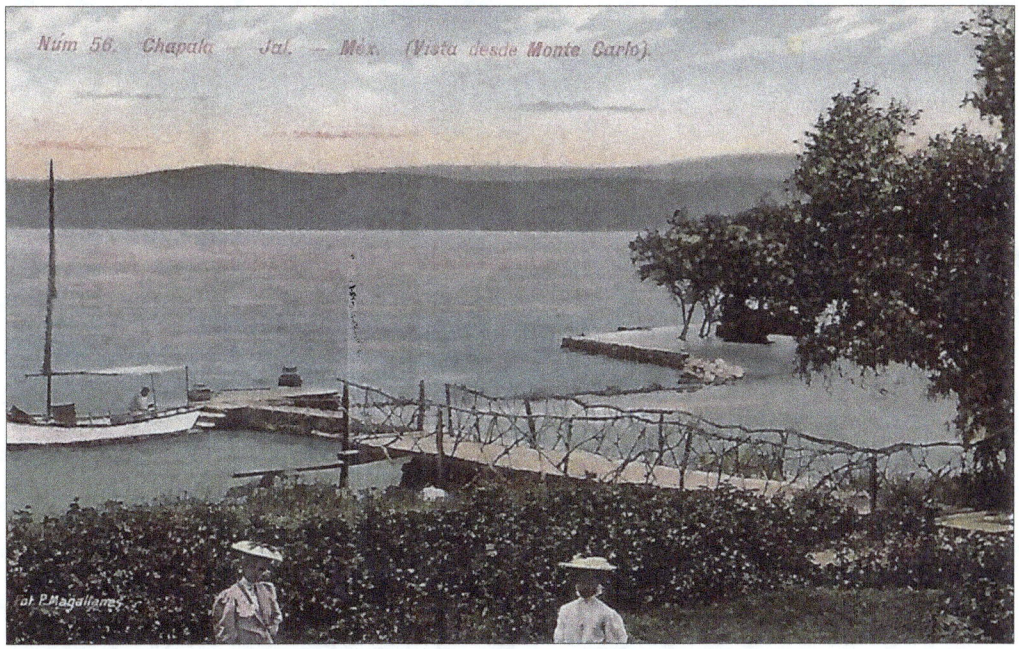

5.23. *Pier at Villa Montecarlo (or El Manglar?), c. 1908. P Magallanes; Alba y Fernández. The Villa was a short boat ride from the pier in Chapala. The stylish dresses and hats are testimony to Chapala's attraction for the rich and famous during the early 1900s.*

on the lake and several sports events, and discussed plans to build a yacht club. The president also swam in the lake and did some hunting.[28]

What happened next?

In hindsight, 1908 marked the height of Chapala's success as a pioneering early tourist destination. What followed over the next decade was unexpected and brought more challenging times to the village.

Ignacio Arzapalo died in 1909, at the age of 72, only a year after the Hotel Palmera opened. Because his son had predeceased him, his granddaughter—María Aurora, then aged 7—inherited both hotels in Chapala as well as property in central Guadalajara, an inheritance worth the equivalent of $7.5 million today. Protracted arguments over her guardianship delayed any meaningful investments in maintaining or expanding the hotels.

In 1910 the Mexican Revolution broke out, causing investors, especially those close to President Díaz, to either flee or keep an extremely low profile. President Díaz, Lorenzo Elizaga and their respective wives escaped to Europe in 1911. Díaz died in Paris in 1915, and Elizaga in Switzerland in the 1920s; their wives, however, both returned to Mexico in 1934.

Several of the other principal players in this account, such as architect George King and Ocotlán photographer Winfield Scott, left Mexico for the US. Scott came back to

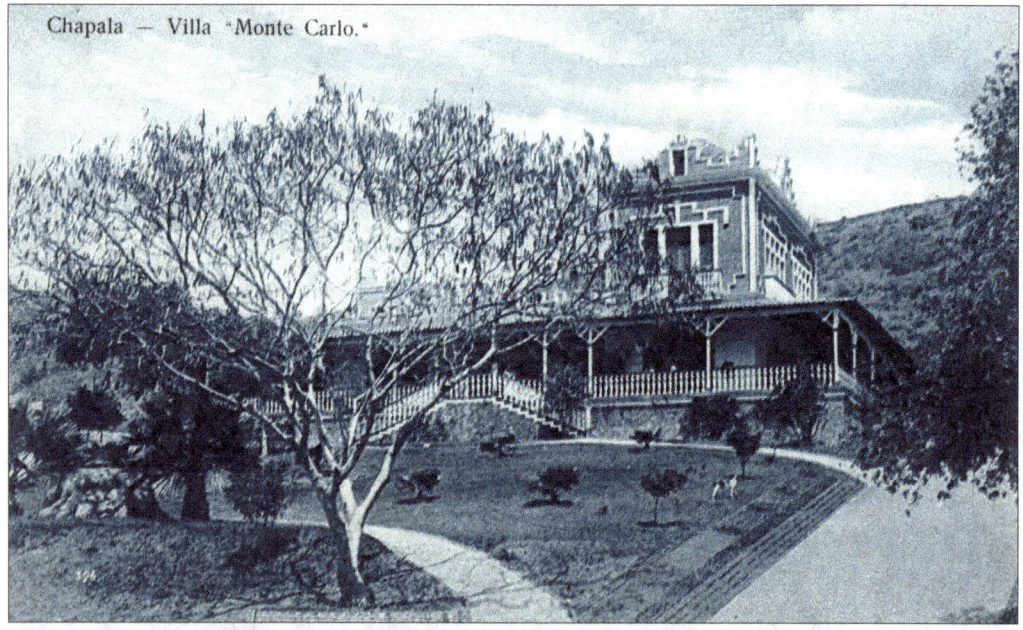

5.24. *Villa Montecarlo, c. 1906. J M Lupercio; M Hernández.*
The *Mexican Herald* described Villa Montecarlo when the Townsends owned it as *"a bright red and white house with a tower which looks as if it came from the old baronial castles of the middle ages."* The image predates the major 1918 remodeling by Angelo Corsi.

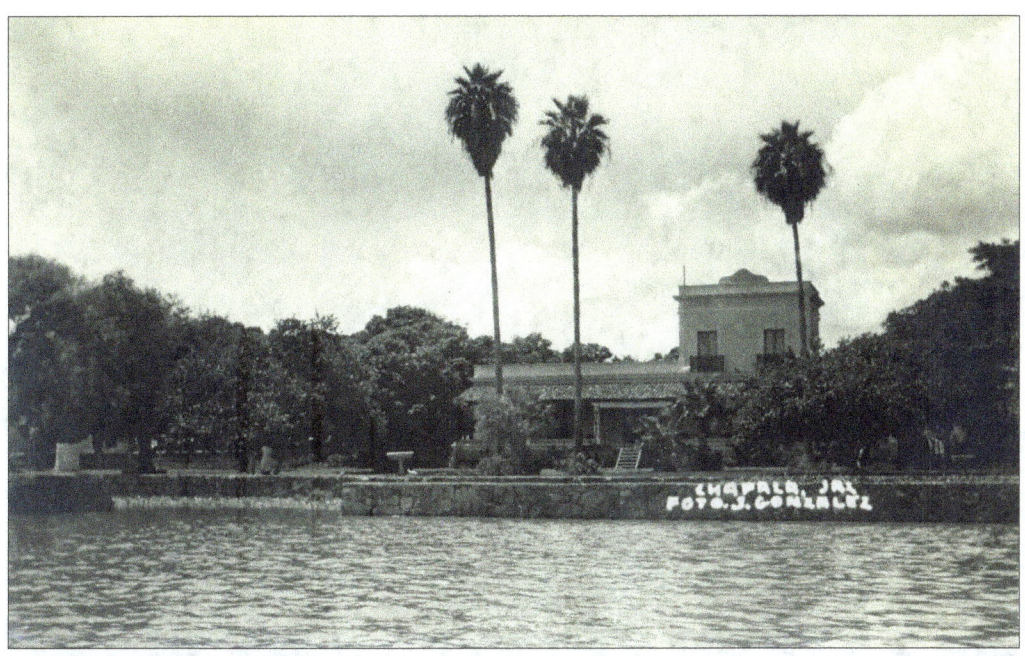

5.25. *El Manglar, c. 1945? J González.*
President Díaz spent Easter at El Manglar in 1905 and 908, visiting his sister-in-law Sofía Romero Rubio y Castelló and her husband, Lorenzo Elizaga, a Mexico City lawyer.

Lake Chapala after the Revolution to manage the Hotel Ribera (chapter 6) and later the Hotel Arzapalo, where he regaled D H Lawrence and his traveling companions with tales of his adventures.

During the Revolution, visitor numbers to Chapala plummeted and hotels struggled. For several years, most of the hotels, if they opened at all, did so only seasonally; there were insufficient tourists to justify them operating year-round. By 1919, as the Revolution petered out and business began to pick up, the Gran Hotel Arzapalo advertised that it had been renovated and was offering French cuisine, special suites for couples, and fair prices. All Chapala hotels were full during Holy Week in 1920.[29]

The road between Guadalajara and Chapala was steadily improved, reducing the travel time (in theory) by 1919 to about two hours each way. Sunday trips from Guadalajara by "rapid and comfortable bus with pneumatic tires" were advertised. The bus left Guadalajara at 8.00am and departed Chapala at 5.00pm; tickets were 4 pesos ($2.00) each way.[30]

The Gran Hotel Victor Huber, later renamed first the Francés and then Gran Hotel Chapala, survived, in one guise or another, until its demolition—along with Villa Ana Victoria—during the major redevelopment of the town center in about 1950.

The Chapala Yacht Club building was completed in 1910 and formally inaugurated the following year. Designed by American architect Charles Strange, the wooden clubhouse was at the end of a 100-meter-long pier. Founder members included British peer and politician William Montagu, the 9th Duke of Manchester, who donated the

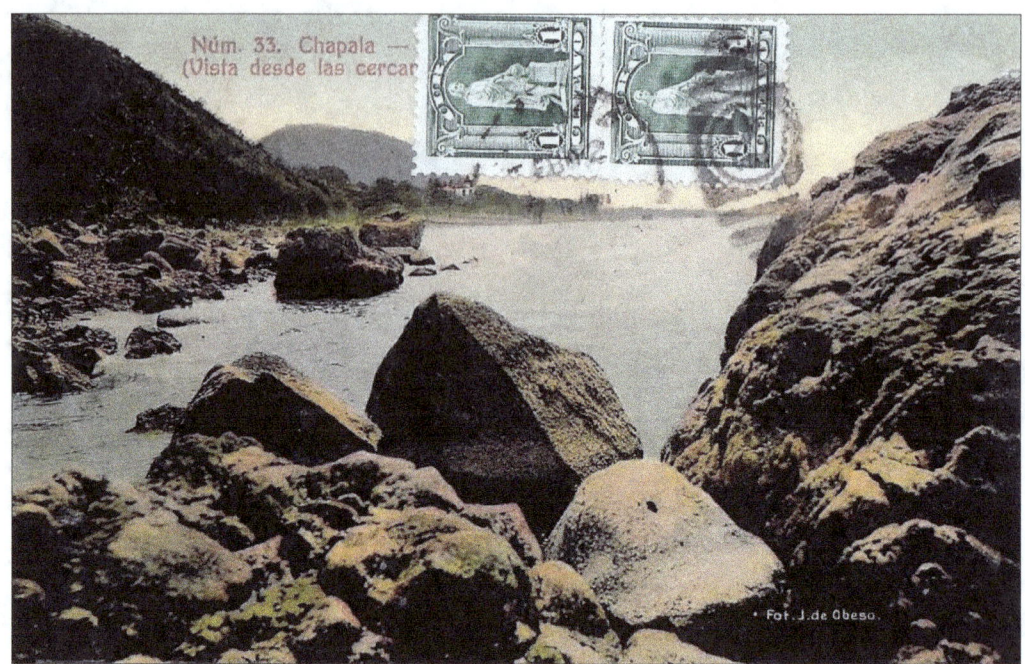

*5.26. View of Chapala from El Manglar, c. 1908. J de Obeso; Alba y Fernández.
With its presidential connection, the El Manglar estate, a few kilometers west of Chapala, was important in establishing the town's growing fame as a resort.*

main trophy for the club's regatta. Because of its close association with (by then former) President Díaz, it was soon abandoned, before being accidentally set on fire in 1916.

By 1920, when Chapala's population had reached 3143 (almost double the number in 1900), several additional villas had been built to infill the lakeshore west and east of the pier. They included Villa Ave María and Villa Niza, the former remodeled by, and the latter designed by, Guillermo de Alba.

The failure of the Jalisco Development Company to achieve its objectives did not deter other individuals from stepping up with equally ambitious plans. The most noteworthy, by far, was visionary Norwegian entrepreneur Paul Christian Schjetnan (1870–1945), who had moved from Mexico City to Chapala with his family in about 1908 and later lived in Villa Aurora (formerly Casa Galván). It was Schjetnan's untiring efforts that eventually resulted in the opening of the Chapala Railroad in 1920.[31] Schjetnan's legacy lives on in the elegant and beautifully proportioned Chapala Railroad Station, now the Centro Cultural González Gallo. (chapter 7)

6

East end: Ocotlán and Hotel Ribera Castellanos

The town of Ocotlán, a short distance downstream from where the River Santiago leaves Lake Chapala, benefited greatly from the opening of the Irapuato-Guadalajara branch of the Mexican Central Railway in 1888. The railroad not only served the needs of the local haciendas, it also significantly reduced the travel time to Lake Chapala from both Mexico City and Guadalajara. All the larger boats on Lake Chapala were imported from abroad, and Ocotlán was by far the most accessible location near the lake where they could easily be launched: a short sail up the Río Grande and these boats were on the open waters of Lake Chapala. The first steamships were launched in Ocotlán in the mid-nineteenth century, followed later by privately owned cruisers.

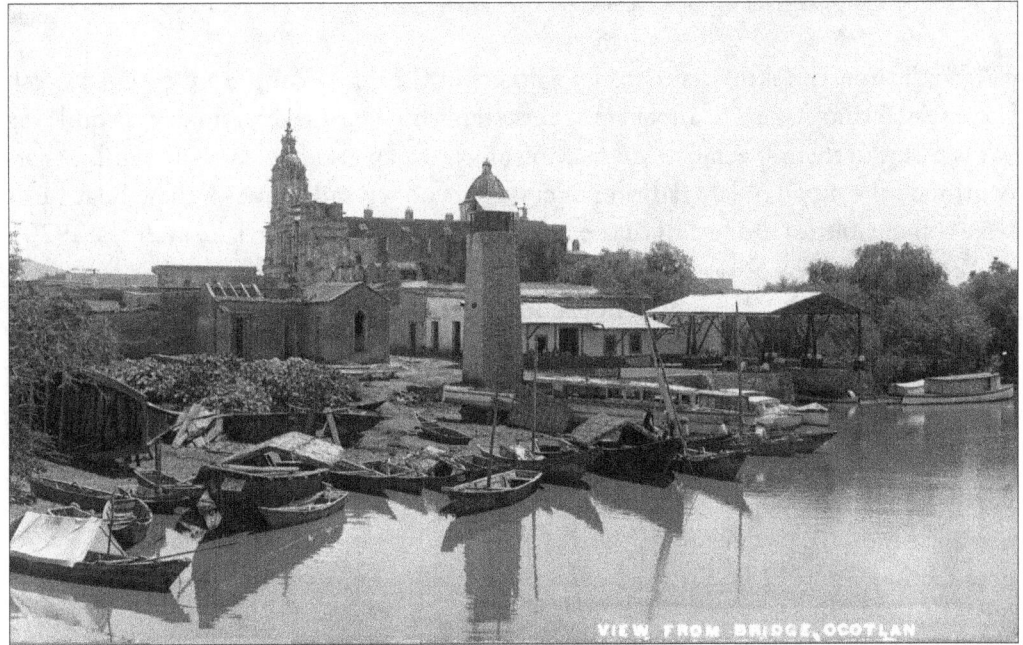

6.1. *View from bridge at Ocotlán, c. 1907. D R Furness.*
Most tourists arrived via the Mexican Central Railway. After alighting at Ocotlán station, they needed to walk or ride only a short distance before boarding a boat for the scenic trip up the River Santiago to Lake Chapala and the Hotel Ribera.

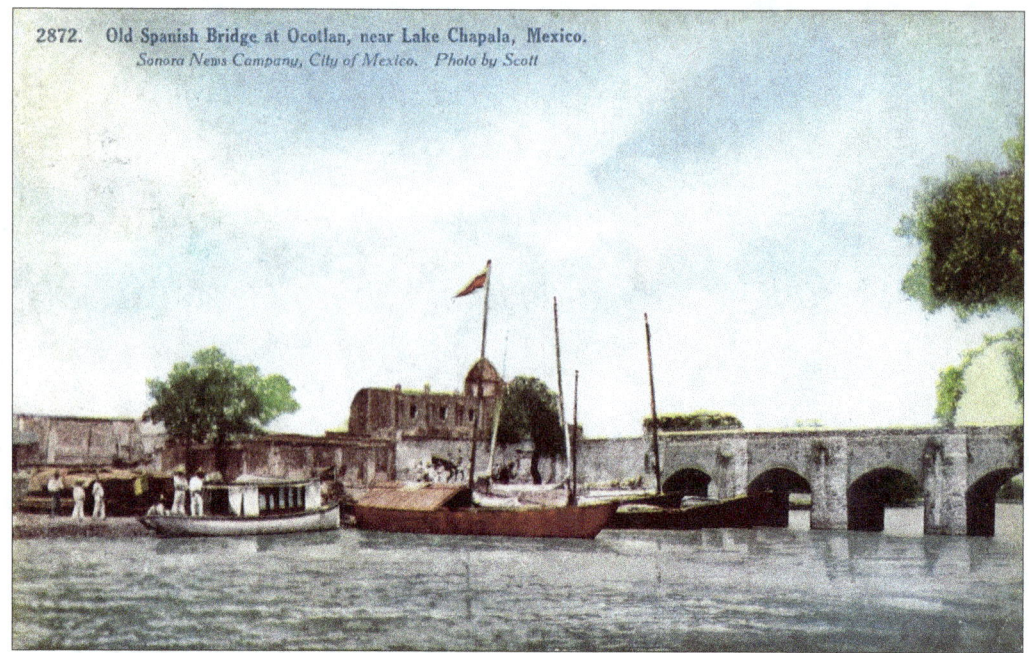

6.2. *Old Spanish Bridge at Ocotlán, c. 1907. W Scott; Sonora News Company.*
This bridge was a familiar sight to most tourists visiting Hotel Ribera. The flag atop the boat mast was added by the publishers. There is no flag on the original photograph, taken by Winfield Scott who lived nearby.

With time, the skills acquired by workers in the repair shops in Ocotlán to keep these vessels shipshape and afloat led to the establishment of several small boat building yards. Some of them specialized in making motorized metal-hulled boats, while others continued the much older tradition of crafting wooden sail canoes.[1] These boat yards were responsible for almost all of the new boats launched on the lake after the 1920s.

Boat houses were also good business for a time in Ocotlán. For example, the wealthy Braniff family built a large boat house in Ocotlán in 1907, with derricks and other equipment for repairing and painting their speedy launch *Reverie* and other boats.[2]

Initially, the needs of travelers, such as those who had to overnight in Ocotlán before taking a train or steamer, were met by several small guesthouses. Then, at the start of the twentieth century, the obvious success of the purpose-built Hotel Arzapalo in Chapala inspired Dwight Furness, a visionary American entrepreneur in Guanajuato, to build an even grander resort, specifically for tourists, on lakefront land he owned near the hamlet of El Fuerte, just outside Ocotlán. The hotel—built on farmland—was Mexico's first greenfield resort.

The Hotel Ribera Castellanos (or simply Hotel Ribera) opened in 1906. Located five kilometers south of Ocotlán, the hotel took its name from the Castellanos family, the influential family who owned this 7000-acre estate prior to Furness, who purchased it from them in 1902 for $100,000.[3]

Dwight Furness (1861–1924) grew up in Furnessville (named for his family), Indiana, and arrived in Guanajuato at age 26 as the representative of a Missouri-based mining company. He soon branched out on his own to buy and trade mineral ore, and was the US consular agent at Guanajuato from 1889 to 1907.[4] He and his wife, Anna Rodgers, a Methodist missionary, had ten children: five sons, one of whom died as an infant, and five daughters.

Furness's business empire grew and grew. In addition to several highly profitable general merchandise and minerals trading companies, which conducted more than $2 million worth of business a year, his financial interests ranged from mines to land and financing, and extended across several states, including Aguascalientes, Durango and Jalisco. Despite all his wheeling and dealing, Furness gained a reputation as a fair and benevolent businessman.[5]

Furness planned to farm most of his newly acquired estate, but recognized the enormous tourist potential of "one of the finest scenic spots in Mexico" and its "nearly three miles of lake and river front," so close to the main Irapuato-Guadalajara railroad. He planned to build a modern "summer colony" alongside an elegant lakefront hotel that would take full advantage of the nearby thermal springs.[6] In a later phase, Furness wanted to bottle and market the spring water, build a sanatorium on the mountainside above the springs, and add a golf links and bowling alley.

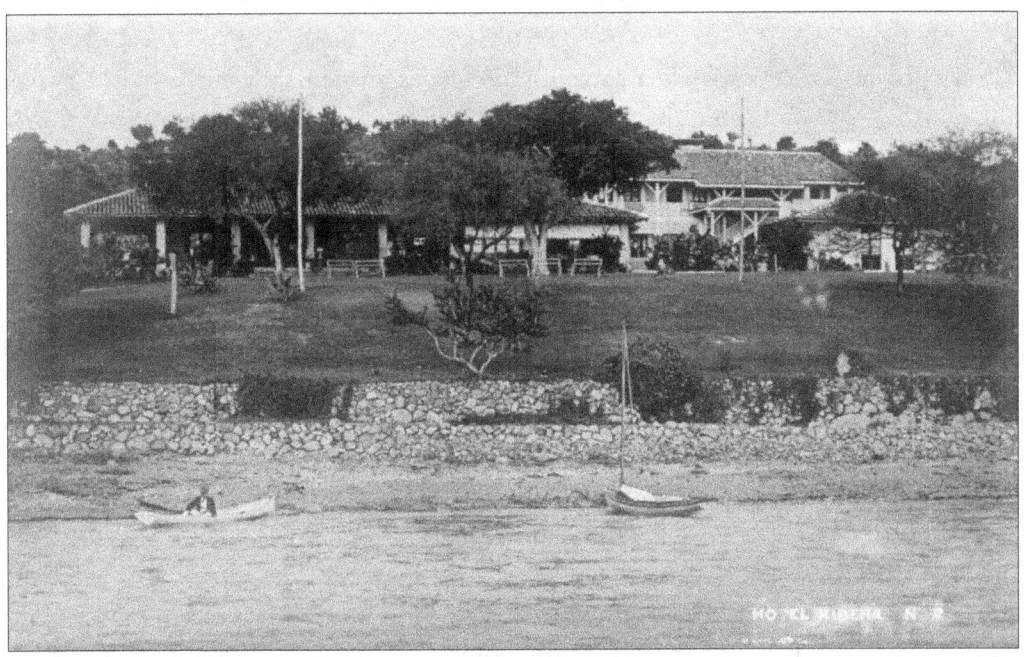

6.3. *Hotel Ribera, viewed from the lake, c. 1907. D R Furness.*
Most hotel guests arrived by boat; it took 30 minutes by steam launch from Ocotlán, or about five hours from Chapala. This was their first view of the well-appointed buildings and beautiful grounds.

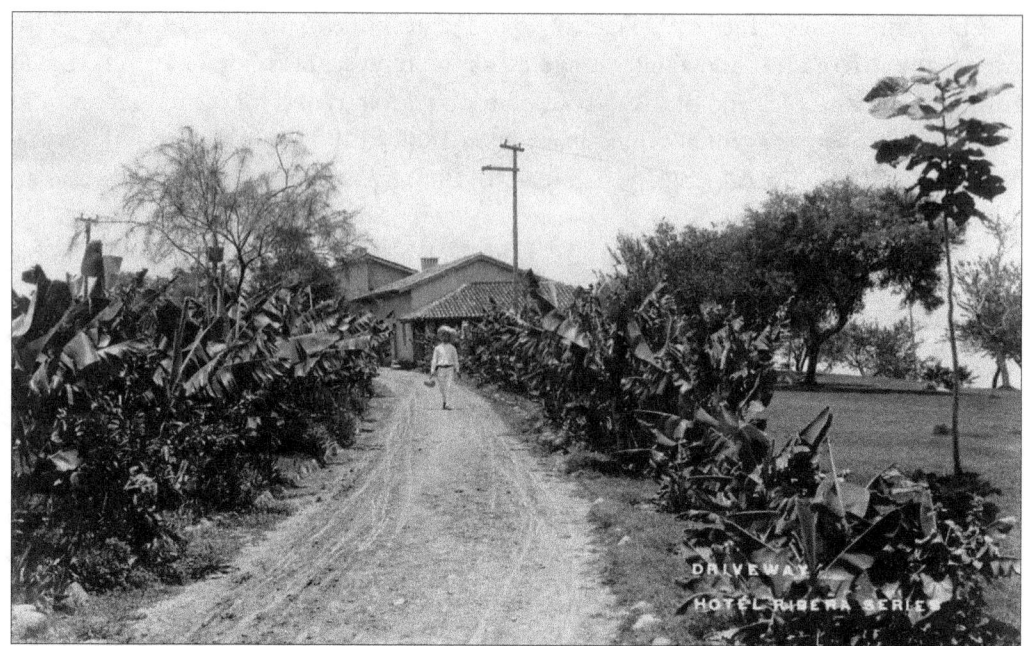

6.4. Driveway to Hotel Ribera, c. 1907. D R Furness.
By road, the hotel was about five kilometers south of Ocotlán and approximately the same distance west of Jamay. However, very few early visitors arrived by road. Of those who did, most were from either Guanajuato or Guadalajara.

The correspondent for *The Mexican Herald* was immediately enthusiastic, pointing out that "in winter months people of the tableland cities go down to Veracruz or Tampico for sea bathing and boating," while summer months could be uncomfortable both in the cities and on the coast. Therefore, a town of "cottages and hotels" on Lake Chapala was an ideal solution, given its wonderful year-round climate:

> There is no finer all-the-year-round climate than that which may be enjoyed along the shores of Lake Chapala. The air is itself a tonic, the lake breezes invigorating, and the worn out business man, or society woman, finds in a few days that the system is generously renewed.[7]

To finance his project, Furness incorporated the Lake Chapala Agricultural and Improvement Company in Phoenix, Arizona, in July 1902.[8] The company quickly raised $600,000 in capital and Furness started selling building lots for a town "laid out in American style." Construction of the first homes and the Hotel Ribera began in the summer of 1904. Among the prominent individuals who built cottages close to the Hotel Ribera was Arturo Braniff, from Mexico City, who imported his own power boat, fast enough to cover the 45 kilometers between Ribera Castellanos and Chapala in less than 90 minutes.[9]

The Hotel Ribera was fully functional by 1907, when banner advertisements for the "Coming Pleasure Resort" used the tagline, "The Riviera of Mexico," a line designed to strike a chord with the well-heeled clientele being targeted. The adverts pointed out how easy it was, with two trains daily each way, for Guadalajara residents to visit for a day, or for a weekend, and enjoy the hotel's "wholesome meals, clean beds." The hotel claimed to be a "Sportsman's Paradise," the perfect base for hunting during the winter season in an area free from mosquitoes and malaria.[10]

Dwight Furness took a close personal interest in the hotel. His eldest son, Dwight Rodgers Furness, used his amateur photography skills for a series of promotional images of the hotel and its surroundings. Published as postcards, these photos offer us an insider's view of the hotel's history, though the quality of their composition and printing is nowhere near as high as that achieved by professional photographers of the time, one of whom—Winfield Scott—lived just down the road at Las Tortugas.

Scott, the official photographer for the Mexican Central Railway, was actually something of a business rival to Furness. After he settled in Ocotlán in 1901, Scott—who was almost certainly the first to advertise the climate on Lake Chapala as the "best on earth"—bought lakeshore property (Las Tortugas) and tried to establish his own hotel and Inland Sea Boating Club, with rowboats, sailboats and houseboats.[11] In a curious twist of fate, Scott, despite not taking the promotional photos of Hotel Ribera, was appointed the hotel's manager in 1919 by then-owner Enrique Langenscheidt. Scott remained there for a couple of years, before moving to Chapala to manage the Hotel Arzapalo.

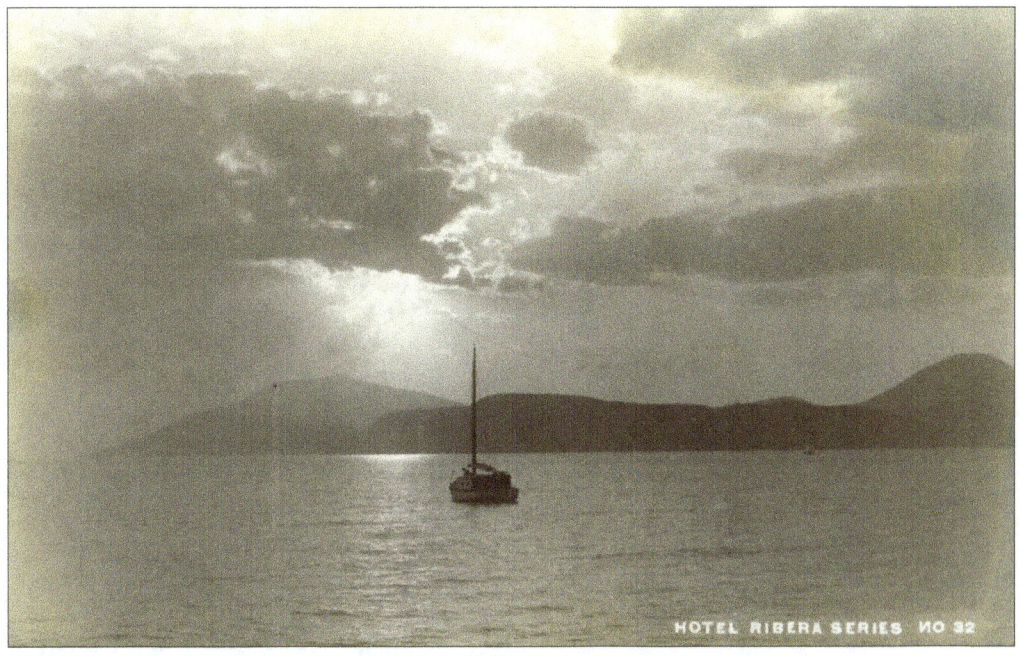

6.5. *Atmospheric shot of Lake Chapala, c. 1907. D R Furness.*
This view, taken from close to the Hotel Ribera, looks west to the hills behind San Pedro Itzicán and Mexcala, two lakeshore villages mid-way between Jamay and Chapala.

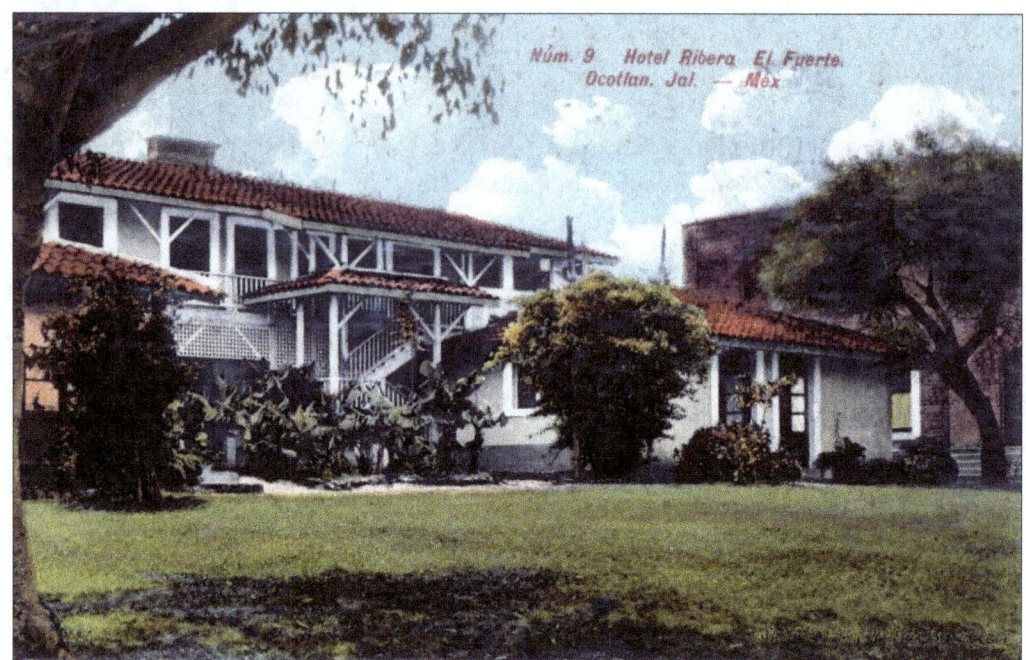

6.6. Hotel Ribera, El Fuerte, Ocotlán, c. 1907. D R Furness ; Alba y Fernández.
This particular card was mailed by the distinguished engineer, historian and academic José López Portillo y Weber, whose former home in Guadalajara is now a museum.

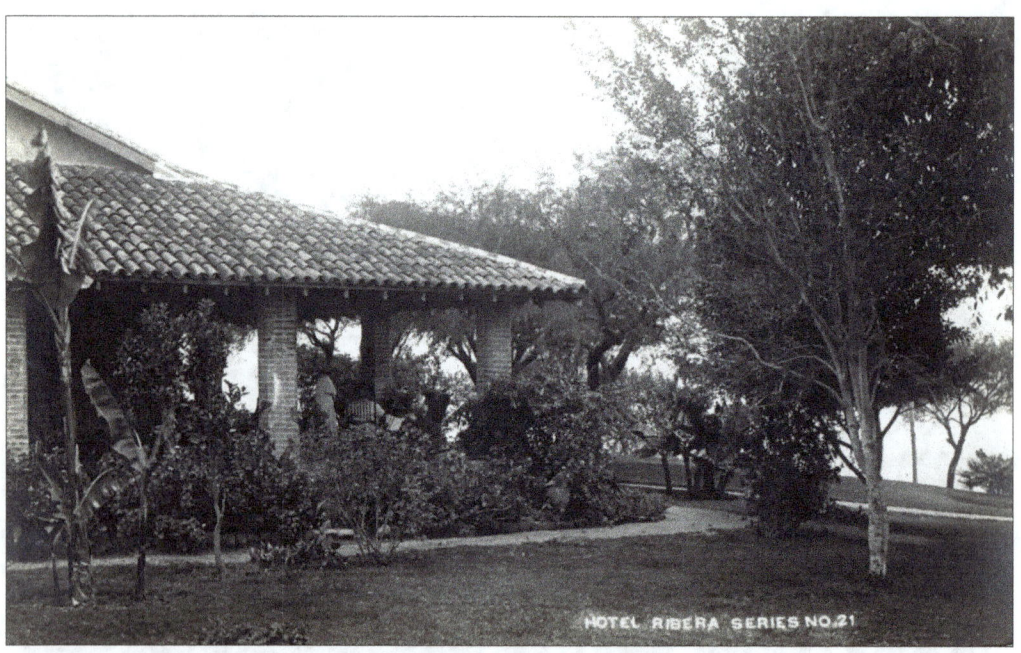

6.7. The hotel's covered terrace overlooking the lake, c. 1907. D R Furness.
Hotel guests could lounge in lawn chairs or hammocks, or be more active and take advantage of the hotel's recreational launches, sailboats, rowboats and horses.

Scott's work appeared in several guidebooks, including *Campbell's New Revised Complete Guide and Descriptive Book of Mexico* and *A Tour in Mexico*. By 1903, Scott had a catalog of 2486 Views of Mexico.[12] The following year two of his Lake Chapala-related photographs—showing Indian women spinning and weaving—appeared in *National Geographic*, illustrating an article by E W Nelson, whose own photograph of a square-sailed boat on Lake Chapala was also included.[13] These three images were the earliest photos of Lake Chapala to find their way into the pages of that august magazine.

The Hotel Ribera, surrounded by its well-maintained gardens, and situated on a bluff overlooking the lake near Ocotlán, had only 17 rooms when it opened in 1906. Rooms with full board cost no more than $2.00 a day.[14] Two well-heeled federal politicians—Vice-President Ramón Corral and Finance Secretary José Yves Limantour—stayed at the hotel overnight in March 1907 before taking a steamer the next morning to spend a few nights in Chapala.[15] Such patronage ensured that the hotel quickly became a highly desirable and popular destination, where all manner of politicians and celebrities would hob-nob over the next decade.

The *Jalisco Times* in 1908, calling the hotel "Mexico's best resort," drew readers' attention to the reduced excursion rates offered by the Mexican Central, as well as to the amenities on offer:

> Hotel Ribera has all modern conveniences: electric lights, American plumbing, tub and shower baths having hot as well as cold water connections. A Brown Swiss

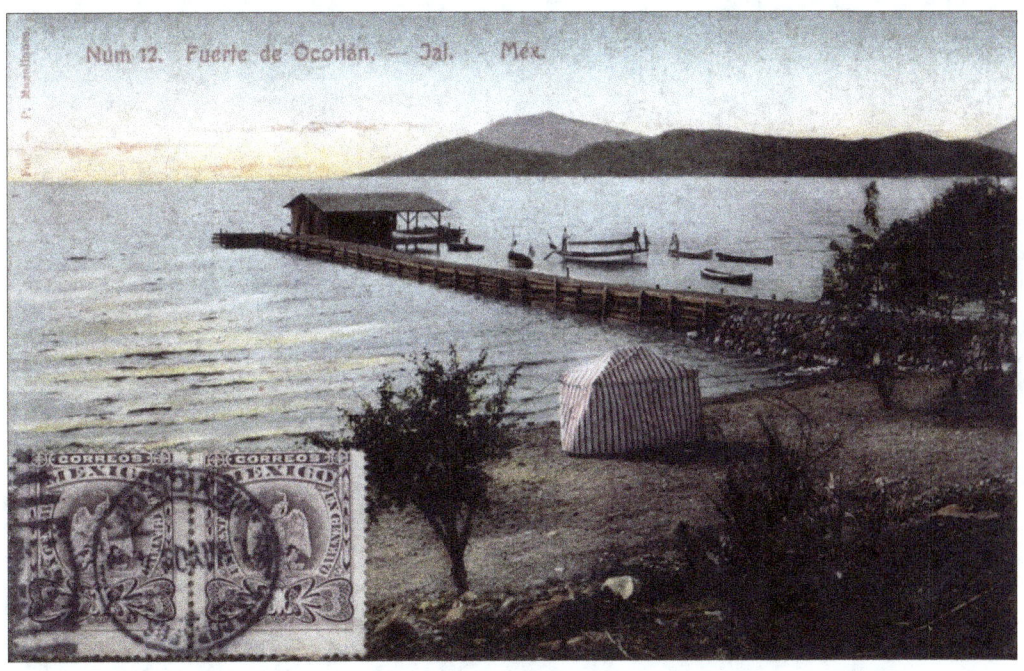

6.8. *The pier at Hotel Ribera, El Fuerte, Ocotlán, c. 1908. P Magallanes; Alba y Fernández Photographer Pedro Magallanes López had close ties via marriage to the extensive and influential Castellanos clan, former owners of this estate.*

herd furnishes milk, cream and butter for the table, and the fruits and vegetables are from the gardens adjoining the hotel. An experienced Chinese cook presides over the kitchen and the cuisine of the hotel is at all times excellent.... Climatic conditions throughout the year are perfect; the lake breezes that blow over Ribera Castellanos are refreshing, exhilarating, health-giving.[16]

The hotel had its own pier, and guests were encouraged to explore the lake by boat. The small village of Jamay, about seven kilometers east of the hotel, was particularly easy to get to. Its plaza boasts one of the largest and most extraordinary religious monuments in Jalisco. Standing thirty-five meters tall, and built between 1875 and 1879, it tells the story of Pope Pius IX. Few towns outside Italy and the Vatican can possibly boast papal monuments on this scale; perhaps none so much resembles the decoration on a wedding cake.

Veteran traveler writer Harry Franck included a photograph of the Hotel Ribera pier in his *Tramping through Mexico, Guatemala & Honduras: Being the Random Notes of an Incurable Vagabond*. Franck had arrived by boat from Chapala and stayed a couple of nights at the hotel, before taking the hotel launch across the lake to La Palma (chapter 4) to continue his herculean hike.

The hotel's growing popularity prompted Furness, in 1909, to add a two-story building with 60 more rooms.[17] Journalist Winifred Martin, who stayed later that year,

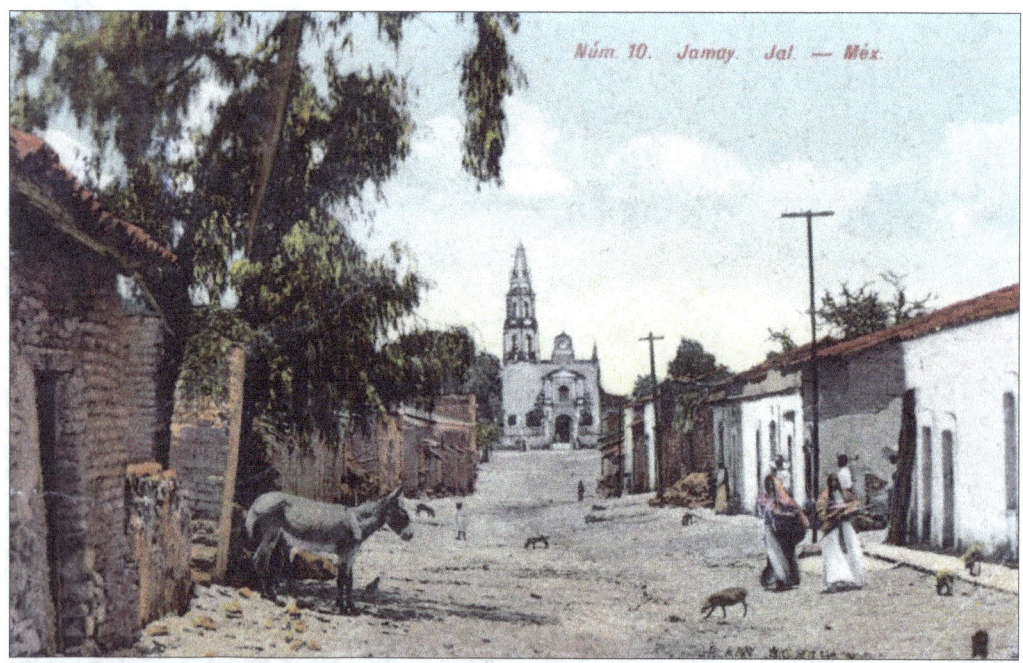

6.9. *Jamay, c. 1908. D R Furness; Alba y Fernández.*
This photo, taken by Dwight Furness, showing a donkey, dogs, children and village folk going about their daily activities, is a classic costumbrista *depiction of village life.*

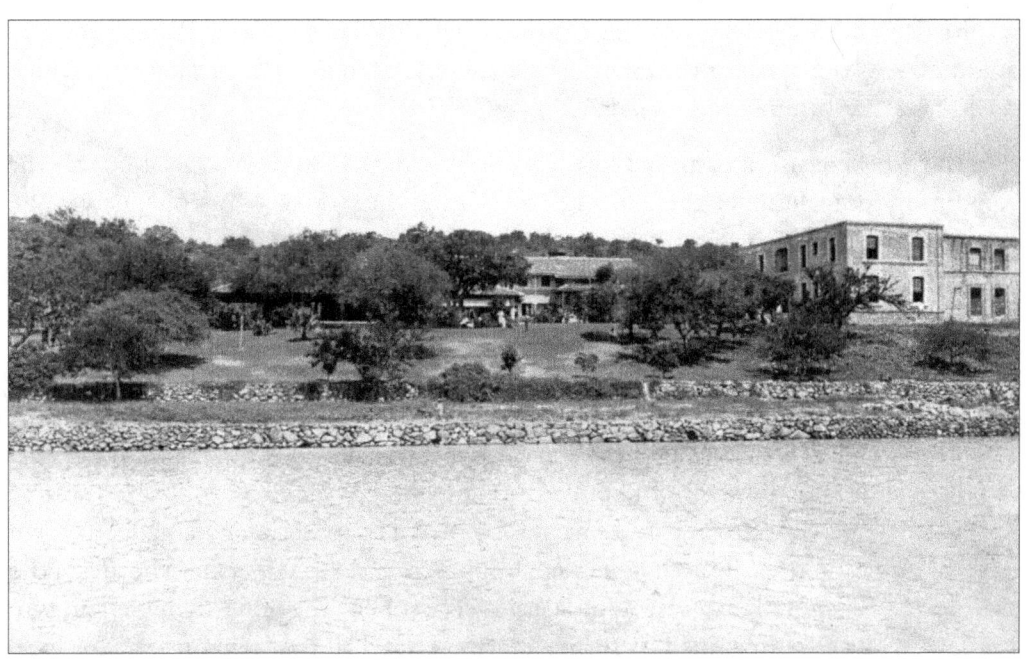

6.10. The hotel as viewed from the lake, c. 1910. D R Furness.
By this time the hotel had more than 75 rooms in operation, making it the largest single hotel on Lake Chapala.

remarked on the colorful flora and fauna and described the hotel as "picturesque and charming with lawns sloping steeply to the water's edge... the long rambling building with its tiled roof fits well into the setting."[18]

An advertisement for the hotel in June 1910, when George J Comedy was manager, quoted a letter from a recent guest, American inventor and writer Frederick Upham Adams: "I have sailed the lakes of four continents but have seen nothing to compare with the superb beauty of Lake Chapala."[19]

Juan Kaiser, the Swiss-born publisher of several of the postcards in this book, was equally impressed when he stayed at the Hotel Ribera in August 1911 to recover from a relapse of malaria.[20]

Two years later, during the Mexican Revolution, the Hotel Ribera Castellanos offered weekend trips by train from Mexico City to Ocotlán for $12.50 round trip, or from Guanajuato for $5.50 round trip.[21] When the unrest of the Revolution prompted Dwight Furness and his family to leave Mexico, he sold the hotel to Enrique Langenscheidt Schwartz, a prominent and well-connected German businessman living in Guanajuato.

In 1919, as the Mexican Revolution was finally drawing to a close, photographer Winfield Scott became manager. Scott later told some disturbing tales about his short time in charge at the hotel, and about how the owner's son, Enrique Langenscheidt Jr., had been murdered there that year by bandits.[22]

British novelist D H Lawrence enjoyed a brief stay at the Hotel Ribera in 1923, and used it as the basis for the Hotel Orilla, described in *The Plumed Serpent*, which he drafted that summer in Chapala:

> The hotel consisted of an old low ranch-house with a veranda—and this was the dining-room, lounge, kitchen, and office. Then there was a two-storey new wing, with a smart bathroom between each two bedrooms, and almost up-to-date fittings: very incongruous.[23]

A few months after Lawrence's visit, President Álvaro Obregón, accompanied by six ministers and several top government officials, stayed in El Fuerte (alongside Hotel Ribera) to convalesce following an illness. As reported in the *Los Angeles Times*, "A tiny fishing village located along the shores of picturesque Lake Chapala in the State of Jalisco is now to all intents and purposes the capital of Mexico."[24]

By this time, regular buses and a newly completed train station had made the town of Chapala far more easily accessible—enabling it to attract the weekend hordes—and the Hotel Ribera gradually lost popularity and clientele. The hotel struggled on into the 1930s, but never regained its former status. Today, all that remains of this once-grand lakeshore resort are a few ruined walls.

7

Chapala 1920–1940: opportunities and challenges

Chapala had 3142 residents in 1920, according to the national census that year. Several luxurious new villas had recently been completed, the Villa Montecarlo had been remodeled, and things were beginning to look up after the uncertain times of the Revolution. During Easter week, the town's hotels were almost fully booked, and two big dances were publicized, one at Hotel Arzapalo, and one at Hotel Palmera.[1]

The architect of Villa Niza, one of the grander new villas, was Guillermo de Alba, who had designed Hotel Palmera a decade earlier. Villa Niza, which makes the most of its lakeshore position, was built for Andrés Somellera, a prominent Guadalajara businessman.[2] The property immediately west of Villa Niza had been bought from

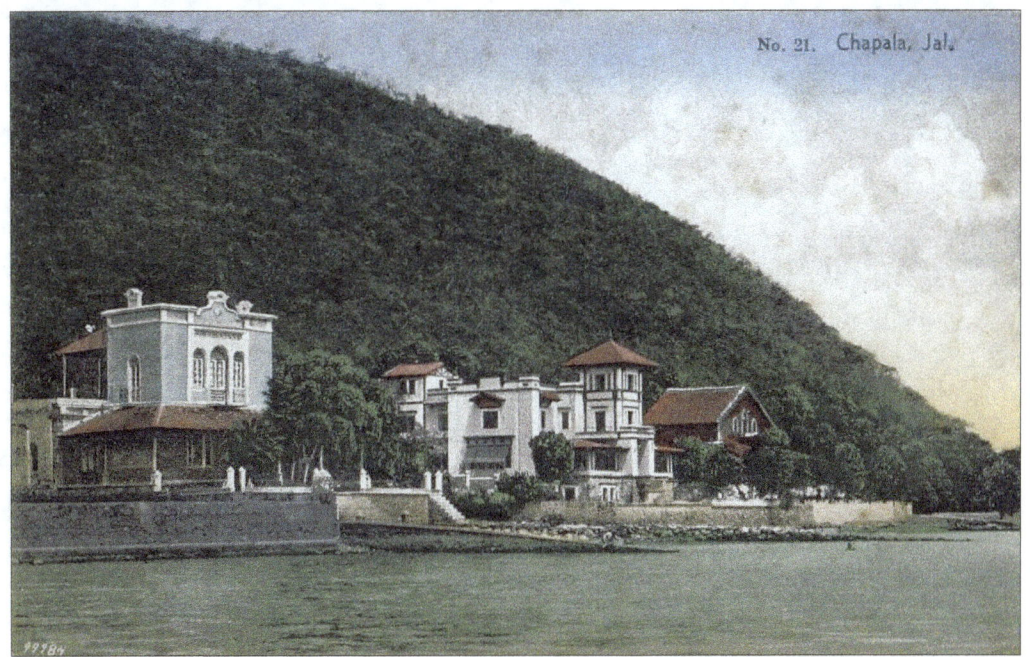

7.1. *Villas Elena (left), Niza and Josefina, c. 1923. Romero; S Altamirano.*
Villa Josefina and Villa Elena, from the 1890s, are older than Villa Niza, completed in 1919. Empty lots on this stretch of shoreline were infilled with more modern residences in the 1940s.

Guillermo de Alba in the early 1940s and developed by Enrique Anisz (1896–1946), a successful Czech-born businessman in Guadalajara, who helped get the massive Celanese Mexicana chemical plant established in Ocotlán.

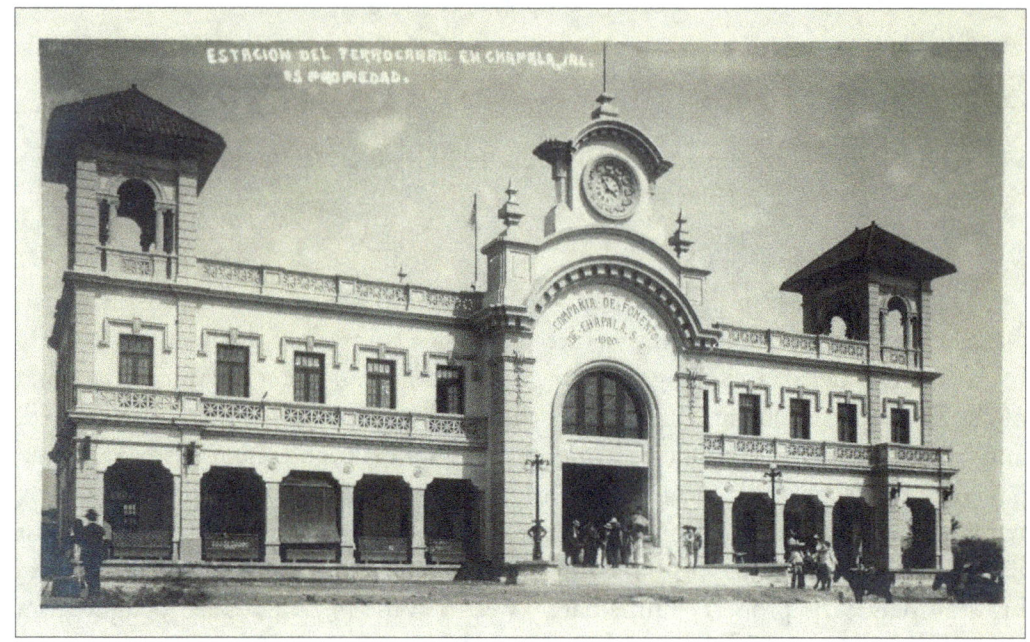

7.2. *Chapala Railroad Station, c. 1923. Romero?*
The station, designed by Guillermo de Alba, opened in 1920. Christian Schjetnan intended the iconic station building to be the hub of a major tourist development; the plans also included a luxury hotel, yacht club and private residences.

Chapala Railroad Station

Guillermo de Alba's crowning triumph was the Chapala Railroad Station which opened in 1920. It marked the culmination of years of work by Christian Schjetnan on behalf of Compañia de Fomento de Chapala (Chapala Development Company), and heralded a new period of optimism as regards tourism.

When Norwegian entrepreneur Paul Christian Schjetnan (1870–1945) first became involved with the Chapala Railroad project, he had absolutely no idea how long the political unrest in Mexico might last, making his decision to proceed with such a grandiose scheme, despite the obvious challenges, all the more remarkable. Schjetnan hired a young Norwegian, Birger Winsnes, as his chief engineer, to be assisted by Guadalajara engineer Juan José Barragán, the brother of modernist architect Luis Barragán. They managed to complete the 26.3-kilometer (16.2-mile) branch line from La Capilla, on the Ocotlán-Guadalajara mainline, to Chapala in three years.

Schjetnan and the Chapala Development Company also launched a passenger steamship on the lake—by remodeling an abandoned ship into the double-decked *Viking*, which could carry 200 passengers—as well as a second vessel, the *Tapatía*, for freight.

The official inauguration of the Chapala Railroad and the Chapala Railroad Station took place on Thursday 8 April 1920. On board the eight-car train, which was given a rousing send-off from Guadalajara at about 9.00am, were some 250 fashionably attired members of Tapatío high society. After a change of train at La Capilla, the Chapala train pulled into the magnificent new station in time for a tour of the building before lunch at the Hotel Palmera.

Regular daily rail service began a few days later. Initially, the train made two daily trips each way, but this was later reduced to a single daily journey. In 1920 the round-trip fare from Guadalajara for a Sunday excursion to the lake cost 5 pesos ($2.50) first class; second class tickets were half that price.[3]

The political upheavals seemed to have come to an end, it finally looked like there were more settled times ahead, and expectations ran high. Sadly, for both Schjetnan and the town, the Chapala railroad never did become profitable. Making matters still worse, there was growing competition from automobiles and buses for passengers headed to and from the lake.

The death knell for the Chapala Railroad came in August 1926 when exceptionally heavy rains swelled the lake to the highest level ever recorded in the twentieth century. The iconic station, built right on the beach, was flooded to a height of more than a

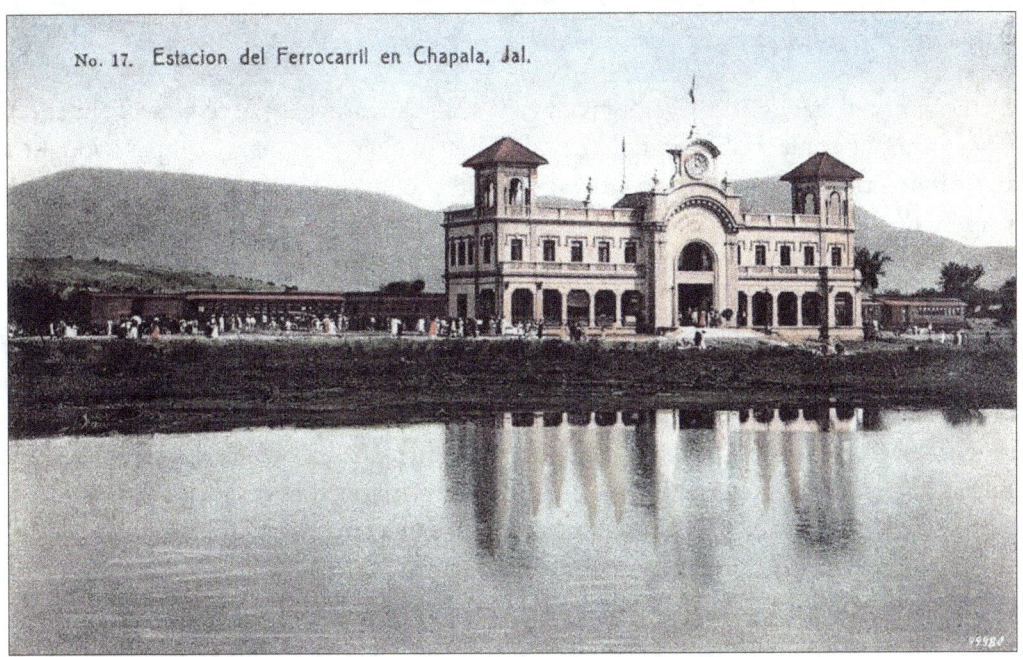

7.3. *Chapala Railroad Station, c. 1923. Romero?; S Altamirano.*
The Chapala Railroad had two locomotives (#25 and #26), three first-class passenger cars with plush red velvet seats, three second-class cars with plain wooden benches, and several extra wagons for baggage and freight. When this photograph was taken, the station was still in service, as evidenced by the passengers milling about on the platform and the train.

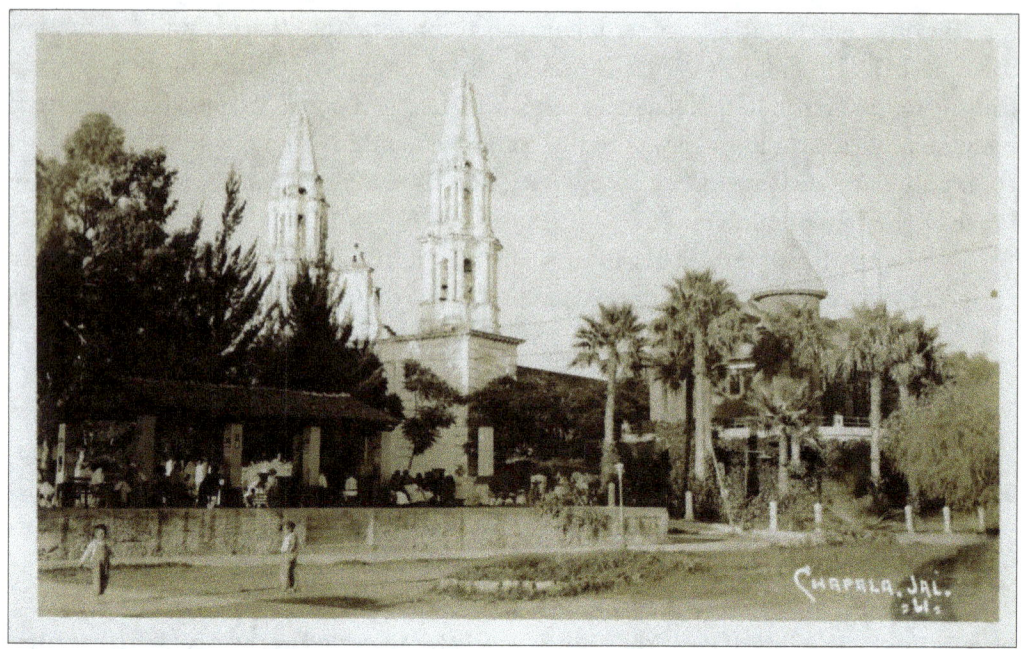

7.4. *Lakefront bar, c. 1925?*
This popular lakefront bar—originally known as Pavilion Monterrey—was later known, following the death of its patrón, *as Cantina de la Viuda Sánchez.*

meter; railroad tracks disappeared from view and train service had to be suspended. A few months later, after labor complaints, the Chapala Development Company sought a court injunction to prevent the confiscation of its property and goods. The Chapala–La Capilla Railroad closed down, its offices and stations were shuttered, and the town of Chapala was set back a decade.

Challenges for tourism

In the same year the Railroad Station opened, Guillermo de Alba had become a partner in Pavilion Monterrey, a lakefront bar in a prime location, only meters from the beach, between the Hotel Arzapalo and Casa Braniff. The co-owner of the bar was José Edmundo Sánchez.[4] Regulars at the bar included American poet Witter Bynner, who first visited Chapala in 1923 in the company of D H Lawrence and his wife, Frieda. Bynner subsequently bought a house near the church.

When de Alba left Chapala for Mexico City in 1926, Sánchez and his wife—María Guadalupe Nuño, credited with inventing sangrita as a chaser for tequila—ran the bar on their own. After her husband died in 1933, María continued to manage the bar, which then became known as the Cantina de la Viuda Sánchez (Widow Sánchez's bar).

Coincidentally, both Sánchez and de Alba were keen and skilled photographers. Unlike de Alba, who apparently never commercialized his photos, Sánchez sold hundreds of his own picture postcards from the bar, which had *"tarjetas postales"* emblazoned proudly across an exterior wall. Sánchez was a prolific photographer and his images provide interesting insights into local life. As well as photographing hotels, villas and scenic views, Sánchez documented local families and fishermen and their humble rustic homes. The earliest Sánchez photographs are believed to date from about 1915. Among his more noteworthy images are several taken during the floods of 1926, when all low-lying areas of the town were under water.

The 1926 floods did not damage only the Railroad Station. The unprecedented high level of the lake also damaged many of the town's older villas, some of which had been built perilously close to the shoreline. Downtown Chapala was flooded, with the water rising well above the elevated sidewalk in front of the Hotel Arzapalo and lapping against several chalets. The flooding near Ocotlán had far more disastrous consequences: twenty-five men, women and children were drowned.[5]

The following year, an even more horrific death toll resulted near La Barca when bandits derailed and set fire to a passenger train, headed for Mexico City, that was packed with people who had spent Holy Week at Lake Chapala. The event was an escalation in the Cristero War (La Cristiada) which had begun the year before in response to anti-clerical laws. The alleged leader of the bandits was El Catorce. The hundred-plus victims on 19 April 1927 included the eldest daughter of former President Obregón.[6] The tragedy heralded several more years of uncertainty for tourism at Lake Chapala.

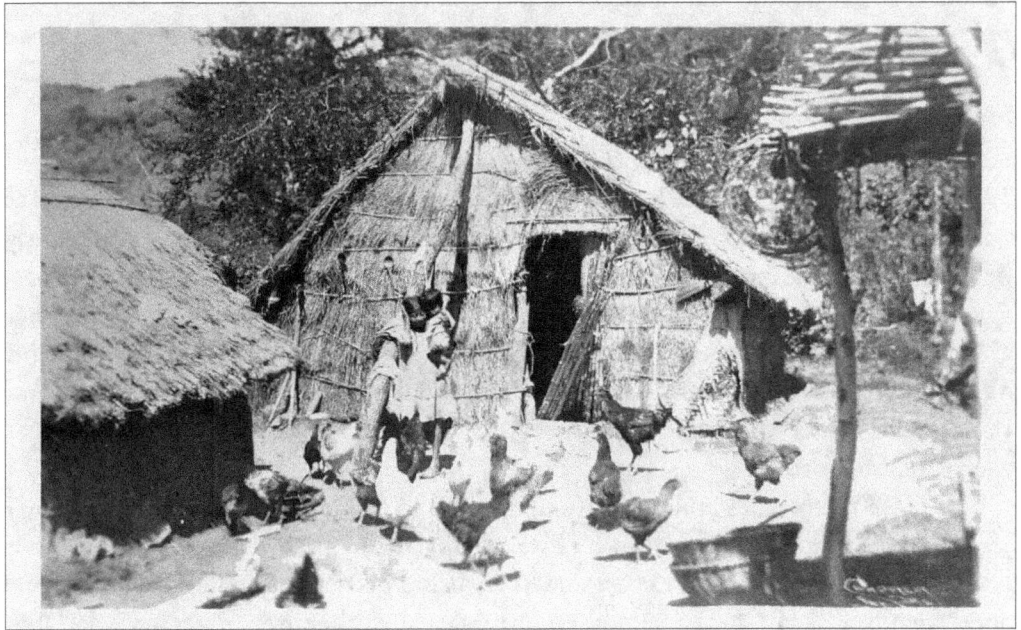

7.5. *Family scene, c. 1930? J E Sánchez.*
This card, mailed to Los Angeles in 1935, had this humorous observation about the hut: "Its construction is simple but well designed & possesses no glass... shatter proof." The sender added that all auto traffic in Chapala ceased at eight o'clock.

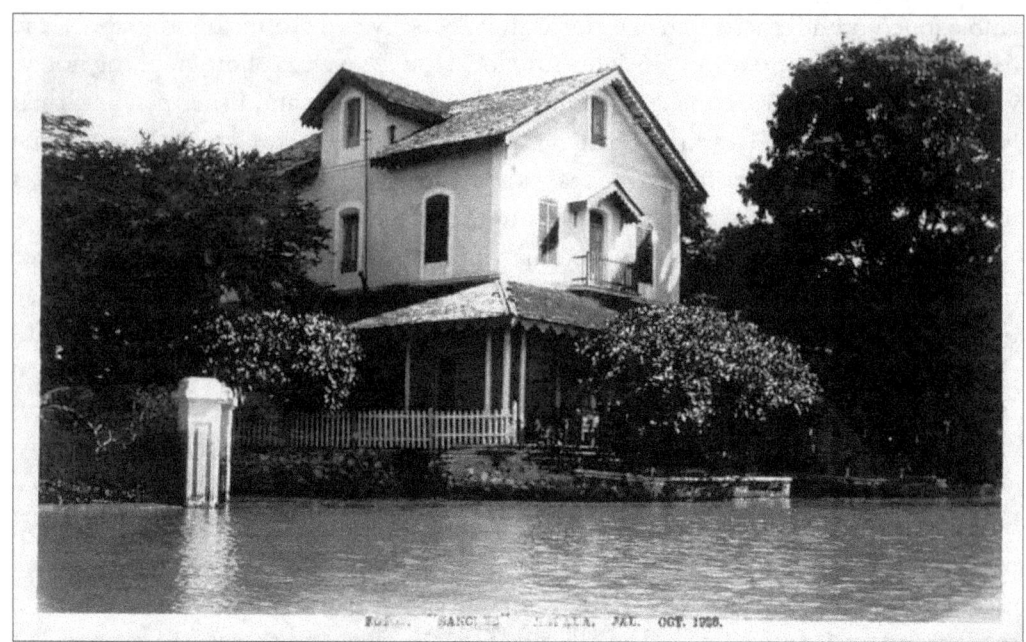

7.6. Casa Capetillo, October 1926. J E Sánchez.
In October 1926 the lake was still dangerously high. Following Manuel Capetillo Sr.'s death in 1922, Casa Capetillo had passed to four of his children, including María Elena, who had married Norwegian railroad engineer Birger Winsnes. The house was rented at the time of the photo by Eduardo Collignon Stephenson (son of the owner of Villa Ana Victoria) and his wife, María de la Peña Arias; they had lost their 10-year-old daughter, Ana Elena, to typhoid only two months earlier.

In order to reverse the trend, a concerted campaign to attract tourists was begun in 1934, spearheaded by hotelier Ramón Nido, owner of the eponymous hotel in Chapala.[7]

The Hotel Arzapalo remained a popular hotel into the 1920s and 1930s, mainly because of its prime location. In May 1923, when novelist D H Lawrence and his wife, Frieda, rented a house in Chapala, their traveling companions—poets Witter Bynner and Willard Johnson—stayed at the Hotel Arzapalo for more than two months. Shortly after they left, Antonio Mólgora (former manager of the Hotel Francés and the Hotel Palmera) took over the Hotel Arzapalo and ran it for about three years as the Hotel Mólgora.

By 1923 the Hotel Francés (formerly Hotel Victor Huber) had been bought by J Jesús Cuevas and renamed the Gran Hotel Chapala. Guests over Easter 1923, when it was fully occupied, included Dr George Purnell and his daughter, Idella, who became good friends of D H Lawrence and his entourage when they arrived a few weeks later. The Hotel Chapala continued in service until the late 1940s.

Cuevas also acquired the Hotel Palmera in the mid-1920s and subsequently divided it into two independent hotels.[8] The northern wing, bought by Luis Cuevas, became the Hotel Niza and operated into the 1940s. The southern wing was purchased in the late 1920s by Ramón Nido and his wife, Sara Fregoso, who reopened it as the Hotel Nido in 1930.[9]

In the 1930s, Villa Montecarlo became a popular choice for private groups seeking upscale hospitality. The villa had been remodeled in 1918 into a most impressive building, Italianate in style and grand in concept, set amidst beautifully landscaped gardens. In 1932 the Club Alemán (German Club) of Guadalajara drove out to the Montecarlo for a banquet; two years later, delegates attending a Banking Convention in Guadalajara had a meal there.[10] In 1935, Jalisco State governor Everardo Topete invited a large number of accredited diplomats to lunch at Villa Montecarlo. Among the guests were the US Ambassador to Mexico, Josephus Daniels, and his wife, who enjoyed the local specialty, caldo michi, as well as mariachi music, a jazz band and folkloric dancing.

Among the more outrageous tourism proposals of the 1930s was a suggestion, by a foreigner whose name (perhaps fortunately) has been lost to history, that the two central blocks of Chapala—including all three of the main hotels, as well as Casa Capetillo and Villa Ana Victoria—be expropriated and replaced with a large public plaza and a single luxury five-story hotel with swimming pool and tennis courts. Fortunately, wiser heads prevailed—at least on that occasion—and this "absurd and ill-intentioned" proposal was totally rejected.[11]

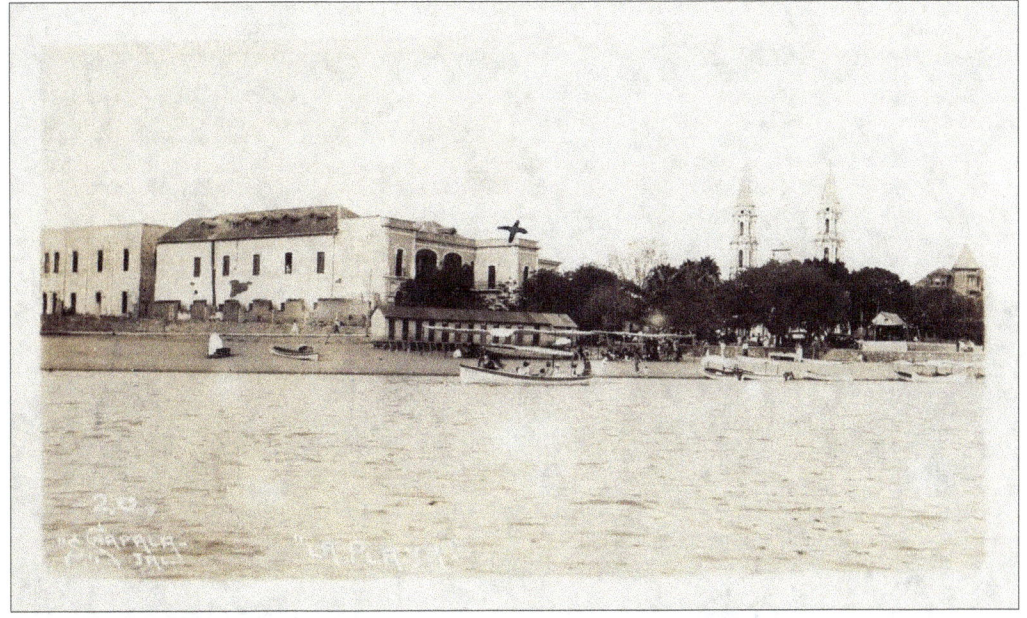

7.7. *Hotel Palmera (left) and Hotel Arzapalo, c. 1920. J E Sánchez.*
The 1920s were fashionable times in Chapala; bathing huts in front of the hotel provided privacy for guests to change into their bathing suits far from prying eyes. This card was mailed to California in July 1923, only a few days after D H Lawrence and his wife left Chapala for New York. The sender added an 'X' to mark his own room.

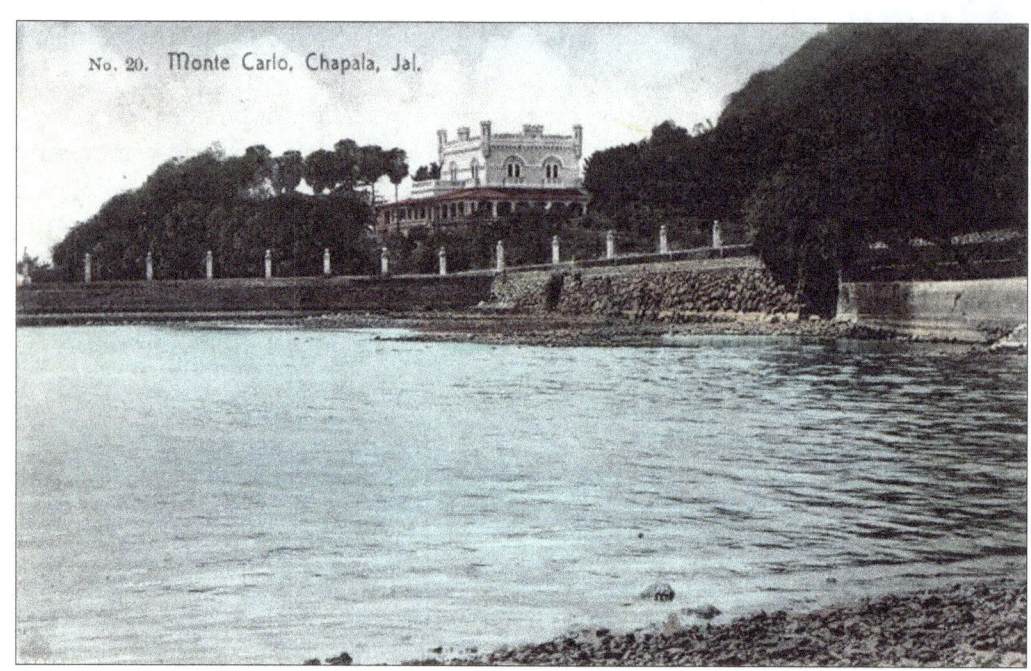

7.8. Villa Montecarlo, c. 1923. Romero?; S Altamirano.
The potential of this site was first recognized by Norwegian-born Englishman Septimus Crowe. Aurelio González Hermosillo later transformed it into this magnificent holiday home.

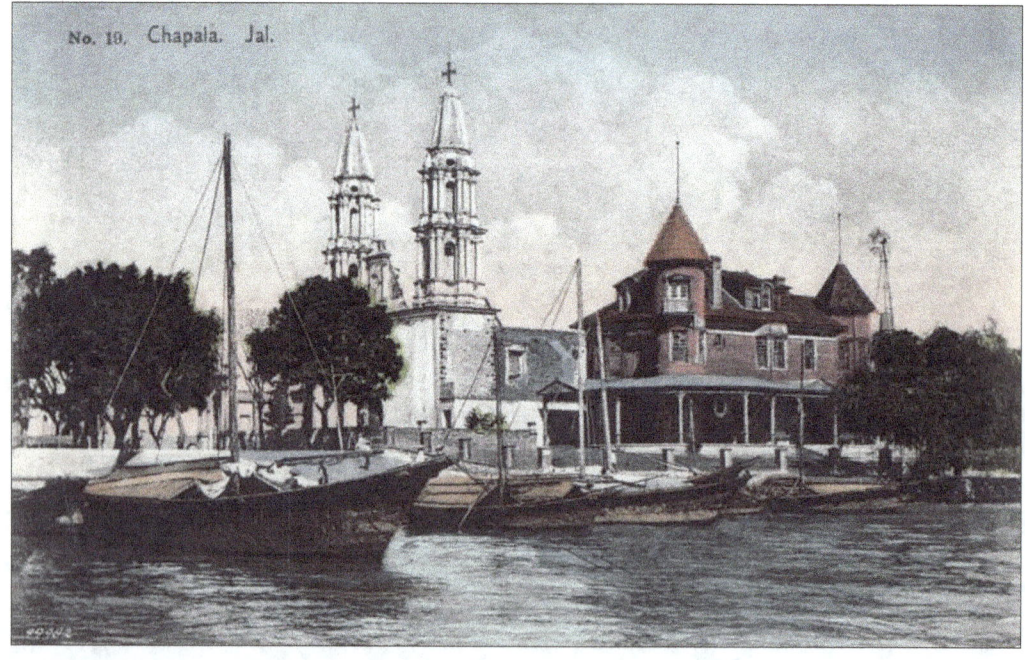

7.9. Casa Braniff, c. 1923. Romero?; S Altamirano.
Prior to being remodeld in the 1960s the two steeples of the imposing parish church of San Francisco were symmetrical and the same height.

D H Lawrence in Chapala

In 1923 the description of Chapala in *Terry's Mexico Handbook*, the popular tourist guide, convinced English author D H Lawrence, then staying in Mexico City, that he simply had to see the town and lake for himself. Lawrence and his wife, Frieda, rented a single-story village home in Chapala from the beginning of May to early July, not far from Casa Braniff, on what is now Calle Zaragoza. The street was known at that time as Calle de la Pesquería (Fishing Street) because it was where local fishermen repaired their nets and strung them out to dry.

Casa Braniff was the elaborately decorated residence begun by Guadalajara lawyer Luis Pérez Verdía in 1904, which became known as Casa Braniff after it was purchased by Mexico City industrialist Alberto Braniff a few years later. The house remained in his family until 1942.

The quixotic design of Casa Braniff was perfectly encapsulated by American poet Witter Bynner, who first saw it in 1923 while walking back to his rooms at the Hotel Arzapalo from the house rented by Lawrence: "We came by a pretentious Victorian brick villa, in the convulsive style of architecture—bay windows, turrets, cupolas, stained-glass windows."[12]

What was Chapala like in 1923? The message on the back of a Casa Braniff card mailed from Chapala to New Mexico in 1923 explained that the sender had paid 50

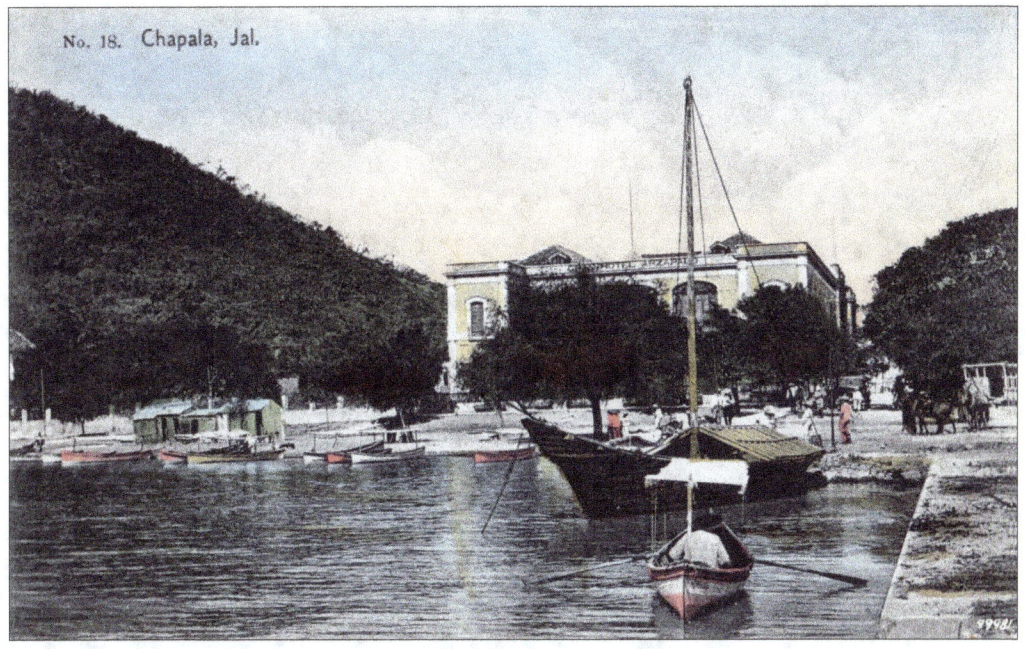

7.10. *Hotel Arzapalo, c. 1923. Romero?; S Altamirano.*
Poet Witter Bynner rented rooms here for several weeks in 1923. Bynner returned regularly to Chapala, wrote some of his best work in Chapala, and bought a home near the hotel in 1940.

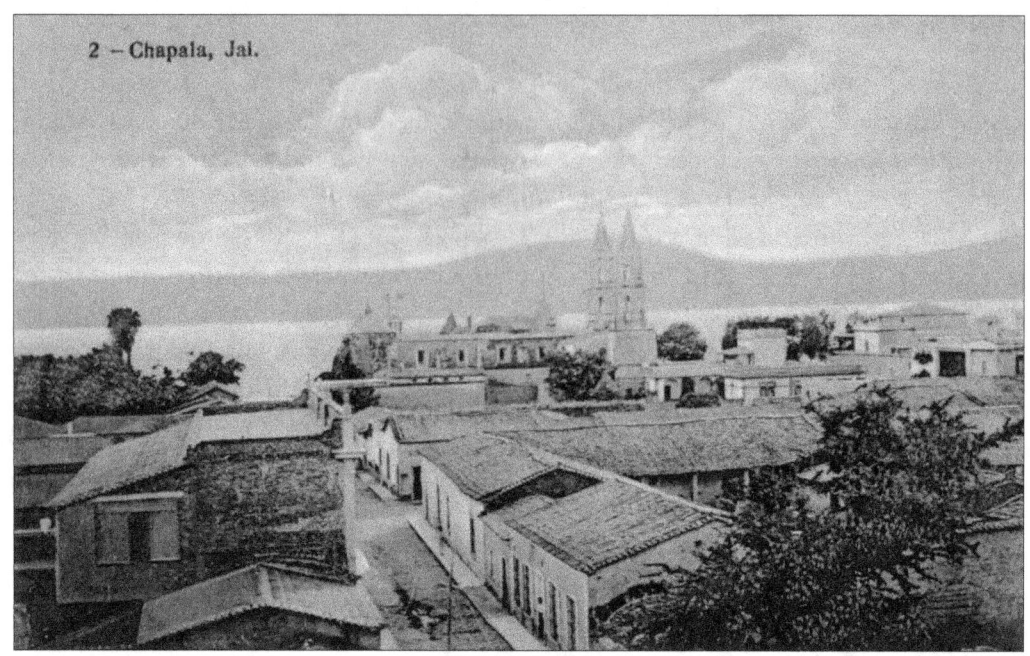

7.11. Calle del Ex-Convento, Chapala, c. 1910. B de Alba.
The single-story homes in this view along Calle del Ex-Convento (now Juárez) are similar to the property rented for several months in 1923 by D H Lawrence on Calle de la Pesquería, the next street to the east.

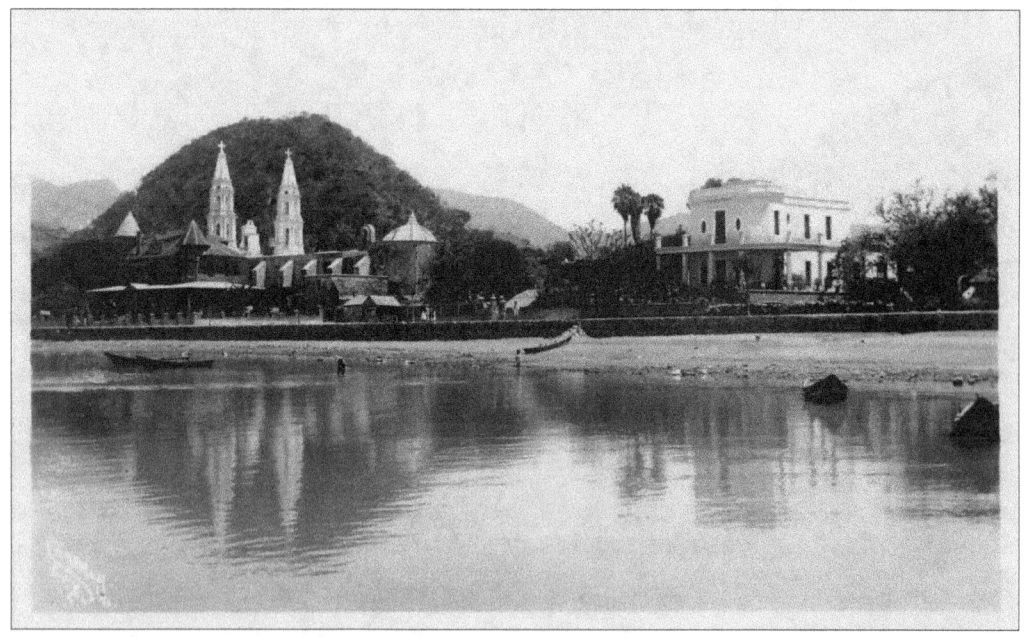

7.12. Villa Robles León, c. 1930. J E Sánchez.
Several aspects of Villa Robles León, including its rounded sides, were apparently inspired by the shape of a boat.

cents for the bus fare from Guadalajara, and preferred Chapala to any of the beach resorts in California or to Palm Beach, Florida. The daily rate at the best hotel, including three meals a day, was $1.50.

Within hours of first arriving in Chapala, Lawrence declared the village 'paradise.' Writing a few days later to friends in Taos, he offered this succinct description of Chapala:

> There are camions—Ford omnibuses—to Guadalajara—2 hours. Chapala village is small with a market place with trees and Indians in big hats. Also three hotels, because this is a tiny holiday place for Guadalajara.[13]

Each morning, the novelist proceeded to sit under his favorite tree on Playa Chacaltita, east of Casa Braniff, hard at work on the first draft of *The Plumed Serpent*. The rented house was the basis for Kate's living quarters in his novel:

> Her house was what she wanted; a low, L-shaped, tiled building with rough red floors and deep veranda, and the other two sides of the patio completed by the thick, dark little mango forest outside the low wall. The square of the patio, within the precincts of the house and the mango trees, was gay with oleanders and hibiscus, and there was a basin of water in the seedy grass. The flowerpots along the veranda were full of flowering geranium and foreign flowers.[14]

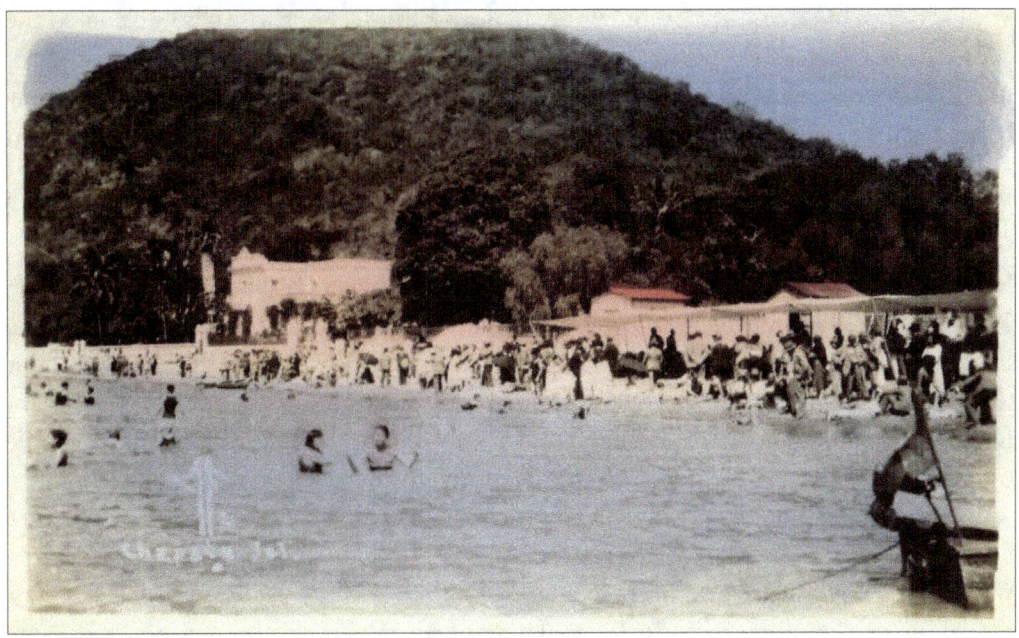

7.13. *The main beach at Chapala, c. 1935? México Fotográfico.*
The beach between Hotel Arzapalo and Villa Aurora (formerly Casa Galván), the two-story house on the left, teems with well-dressed tourists. To the right of Villa Aurora, Casa Capetillo is completely hidden by the massive tree.

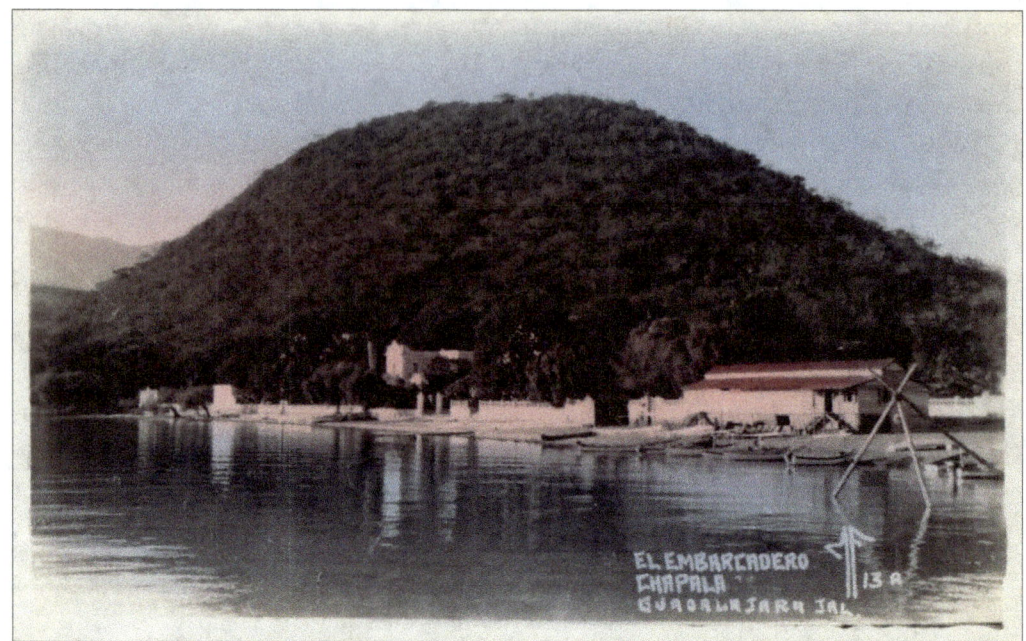

7.14. The main beach at Chapala, c. 1935? México Fotográfico.
Fishing and tourist boats are pulled up on the beach. The publisher of this card was México Fotográfico, a Mexico City firm active from the 1920s to the 1970s.

Lawrence liked his privacy and wrote in near solitude. For those who welcomed the company of others, the main beach by the Hotel Arzapalo attracted huge throngs of tourists on weekends and holidays. Though their precise date is unknown, two crudely colorized cards, published by México Fotográfico, show this beach—both with and without tourists—at a time when the lake level was relatively high.

The 1930s

Several of the buildings fronting onto Playa Chacaltita were built or remodeled in the 1930s by engineer-architects who were graduates—as was Guillermo de Alba—of the Escuela Libre de Ingenieros in Guadalajara. These talented individuals included Pedro Castellanos Lambley, Ignacio Díaz Morales and, most famous of all, Luis Barragán. Díaz Morales and Barragán combined to design Villa Robles León, readily identifiable by its highly distinctive rounded sides. Apparently inspired by a boat, its front boundary wall has long, thin bricks arranged as a series of 'V's, to form a geometric wave design. Sadly, the building, which lost direct access to the beach when Paseo Ramón Corona was built, is now vacant and in disrepair.

Many of the older villas in Chapala changed owners in this period, and some changed name. Chalet Paulsen was renamed Villa Paz in the late 1920s when it was bought by Ignacio E Castellanos and his wife, Paz González Rivas.[15] Castellanos was the son of poet Esther Tapia de Castellanos and Ignacio E Castellanos, former owners of the prime agricultural land near Ocotlán that had been developed as the Hotel Ribera

Castellanos. Villa Tlalocan, which had come into the possession of Manuel Cuesta Gallardo (1873–1920), a godson of President Díaz, was subdivided in the 1930s by his descendants into two large sections, respectively to the north and south of the current highway. The Cuesta Gallardo family had extensive business interests ranging from agriculture and irrigation to the hydroelectric power station at Juanacatlán; they were the prime movers behind the deplorable draining of the eastern third of Lake Chapala in the first decade of the twentieth century.

Cerro San Miguel and villas to the west

For day-trippers and tourists alike, the short hike up Cerro San Miguel, to get the view over Chapala and across the lake, remained a popular activity in the 1930s. This short climb was made even easier in 1931 when Guillermo de Alba was commissioned to improve the path and build various look outs and shelters from where the panoramic views could best be appreciated.[16]

The views from the summit revealed just how large Chapala had become. To the west, an almost unbroken line of villas, some of them with significant artistic and literary connections, extended well beyond Villa Tlalocan.

A prime example is Villa Virginia, built by Victor and Elizabeth Hunton, which dates back to 1905. Even in the 1920s, Villa Virginia had no electricity or running

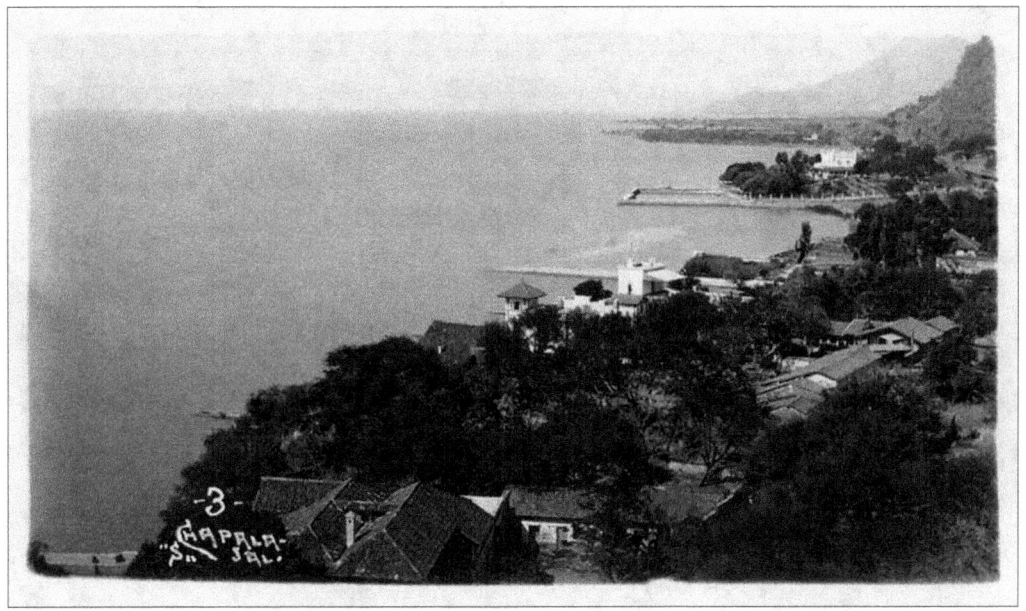

7.15. *View west from Cerro San Miguel, c. 1931. J E Sánchez.*
The improved access up Cerro San Miguel may have prompted de Alba's former business partner, José Edmundo Sánchez, to carry his camera and tripod up the hill to take this view showing the rapid spread of villas to the west of Villa Tlalocan, the building in the foreground. The white building near the center of the image is Villa Elena.

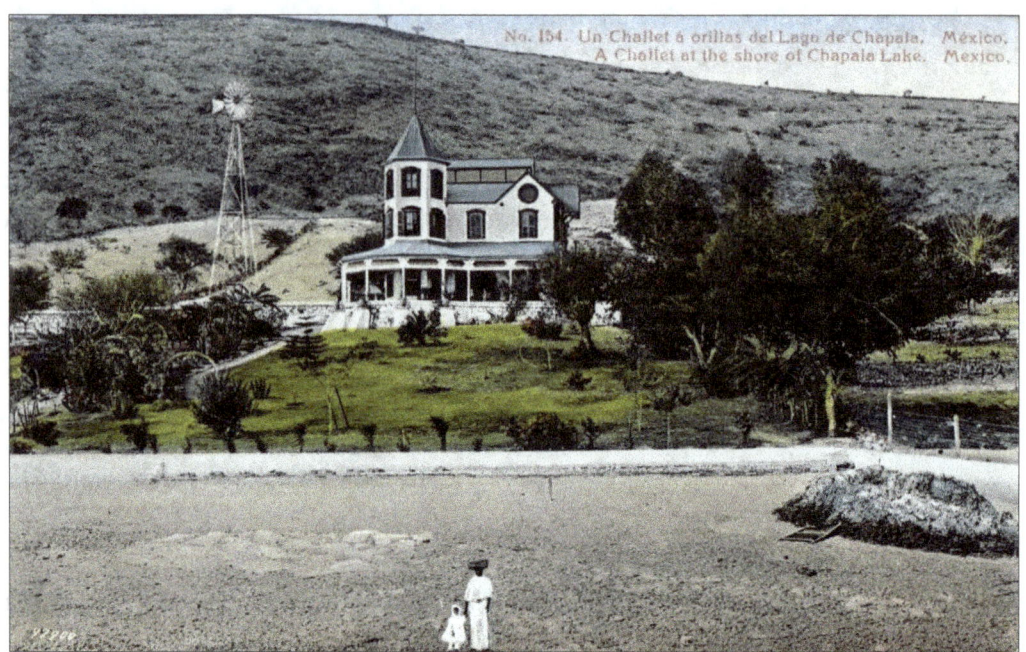

7.16 Villa Virginia, c. 1930. F Martin.
The gardens of Villa Virginia and many other lakefront properties have been greatly extended over the years by reclaiming parts of the beach whenever the lake level is low.

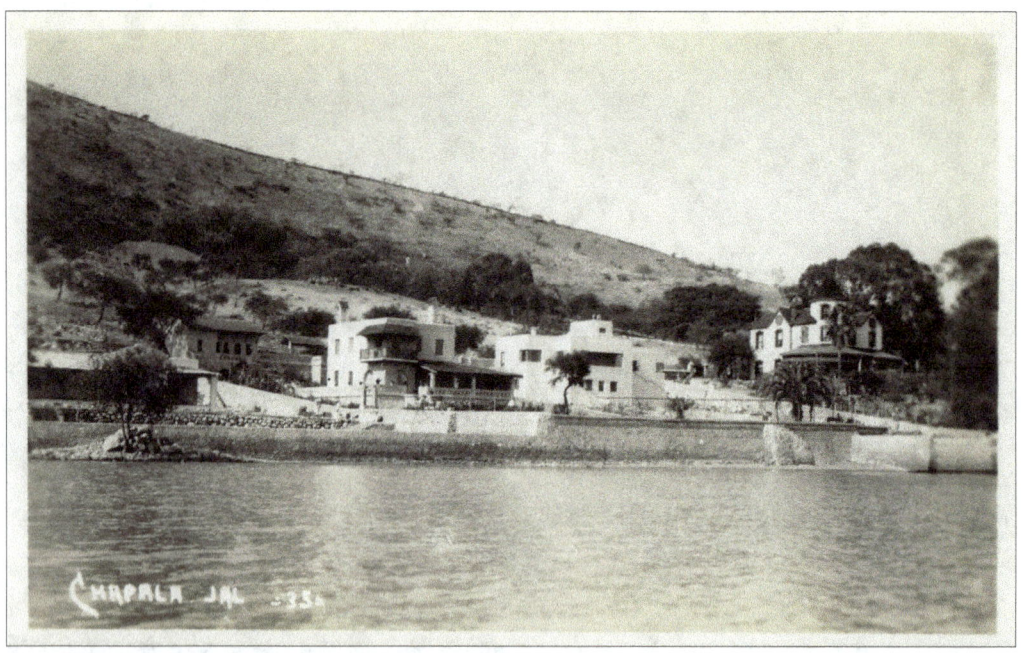

7.17. Villas west of Villa Virginia, c. 1930?
As Chapala spread west, new buildings were erected alongside the old. Three modernist-looking homes stand in stark contrast to the elaborate Porfirian style of Villa Virginia.

water, and breakfast would not be served until each member of the family had gone down to the lake to fill a demijohn with water.[17] The house displays some similarities in style with Casa Braniff (designed by George King) and Villa Reynera; King (or one of his associates) may have had a hand in all three projects.

Villa Virginia became known to most locals as Villa Negra or Casa Negra, following a terrible accident in 1909 when one of the Huntons' daughters and her governess were drowned while swimming in the lake. Two younger children, Pepe and Isabel, were educated in the UK, but retained close ties to the Chapala area for the remainder of their lives. In 1956, Isabel and her husband opened a motel, the Posada Rancho Santa Isabel, at the eastern edge of Ajijic.

After Victor Hunton died in about 1930, his wife continued to live in Villa Virginia, tending her garden, one of the finest in the area. Strong-willed, opinionated, and sometimes obstinate, she was described by Neill James in *Dust on my Heart*. Mrs Hunton was a good friend of poet Witter Bynner, and has the unusual distinction of being the inspiration for characters in two full length novels. Sybille Bedford, in *A Visit to Don Otavio*, transformed her into Mrs Rawlston, an elderly widow living alone in a "large, dark, ugly, disheveled house." Arthur Davison Ficke, who visited Bynner in Chapala, went one step further and used her as the basis for the title character of his only novel, *Mrs. Morton of Mexico* (1939), set entirely at Chapala. In the same novel, Ficke praised Widow Sánchez as a "very famous cook."

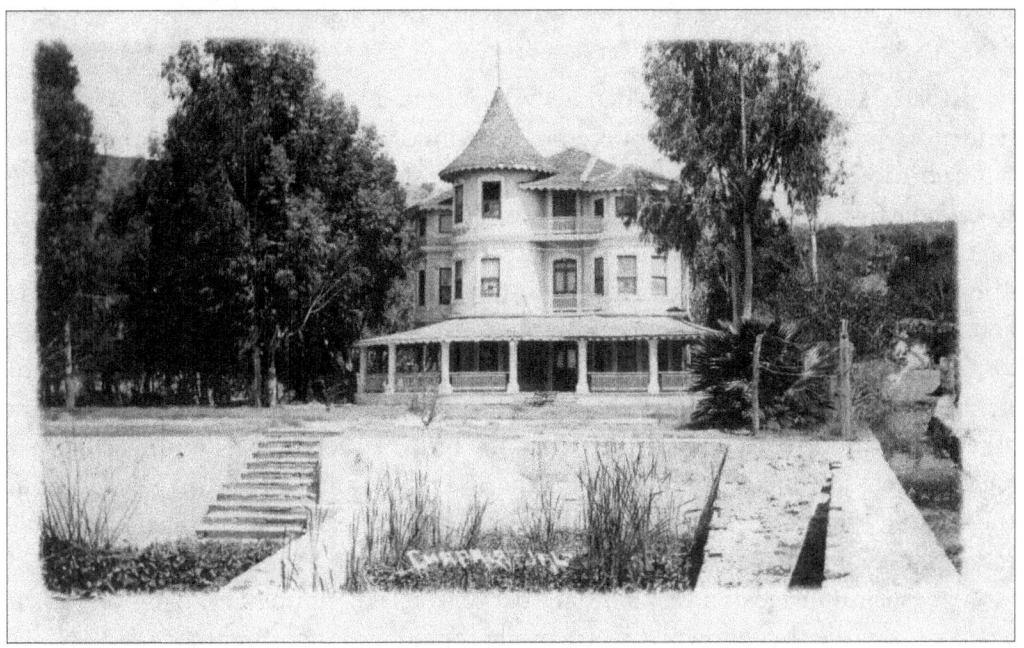

7.18. *Villa Reynera, c. 1925?*
This picturesque lakeside home inspired Zara Alexeyewa in 1925 to write two original ballets: Princess of the Moon *and* Nauollin, *first performed publicly half a century later.*

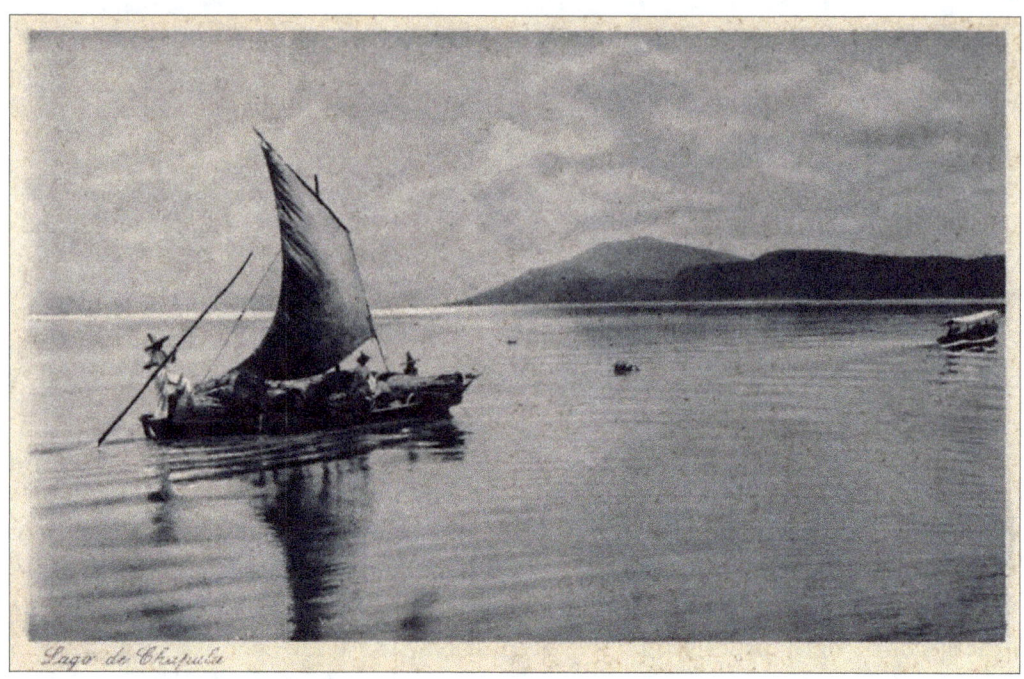

7.19. Boat on Lake Chapala, c. 1920. H Brehme.
This evocative photograph, taken in about 1920, was used for several postcards and was published in Modern Mexico *in 1943. Brehme's outstanding technique and composition captured all manner of scenes; some of his images are hauntingly beautiful, reminding us of a bygone age that we can never hope to regain.*

Broadly similar in style and date to Villa Virginia is Villa Reynera, an imposing, residence with high ceilings and numerous bay windows. Its ground floor rooms opened onto a broad covered terrace that hugged the lake side of the house. This is where the so-called Russian dancers—Zara Alexeyewa (born Eleanore Saenger) and her dancing partner, Holger Mehnen—lived, while preparing to perform in 1925 at the Degollado Theater in Guadalajara.[18] This was the beginning of their close association with Chapala and Ajijic that lasted the rest of their lives.

Zara and Holger were devotees of the Self-Realization movement headed by Swami Paramahansa Yogananda. After the funeral of her father in New York in 1929, Zara asked Yogananda to accompany her when she returned to Chapala with her mother and Holger.[19] The striking photograph of the Swami, standing on a broad-sailed boat in the middle of the lake, that is still regularly used in Self-Realization publicity materials today, was taken during this trip.

A beautiful image of a very similar boat on the lake (figure 7.19) had been taken a few years earlier by renowned German photographer Hugo Brehme (1882–1954), who visited Lake Chapala on several occasions.

8

Fishing and environmental change

Prior to 1910, large-scale haciendas controlled almost all the agricultural land along the lakeshore. The limited amount of land available to most families for producing food meant that the lake—with its abundant fish and fresh water—played a vital part in their lives. Even after haciendas were broken up, and some of their land redistributed to *campesinos* via *ejidos*, fishing remained a mainstay of the local economy, and fish remained a healthy, protein-rich source of nutrition.

The biodiversity of fish stocks in Lake Chapala decreased during the twentieth century. The lake once teemed with unique native fish; about one-third of the forty or so species now found in the lake have been introduced.[1] One native fish, popocha,

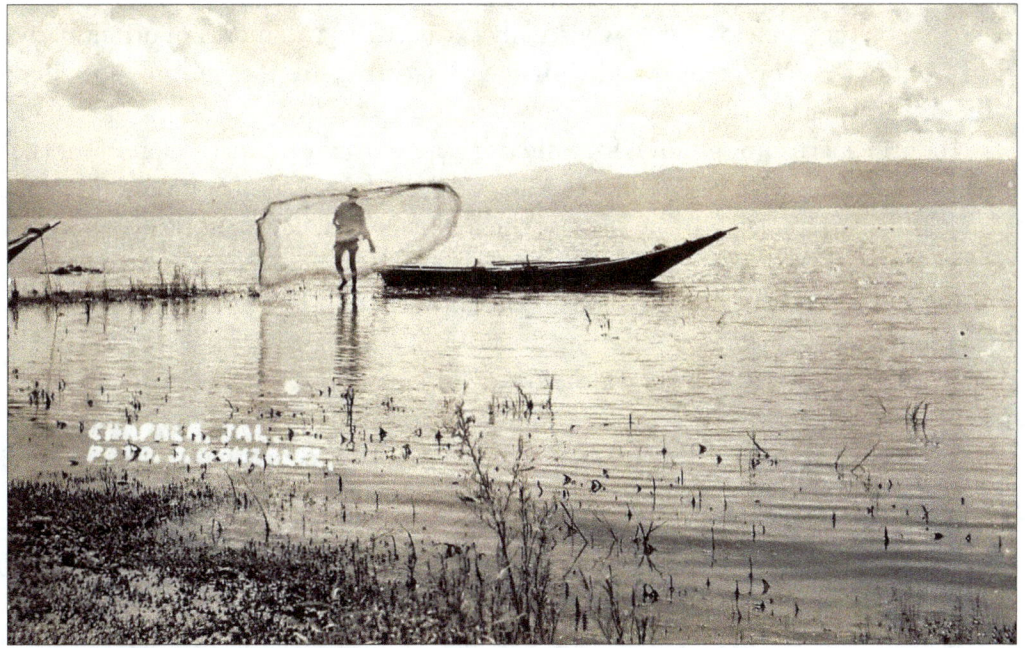

8.1. *Fisherman, c. 1945. J González.*
Close to the shore, a fisherman casts his atarraya *(circular cast net) while standing alongside a traditional* canoa, *built of rough planks, calked with rope and pitch, and powered by wind or oars. Newer* canoas *are fiberglass and have outboard motors.*

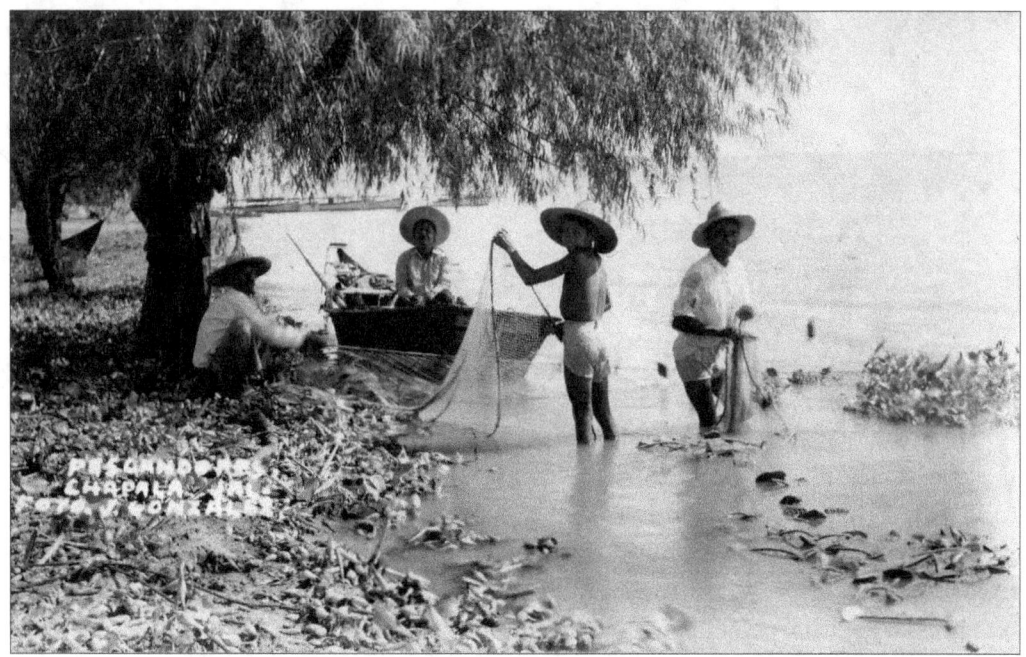

8.2. Fishermen, c. 1945? J González.
The atarraya *is well suited to netting fish in the shallow water close to the shore. Though safe and easy, it is not always the most productive.*

once sold by the canoeload, is now virtually extinct. The two most important native fish, from both a commercial and culinary perspective, are the multiple species of whitefish and charal.

The principal fishing grounds for whitefish were along the southern shore of the lake from San Luis Soyatlán to Tizapán el Alto and La Palma, as well as around Mezcala Island and Scorpion Island. The catch of the highly prized, delicate-tasting, whitefish peaked at 150 tons in 1946. Stocks of whitefish have declined dramatically since, due both to declining water quality and to the introduction of aggressive carnivorous carp that decimated whitefish eggs and fingerlings. The charal catch peaked in 1968 at over 3000 tons.[2] Surprisingly, biologists identified a new native species of charal in Lake Chapala—the Ajijic silverside—as recently as 2002.

Fishing at the lake had its own daily rhythm, remarked upon by Chicago-born Edna Mae Stark, a publicity agent for Grace Line, in the 1930s:

> Early morning unfolds a shadow picture of men hastening to the waterfront, scrambling into their battered boats and setting out for the catch. Midday lights up a scene in which mounds of fish appear along the shore glinting in the sun like piles of gleaming armor, and village streets are walled with nets stretched on poles like giant cobwebs hung with dew drops. And day fades out on interesting closeups of the villagers repairing old nets, or making new, their hands flying like shuttles over the shapeless mass of cords.[3]

Many fishermen had their thatched roof homes or storage huts very close to the shore. Some visitors found them interesting, even romantic, and admired the simplicity of their construction; others remarked on the evident disparities between these huts and the fine stone villas built nearby. British author Maud Pauncefote visited Chapala in about 1899 and was one of the few to comment on the pros and cons of fishing huts:

> Very picturesque are these Indian fishermen.... In that climate no fires are necessary, so their shanties are merely huts of adobe and thatch, adobe being a sort of clay plastering together a few wooden posts. Not an expensive style of building, surely, and about architecture they do not worry... one or, at most, two compartments make a house. Sleeping in the open air wrapped around by the serape, a striped, colored rug, is much in vogue among the men, and right they certainly are, as it is more healthy than those awful huts where... the pig, the hens, and most of the live stock share the house with the proprietor.[4]

Fishermen supplemented their diet by hunting ducks. The traditional method required patience, not gun shots. They first accustomed the ducks to swimming among dry hollow gourds floating in the lake. Then, with their heads camouflaged with gourds, they swam out and grabbed the ducks' webbed feet under water before they could take flight.[5]

The methods used to catch charal, the small silverlings, were equally ingenious, as explained in the 1940s by writing duo Dane Chandos:

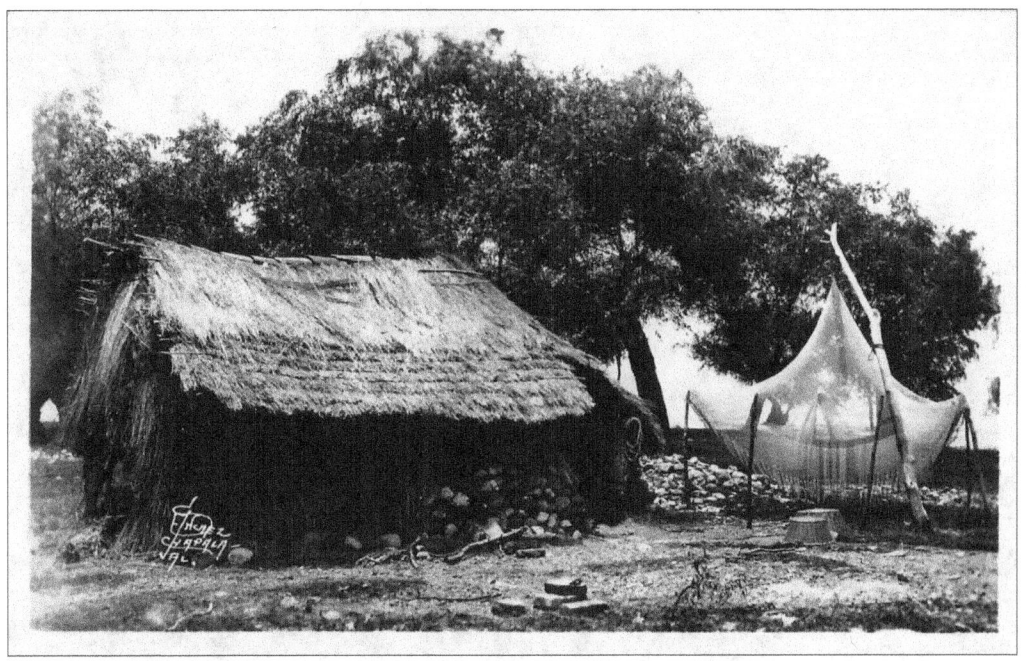

8.3. *Fisherman's hut, c. 1930. J E Sánchez.*
This atarraya, *extended between poles to dry, has a fine mesh designed to catch charal. Such nets could take several months to make. Nets for catfish and carp had a more open mesh.*

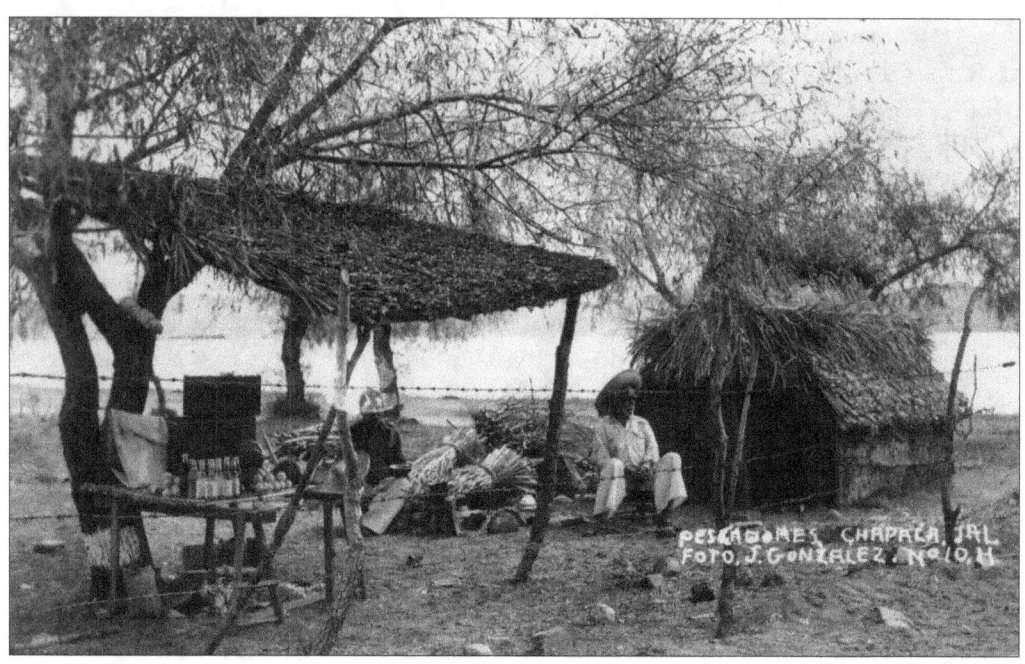

8.4. *Hut and drink stand, c. 1945? J González.*
Small stockpiles of firewood and thatching material are kept behind a barbed wire fence for protection against hungry horses or wandering cattle. These fishermen make a few extra centavos by selling drinks.

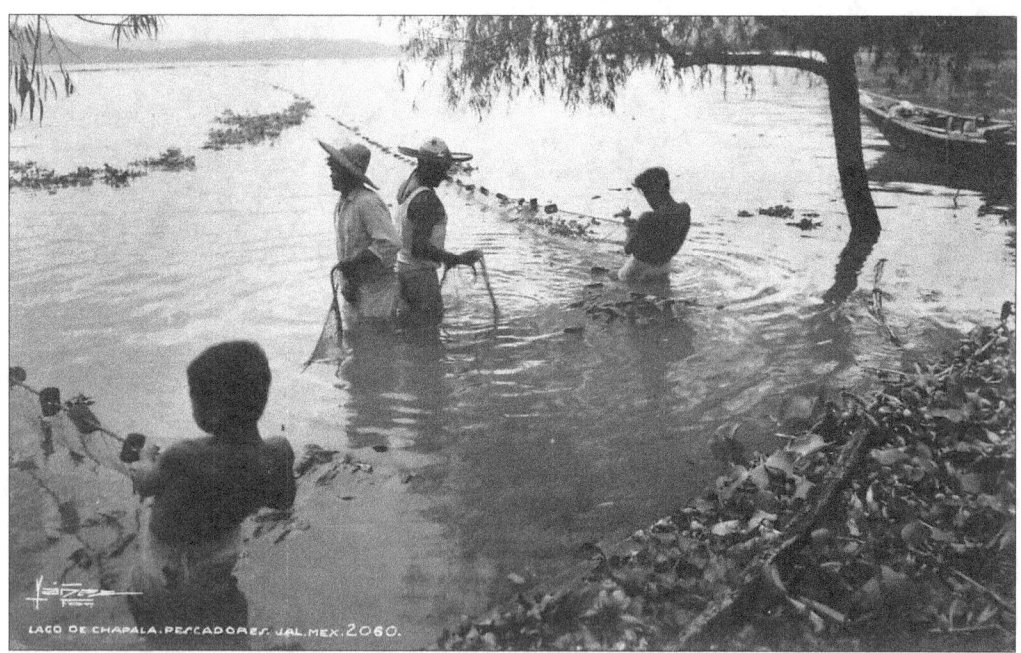

8.5. *Casting net, c. 1935. M Yañez.*
The use of large nets required an arduous and cooperative effort on the part of fishermen, though there were always some tasks that children could assist with.

All along the shore the fishermen have been building little promontories of rock, about ten yards apart and jutting a few feet into the lake. Now the whole shore is divided into neat compartments. These are very handy for those who fish with the atarraya, the circular hand cast net, for throwing it into one compartment will not disturb the fish in the next. Behind the fishermen's promontories are built little piles of dry dung, about one pile to every five or six compartments. As dusk falls they set light to these piles. They do not flame, but sparkle and glow and send up pillars of gray smoke.

— 'Yes, señor,' said an old fisherman in a shower of diminutives, 'the little smoke and the little fire attract the little charal.'[6]

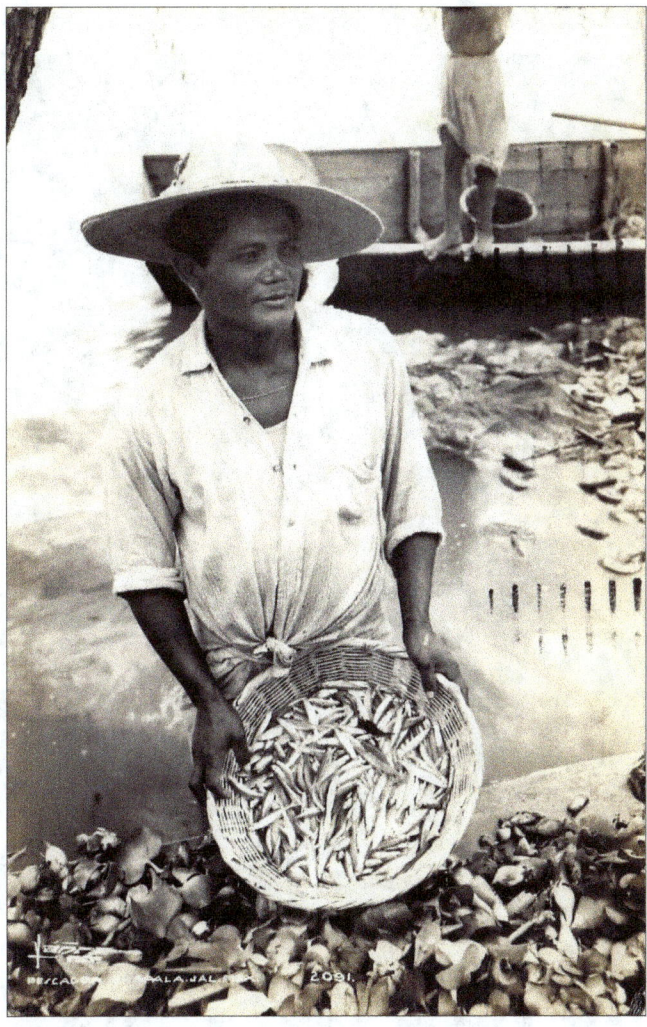

8.6. *Charales, c. 1935. M Yañez.*
Fisherman poses with a round basket full of freshly caught, still-quivering charales. Fried charales are a tasty and inexpensive local treat.

This system, utilizing bonfires to attract spawning females to shallow calm water protected by lines of rocks, may date back hundreds of years. Provided that no eggs or fry are disturbed, these charal farms (*ranchos charaleros*) can be highly productive. Moreover, the entire family is able to contribute to their maintenance and success.

Charales are very tasty, whether sun-dried or, as Dane Chandos described, fried:

> The charal is tiny, a sort of fresh-water whitebait, and if fried exactly like whitebait and served dry enough to be eaten with the fingers, charales are excellent. Dip them in mayonnaise, or tartare, or white sauce stung with English mustard, and see.... Twenty centavos will buy enough for three or four people. [7]

Large scale commercial fishing required much bigger nets than the hand-thrown *atarraya*. For charal, a *mangueadora* (a type of seine net) was used. They could be up to

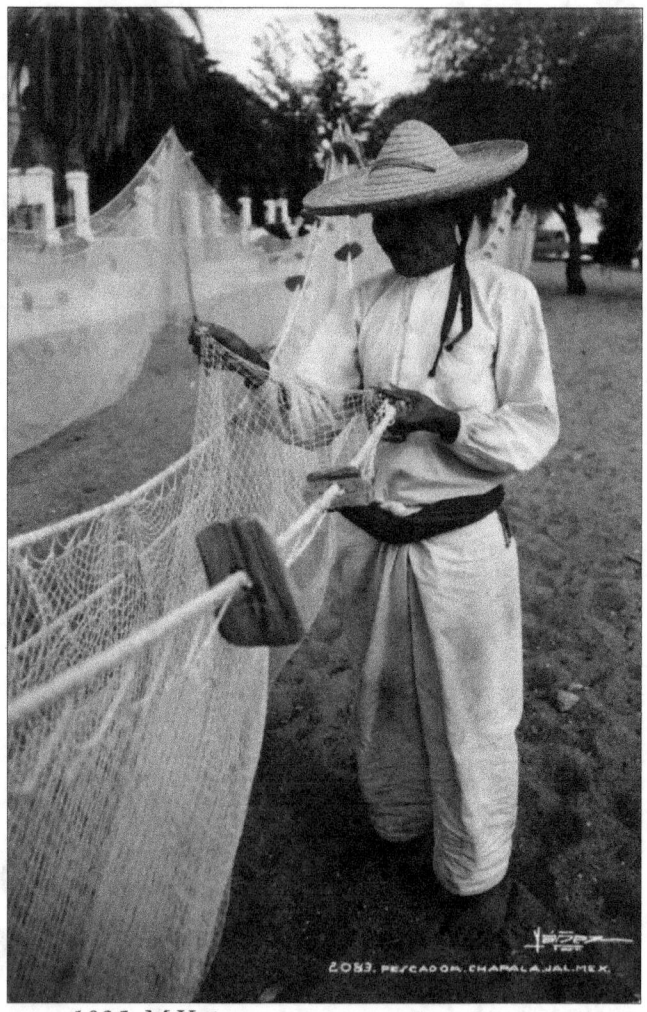

8.7. *Checking a net, c. 1935. M Yañez.*
Mexican photographer Mauricio Yáñez published several beautifully composed postcards in the 1930s of Lake Chapala fishermen going about their daily tasks.

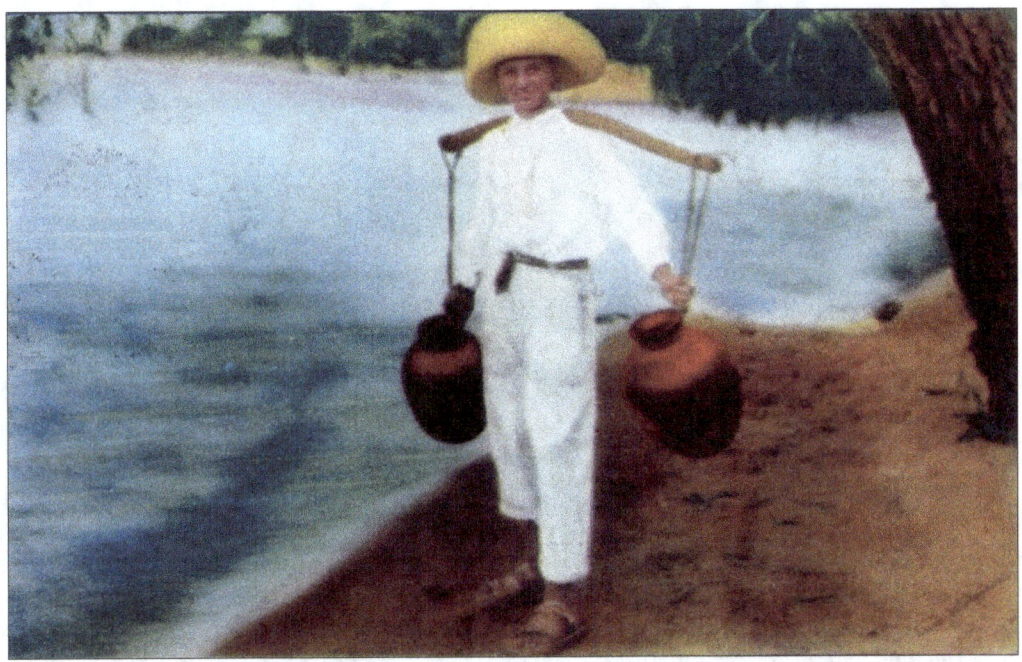

*8.8. Water carrier (*aguador*), 1937. L Márquez; Publicaciones Fischgrund.*
The costumbrista *appeal of this card, a colorized version of a photograph by Luis Márquez Romay, whose work was published in* National Geographic, *is enhanced by the young man's white cotton clothes, broad-rimmed sombrero and open-toed huaraches.*

200 meters (600 feet) long.[8] The *mangueadoras* used in the 1950s, made of thick cotton thread, were known as *redes penales* because many of them were made by prisoners in Guadalajara.[9] Nylon nets were introduced in the 1960s.

For larger fish, such as carp, gill nets (*redes agalleras*) were used, some of them 100 meters (300 feet) in length. These had wood, cork or plastic floats, and stones or rocks as weights. Prior to about 1970, they were normally made of cotton, often by the fishermen themselves. These nets were removed from the water daily to be cleaned, dried and repaired. Prefabricated nylon nets later became widely available.

Drying large nets required an extensive area of beach. Among the many significant adverse impacts of the rash of shoreline invasions that have occurred in the past century is the great reduction in the area available to fishermen for drying and mending their nets. Missing floats or weights and tears in the mesh, however small, require rapid replacement or repair. However long the nets, their drying, checking and repairing is an essential daily task.

Fish was not the only valuable commodity offered by the lake. Fresh water was also otherwise in limited supply. Prior to the 1940s most residents of Ajijic, for example, acquired whatever water they needed for domestic use from either the lake or the spring (Ojo de Agua) above the village. A small number of residents had their own wells. In the 1950s spring water was piped down to the main plaza, where it was stored in a

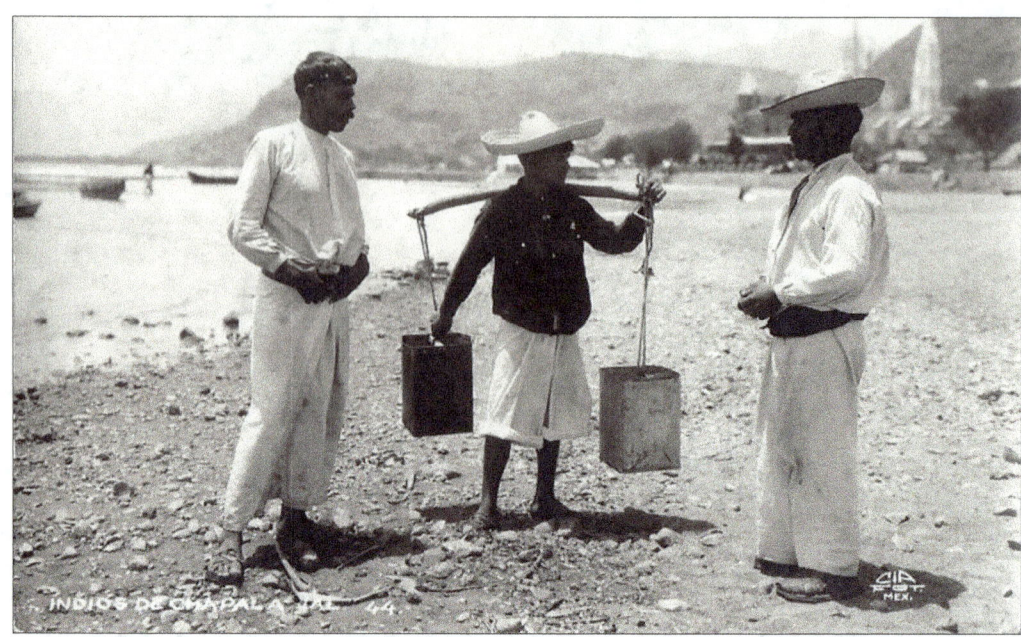

*8.9. Youthful water carrier (*aguador*) at Lake Chapala, c. 1945? Cia. Fotográfica Mexicana. Relatively few early postcards portrayed everyday life in Chapala.*

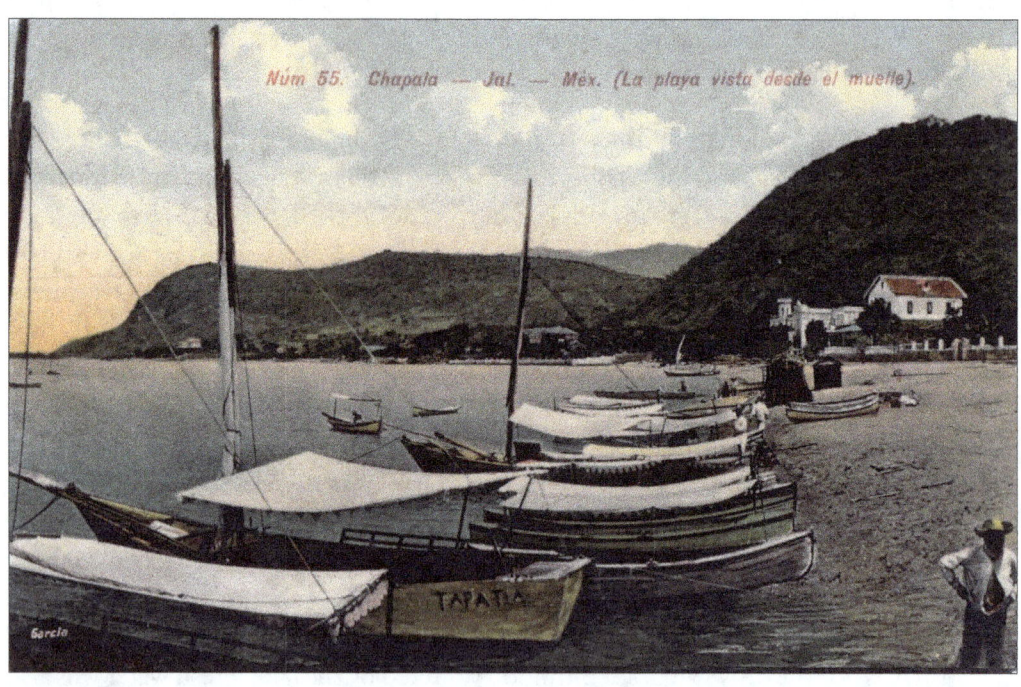

8.10. Canoas on Chapala beach, c. 1907? L V García; Alba y Fernández.
A portable set of wooden steps and the awnings over these canoas identify them as (primarily) tourist boats. From right to left, the residences are Casa Capetillo, Casa Galván, Chalet Paulsen and Villa Tlalocan, with Villa Montecarlo on the extreme left.

holding tank for public use. Getting water from the lake, though, was not as easy as it sounds, because of the lake's shallowness and silty floor.

As in many other parts of Mexico, at Lake Chapala professional water carriers hawked water around the villages. Foreign tourists, in particular, considered this practice to be quaint, charming and photogenic. Most carriers would balance two containers, either ceramic urns or old petrol cans, from a yoke across their shoulders.

The attire of the individuals portrayed on cards of water carriers is interesting in itself. In figure 8.9, for example, the *aguador*, white sombrero on his head, wears a dark long-sleeved shirt and long white pants rolled up to his knees, appropriate for wading into the lake to scoop up lake water. The two men in conversation with him are dressed almost entirely in white, with long-sleeved shirts and long pants. All three men are wearing plaited leather sandals (*huaraches*). While all-white cotton manta clothing later became something of a tourist attraction in indigenous communities, its use in earlier times was highly controversial. During the lengthy regime of President Díaz it was regarded as a sign of economic and social backwardness.

The wearing of "wide-flowing, pajama-like *calzones* which were tied crosswise at the waist and bound with red cotton sashes"[10] caused particular concern. From the end of the nineteenth century, muleteers and other travelers wearing *calzones* were prohibited from entering many larger towns and cities and were fined or made to change into long pants. In Sayula, for example, 1888 regulations mandated a $0.50 fine or eight days of community service for anyone wearing *calzones* on the plaza.

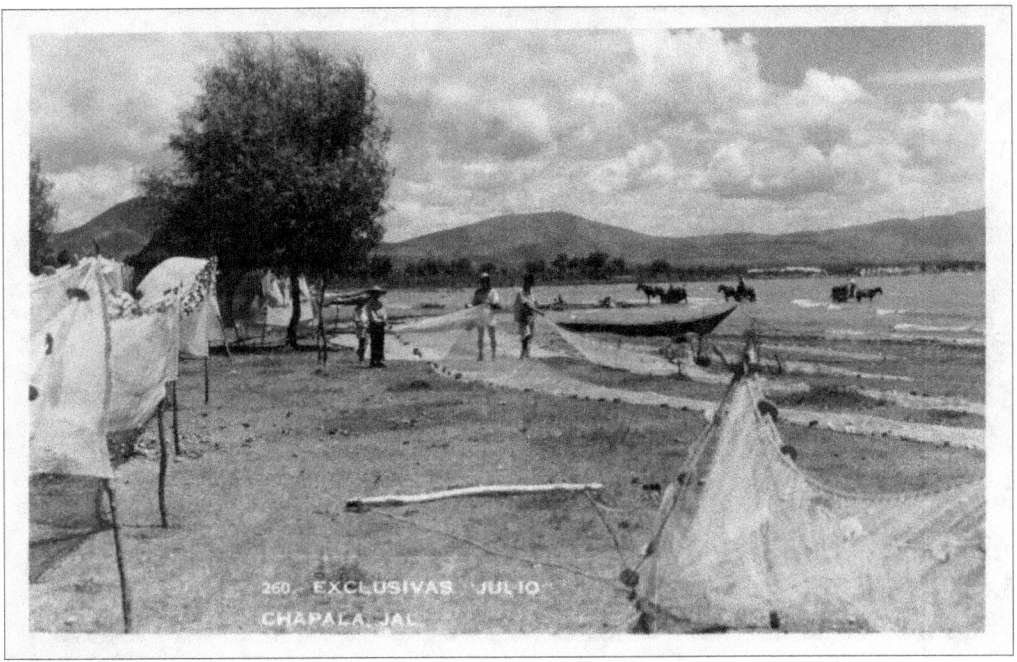

8.11. *Fishermen at work on the beach, c. 1940? Exclusivas Julio.*
Such aesthetically pleasing scenes have inspired numerous artists over the decades.

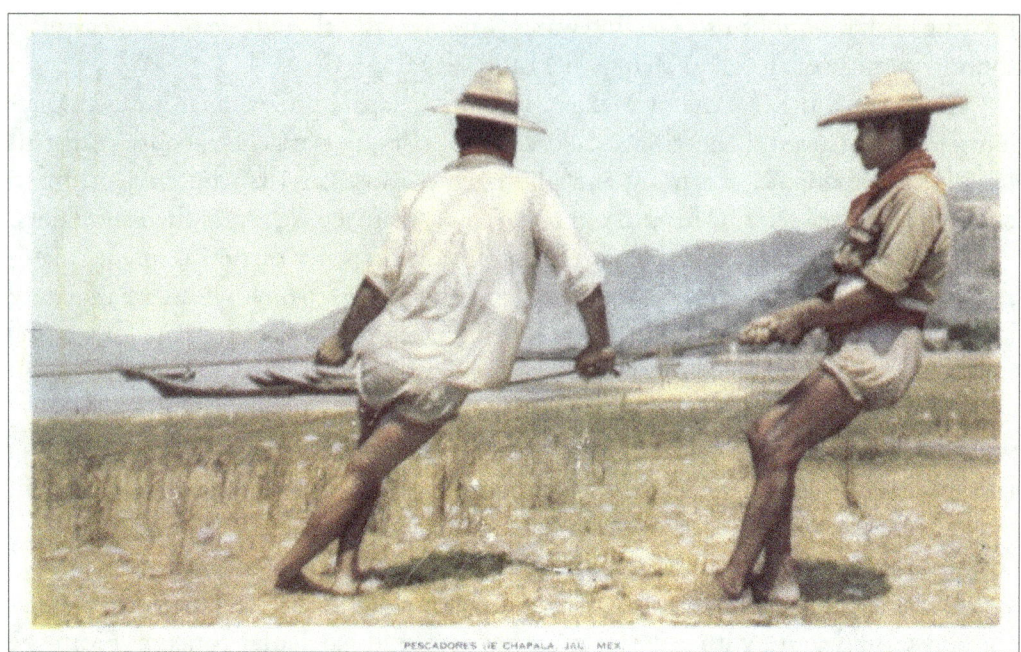

8.12. Fishermen pulling their net ashore, c. 1946. Lotería Nacional.
Published by the National Lottery (Lotería Nacional para la Asistencia Pública), the reverse side of this card pointed out to potential punters that "You could lose $5,000,000.00 [about $1 million] if... you don't play the Lottery on 16 September."

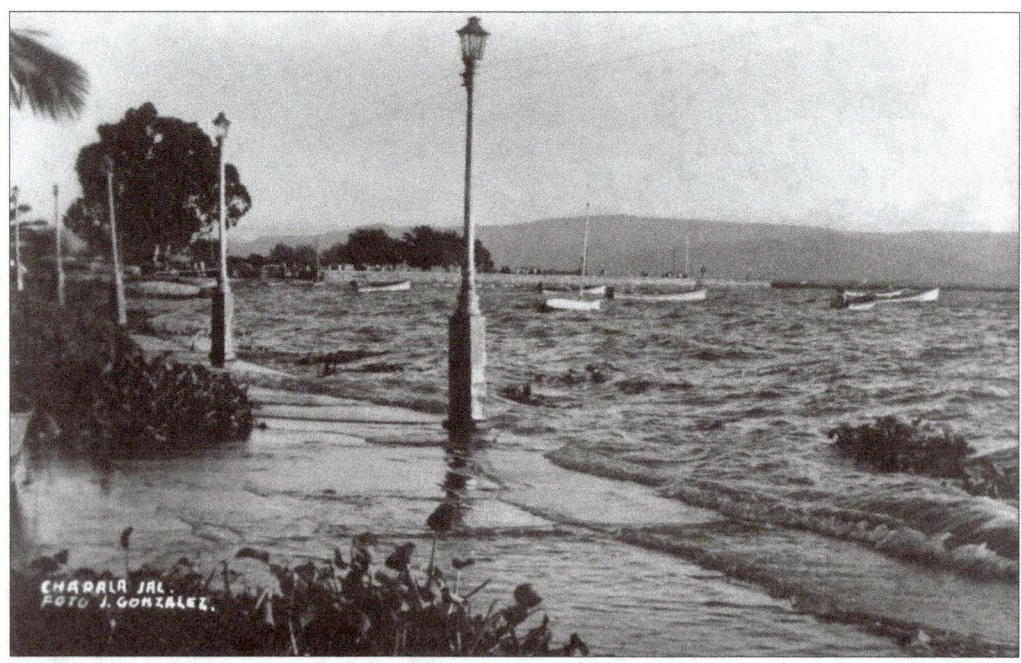

8.13 Storm waves hitting Chapala malecón, c. 1943? J González.
Fishing boats bob up and down as afternoon storm waves hit the malecón west of the pier. Clumps of water hyacinth (lirio) have been washed up onto the promenade.

Such bans on white cotton *calzones* extended to Jocotepec (1901) and Chapala and continued long after Díaz had entered exile in Europe. Kate, a character in D H Lawrence's novel *The Plumed Serpent*, set in a fictional version of Chapala, attributed the ban to a sexual motive: "She understood why the cotton pantaloons were forbidden on the plaza. The living flesh seemed to emanate through them."[11]

Postcard publishers knew that the images of most appeal to tourists, as mementoes of a visit or to mail to friends and family, were quaint, cute, pretty, stereotypical *costumbrista* images of people and scenes. It was of no consequence that such idealized cards were nothing more than a glimpse into the complex reality of life in these villages. One of the stereotypical views of Chapala was of one or two individuals alongside rustic fishing boats, the sandy beach, and several fine villas.

Another of the stereotypical views was of fishing nets strung up on poles along the beach to dry. The ever-shifting colors and patterns of light and shadow of the lake, fishermen and fishing nets billowing in the breeze have exerted a powerful impact on dozens of famous artists and photographers over the decades. The prime example is noted abstract expressionist painter Stanley Twardowicz (1917–2008), whose series of eye-catching photographs of fishermen and their nets in Ajijic, taken in about 1948, was exhibited to wide acclaim in New York three years later.[12]

Fishing and other uses of the lake are not without their challenges, which include unexpected squalls and storms. Changes in wind direction are frequent, and the fishermen have their own names for the winds from different directions, such as El Colimote

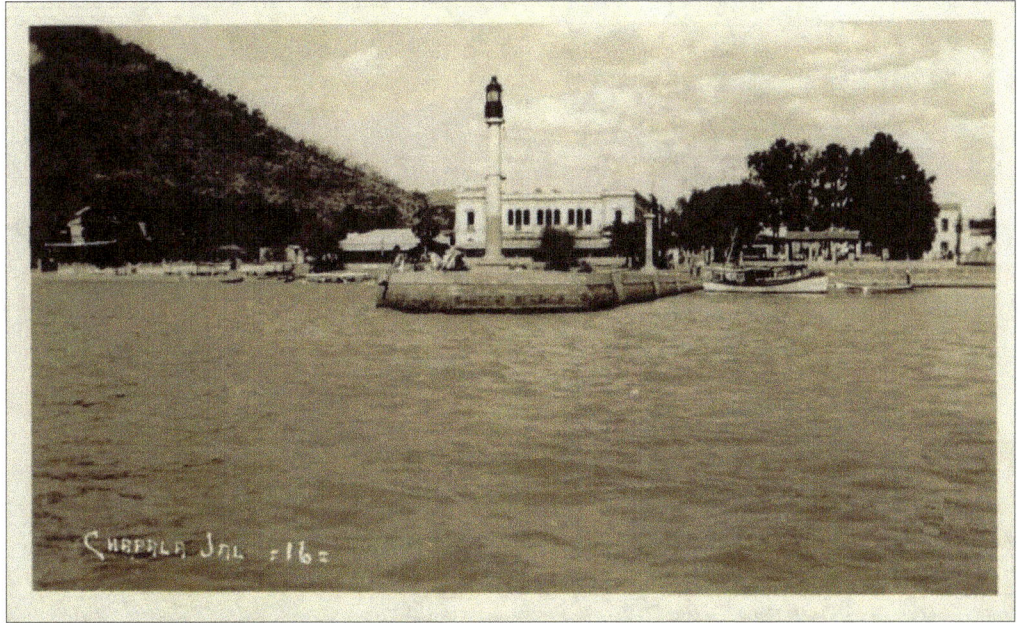

8.14 Lighthouse in Chapala, c. 1940?
This was one of the first four strategically located lighthouses that helped guide fishermen and others to safety.

(from Colima), El Mexicano (from Mexico City), El Tapatío (from Guadalajara), El Abajeño (from the west) and so on. Seasonal and diurnal changes in wind direction are predictable. But sudden afternoon squalls are particularly hazardous and no one is exempt. Following a banquet in his honor on Mexcala Island in 1896, the boat carrying President Díaz got into serious trouble on its way to Ocotlán, where the presidential train was waiting to whisk the president and his entourage back to the capital. Even large sternwheelers, like the *Libertad*, have capsized.

Navigation on large lakes is also tricky. It was all too easy for fishermen to lose their bearings when the shoreline was distant, especially at night. Mezcala Island was

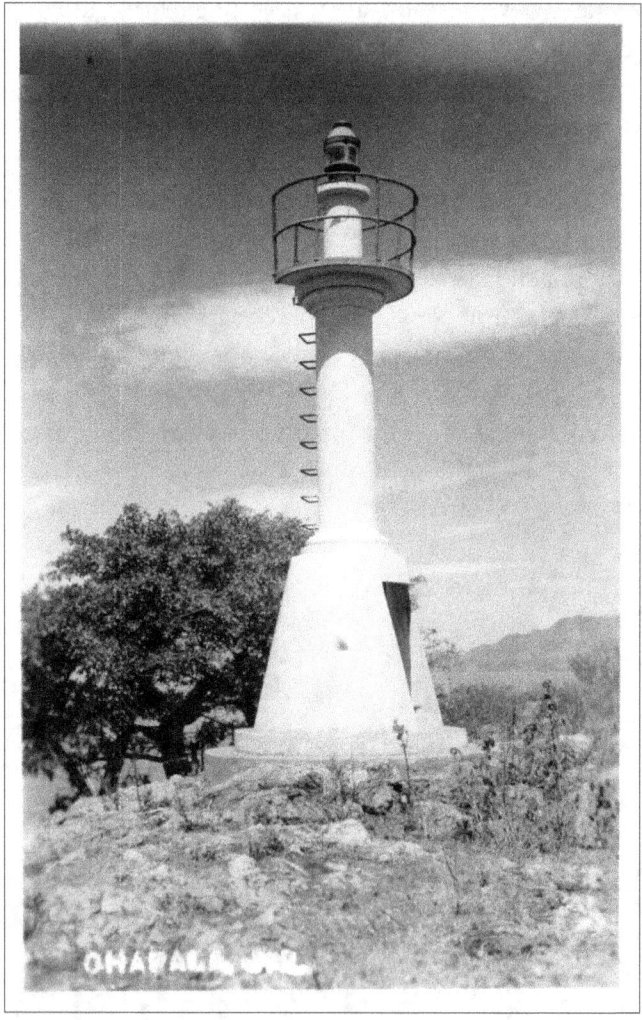

8.15. Lighthouse on Isla de los Alacranes, c. 1955?
The island, a sacred site of the Huichol people, was bought by Luis Pérez Verdía from the federal government in 1896 for $21.00. Later owners included Arturo Braniff, who planned to turn it into a luxurious private home. Following the Revolution, all private claims to the islands in the lake were revoked.

a welcome refuge on occasions when sail boats were out too late to return home safely. Despite the risks, night time journeys by sail canoas and steamers were fairly common. Regulations were introduced to stipulate that boats had to display lights at night, and several lighthouses were established to help guide nocturnal mariners safely home.

In addition to the light in Chapala, there were lights where the River Santiago left the lake near Ocotlán, in Tizapán el Alto and on Mexcala Island. Maintenance of the lights, fueled by acetylene gas, was centralized in Ocotlán. Whenever a flame blew out, usually as a consequence of westerly winds, a boat was dispatched to reignite the light.[13] Numerous additional lighthouses were later added, including one on Scorpion Island (Isla de los Alacranes).

Equally as problematic as the deliberate introduction of exotic fish, such as carnivorous carp, was the accidental introduction of water hyacinth (*lirio*) to the lake at the end of the nineteenth century. The water hyacinth was apparently introduced during an experiment (which went badly wrong!) carried out by the distinguished naturalist Mariano Bárcena.[14]

In a single year, twenty-five *lirio* plants can multiply to become two million separate plants, covering up to 10,000 square meters of water surface. Some years these masses cover up to 20% of the lake surface. The plant blocks channels, hinders navigation and decreases the amount of dissolved oxygen in the water.

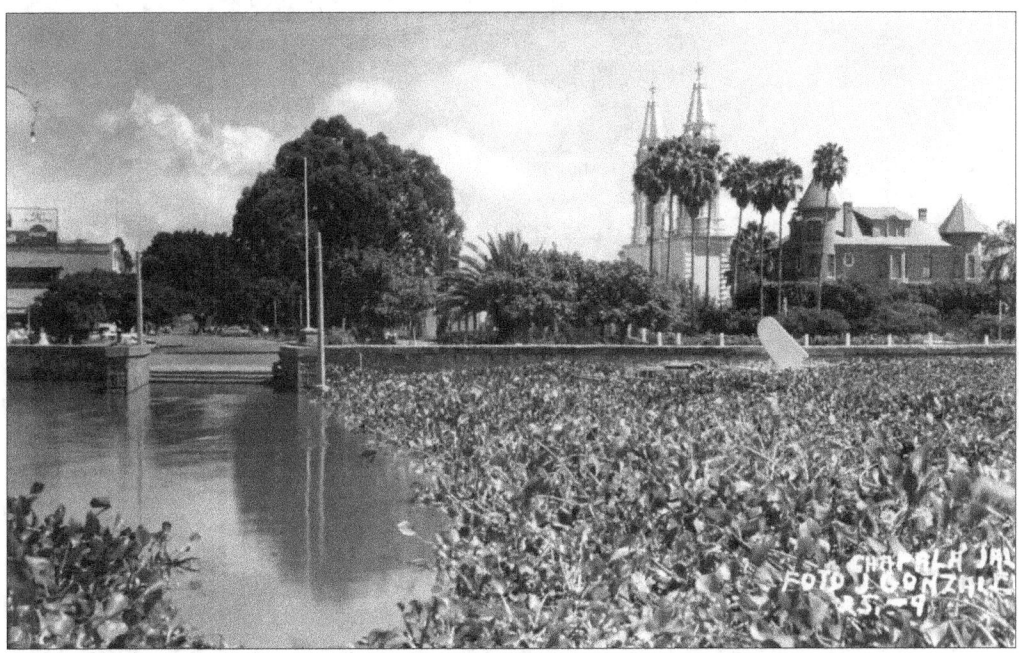

8.16. *Masses of lirio near Casa Braniff, c. 1945? J González.*
Besides hindering boats and fishermen, the presence of so much lirio near the pier harmed tourism, both from an aesthetic standpoint and from a health standpoint—dense mats of lirio are ideal breeding grounds for all manner of insects, including mosquitoes.

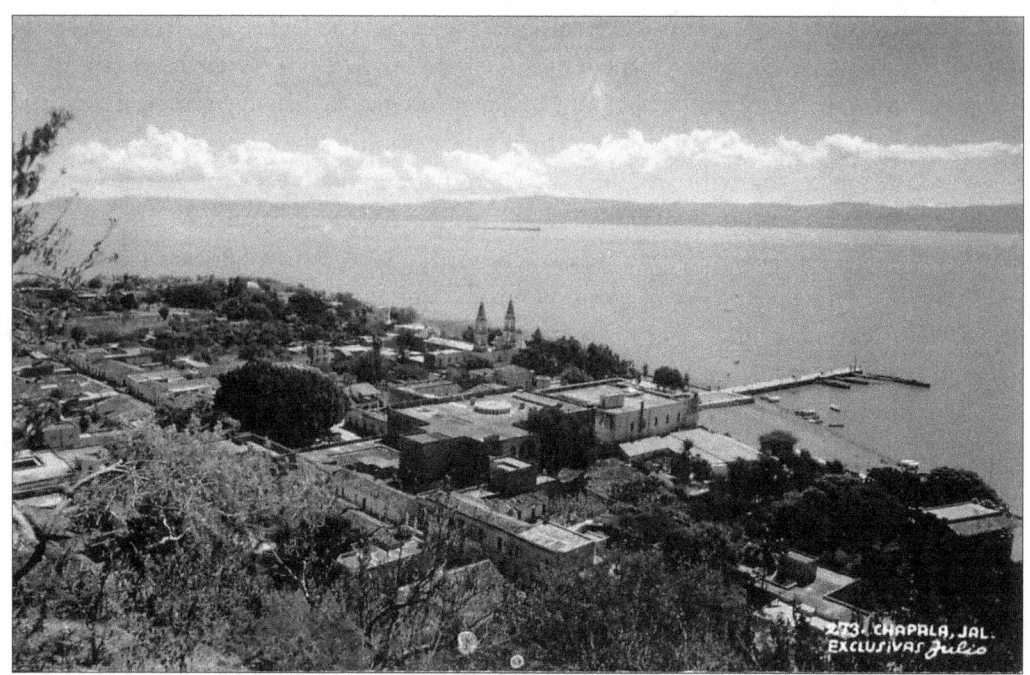

8.17. *Panorama from Cerro San Miguel, c. 1940. Exclusivas Julio.*
The lake level was high, and the pier easily accessible to all boats.

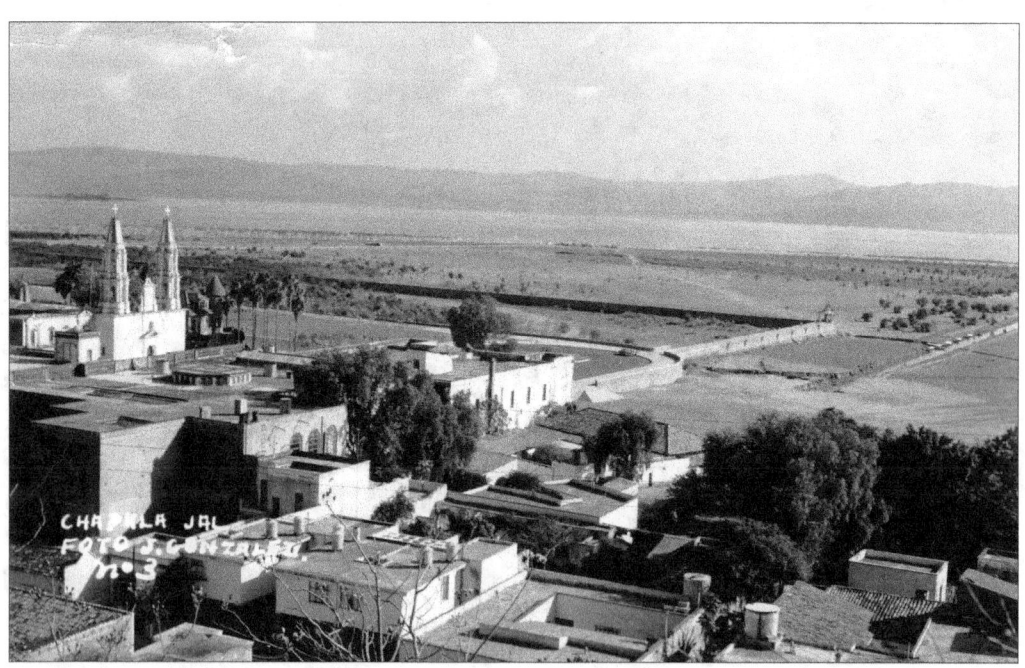

8.18. *Panorama from Cerro San Miguel, c. 1950. J González.*
A decade later the pier was useless and fishermen had a lengthy trek across pastureland to reach their boats.

By 1905 the plant was already recognized as a serious problem. That year a $150,000 prize was offered to anyone who could find a way to rid the lake of the noxious weed.[15] In succeeding years various chemicals were tried in ultimately futile efforts to eradicate it completely.

Coincidentally, also in 1905—far to the south in Argentina—advertisements appeared for a wrinkle-removing compound called Xilitipa, said to be an entirely natural product derived from the aromatic juices of tropical plants growing on the shores of Lake Chapala.[16] For only $4.00 a bottle, all wrinkles were guaranteed to disappear. One can only guess at how much money these Argentinian scammers made from their get-rich scheme.

None of the methods tried at Lake Chapala to control the *lirio*, including herbicides and manual or mechanical removal, has ever been more than partially successful. Even the introduction of five manatees (another exotic species) in 1964 to eat the lirio was a tragic failure; none of them survived more than a few weeks.[17]

The dense masses of floating water hyacinth, constantly shifting position in response to changes in the wind and waves, were a massive problem for smaller fishing boats. Out on the lake, boats could become entangled with the *lirio*; near the shoreline, mats of *lirio* regularly prevented boats from reaching the pier or the beach. Masses of *lirio* tend to be localized: on any given day, Chapala might be suffering, and Jocotepec not, or vice versa. In any one location, *lirio* can appear one day and be gone the next.

A much longer-term challenge for fishermen and other uses of the lake is to adjust to changing lake levels. The highest levels of the lake (since 1900) were in 1926—when the Chapala Railroad Station was flooded—and in 1935. On top of regular annual changes in level in response to the rainy season and dry season, there have been some enormous multi-year fluctuations.

The two panoramas opposite were taken from Cerro San Miguel approximately a decade apart. The diference in the level of the lake in the two photographs is stark: the lake fell approximately 5 meters (16.5 feet) between 1940 and 1950. Shortly before the second photograph was taken, the block of buildings that included Villa Ana Victoria and Gran Hotel Chapala (formerly Hotel Victor Huber), west of the church, had been razed to create Avenida Madero.

The low rainfalls that caused this drop in lake level had forced authorities in Chapala to close municipal washing places in 1948; they reported that the local spring had slowed, leaving barely enough for municipal service to homes.[18] Two years later, they dredged the shoreline, which had become far too shallow for any boats to reach the beach, and extended the pier. The material dredged up was used to infill land east of the pier as a park.

As shown in figure 8.18, the lake level continued its fall. The lowest level of all during the great drought of the mid-1950s was in summer 1955, by which time not only had the lake shrunk significantly in area but its mean depth had fallen to less than 1.5 meters (5 feet).

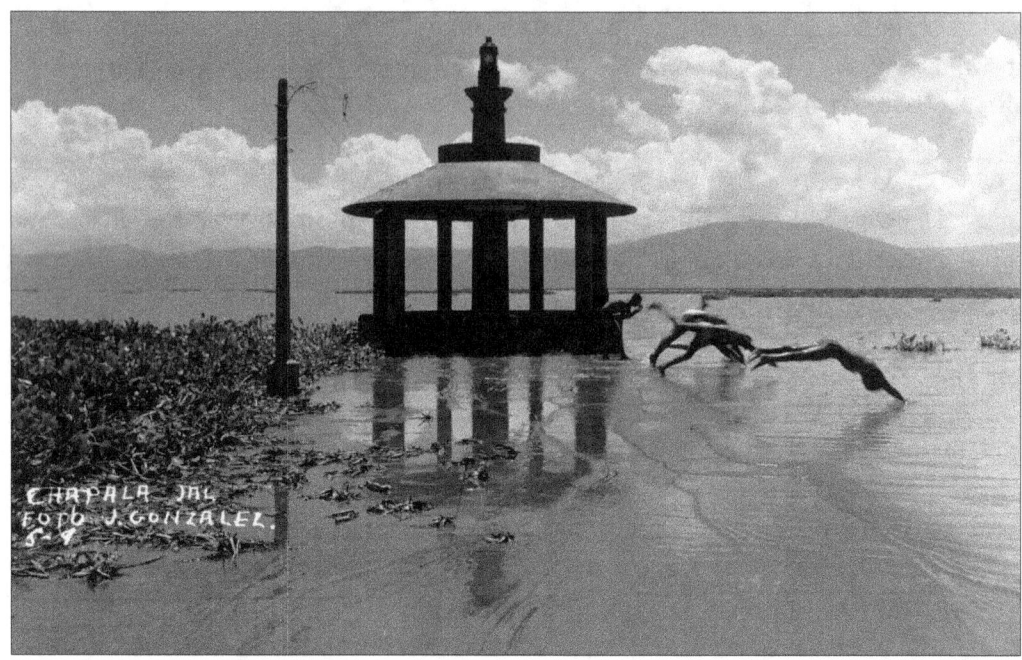

8.19. Diving from Chapala pier, c. 1967. J González.
On a calm day, as tiny ripples swash gently over the pier, swimmers dive into clear water. A floating mass of water hyacinth has accumulated against the left side of the pier.

Such extreme low water levels had all manner of serious consequences, one of which was prompting owners of lakefront properties to extend their use of the federal concession zone that surrounds the lake. Concessions to use this zone are granted, in theory, only for certain specific non-permanent uses. This has become a particularly serious bone of contention in recent years. But abuse of the federal zone is not a new phenomenon; early photographs of the lakeshore show that many properties (including one owned by Septimus Crowe in the 1890s) had permanent wharves and jetties jutting out into the lake. Later panoramas reveal that a large number of homes, originally only a few meters from the lake, had subsequently extended their gardens by reclaiming land from the lake, building stone and concrete breakwaters to protect their newly acquired additional property.

The highest levels of the lake since the big drought were in the period 1967–1977. The peak level was reached in 1967, when Chapala was called Little Venice in one report. Its pier was under water, and several streets were flooded, damaging homes and schools. The water rose so high up the walls of the Chapala Railroad Station building that one occupant was forced to abandon his second floor apartment there clad only in his bathing trunks.[19] Similarly high levels and floods were recorded in 1971, 1973 (when the water almost reached the doors of the parish church) and 1976.

9

Chapala 1940–1960: tourism and redevelopment

Before all-inclusive coastal beach resorts became popular and affordable, many Guadalajara families were accustomed to spending weekends and vacations in Chapala. Its principal attractions have always been the lake, beach, shallow water, boat rides, scenery and fine cuisine. The local authorities in the early 1940s recognized the importance of keeping the water as pristine as possible: bathers on the stretch of beach between the pier and Villa Tlalocan were prohibited from using soap because of complaints about the bad impression it gave national and foreign tourists.

For many families an additional appeal of a trip to the lake was the opportunity to have their portrait taken. The most prolific of all the professional photographers

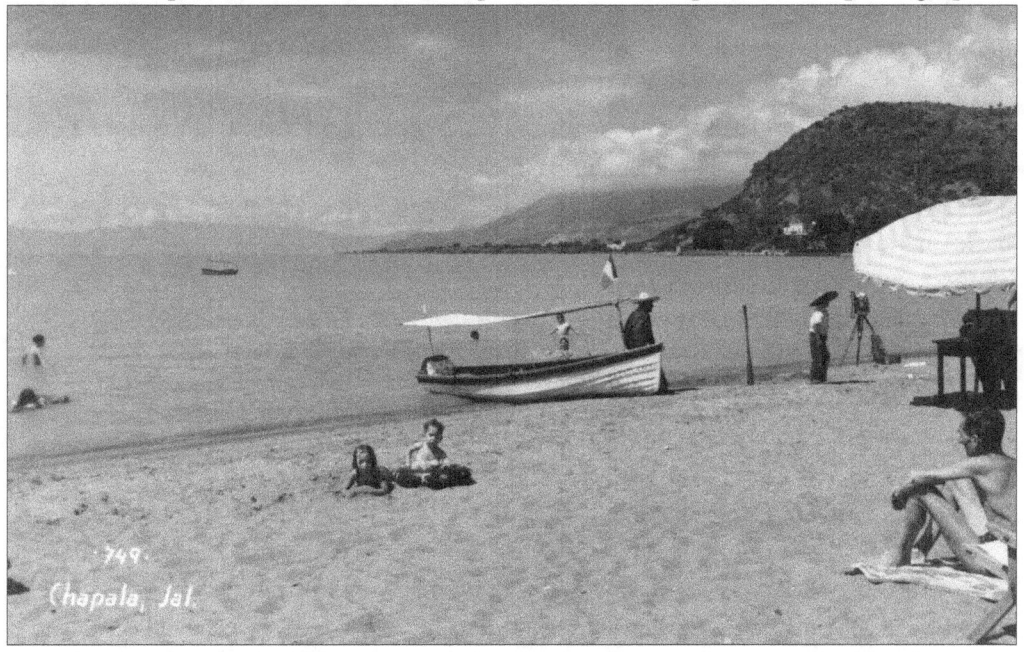

9.1. *Chapala beach, c. 1945?*
Note the camera tripod at the water's edge. Before inexpensive point-and-shoot cameras were common, enterprising photographers frequented popular locations offering to take family and individual portraits.

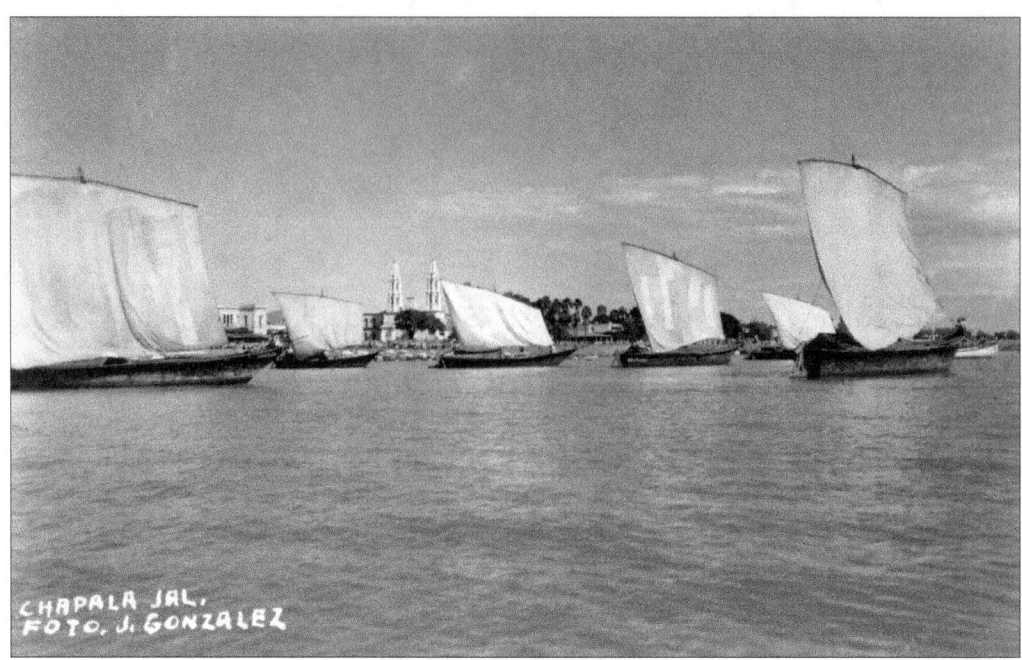

9.2. *Sail canoes, c. 1945. J González.*
This powerful image of large cargo-carrying sail canoes, their trapezoidal sails unfurled, probably coincided with an event such as Día de la Marina (Navy Day, 1 June).

working in Chapala from 1940 onwards was Jesús González Miranda (1898–1995). For more than forty years he specialized in taking portraits of the famous, and the not-so-famous, enjoying themselves near the jetty or by the Beer Garden, the quintessential restaurant-bar overlooking the beach. His business was especially brisk on weekends and holidays. González also published hundreds of real photo postcards featuring local buildings and views.

Watersports at Chapala have waxed and waned in popularity over the years. The first swimming, rowing and yacht races were held in the early years of the twentieth century. Perhaps the most international regatta ever held at Lake Chapala was in November 1947, when several classes of speed boats competed in an event sponsored by the state government and approved by the American Power Boat Association. The winner completed the eight-kilometer course in just under six minutes.[1] Most of the 39 competitors came from the US; they also competed in a similar event in Acapulco.

The annual commemoration of Navy Day is on 1 June. Following a shoreline ceremony, a small flotilla of vessels leaves the port to lay a memorial wreath on the water in honor of all those who have lost their lives in Mexico's largest natural lake.

In addition to vacationers, Lake Chapala also began to attract more foreign settlers. The outbreak of the second world war in Europe in 1939 triggered a steady influx of foreigners seeking temporary or permanent residence at Lake Chapala. Some fled Europe voluntarily ahead of the war; others were political refugees displaced from their homeland. The US entry into the war in 1941 prompted many Americans to move to Mexico; some were draft dodgers, others were the wives or partners of military personnel serving overseas.

As this message on a postcard mailed in 1940 to an upper crust family in Rhode Island reveals, a stay at Lake Chapala offered a welcome respite from world problems:

> You are good to write and I do enjoy your letters. This is not an answer but a message from the tropics where gay flowers and trees in blossom assure you there is still spring over the horizon.... The little resort is completely primitive & accommodations are comparably simple. The girls love the swimming! And we revel in beach idling—world wars and all the consequences seem to belong to another planet.

In the 1940s, Villa Montecarlo became closely associated with artists and writers. Swedish painter Nils Dardel and his partner, American author Edita Toll Morris, loved the Montecarlo and wrote to friends in 1941 that their garden was the largest and most beautiful in all of Chapala.[2] The Montecarlo was also the venue for several important art exhibitions, and Sybille Bedford stayed here in 1946–47 prior to writing *A Visit to Don Otavio*, her impressionistic travelogue about Mexico. The following decade saw Villa Montecarlo listed in national guidebooks as one of Chapala's established hotels.[3]

After the hotel was sold in the early 1960s, the beautiful Italianate building designed by Angelo Corsi was torn down to be replaced by a generic Holiday Inn lookalike.[4] The

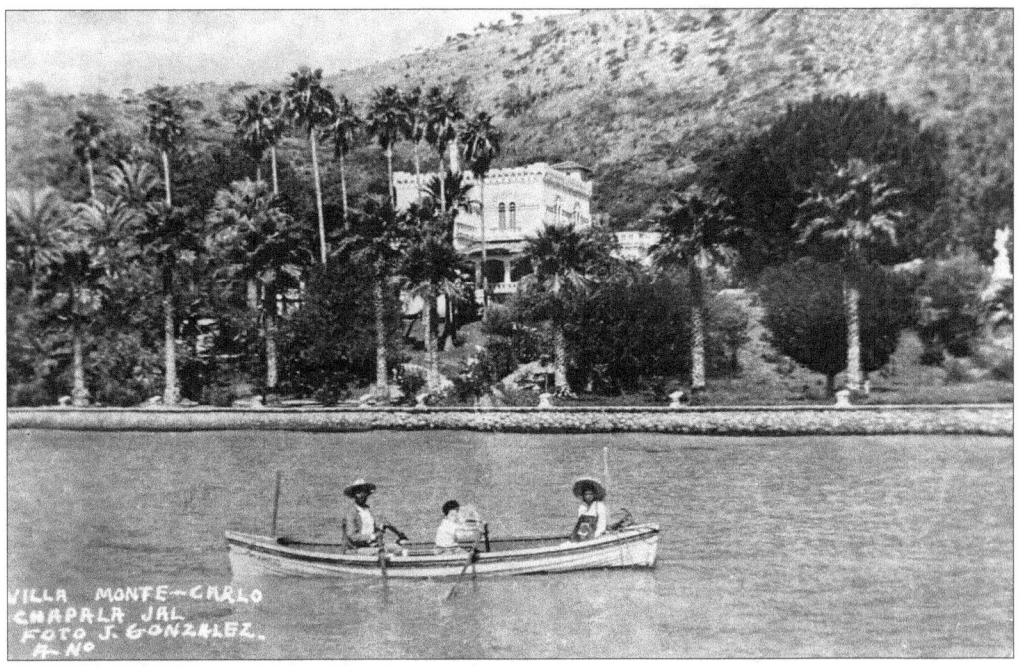

9.3. *Villa Montecarlo, c. 1945? J González.*
Famous Swedish painter Nils Dardel rented the Villa Montecarlo for several months in 1941 to complete paintings for a major exhibition in New York.

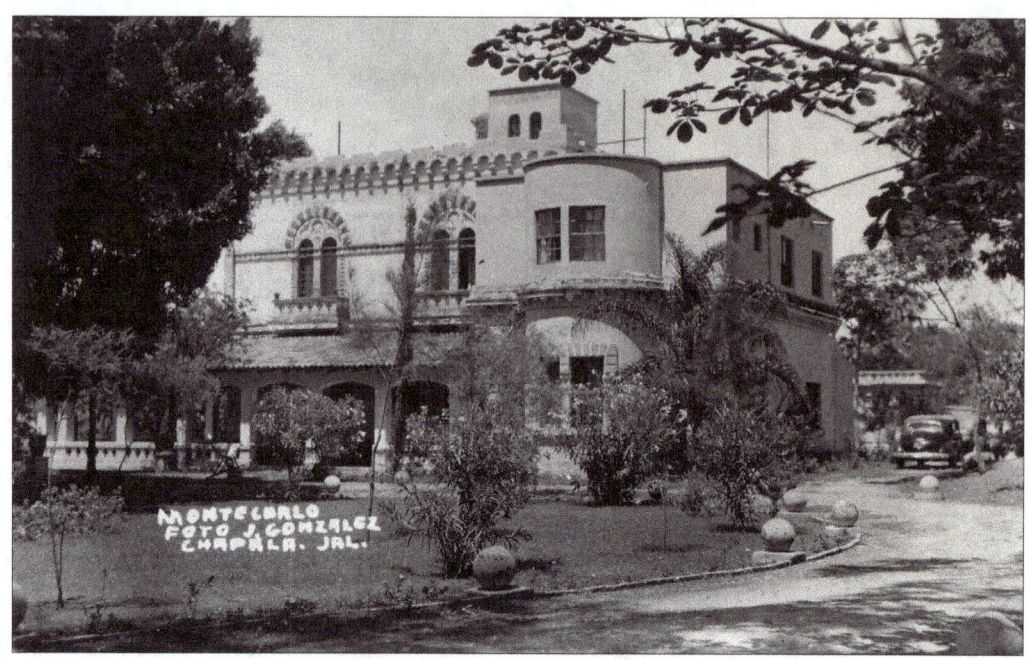

9.4. *Villa Montecarlo, c 1945? J González.*
The Italianate Villa Montecarlo was remodeled many times over the years before being demolished in the 1960s to be replaced by a generic, ill-considered two-story hotel.

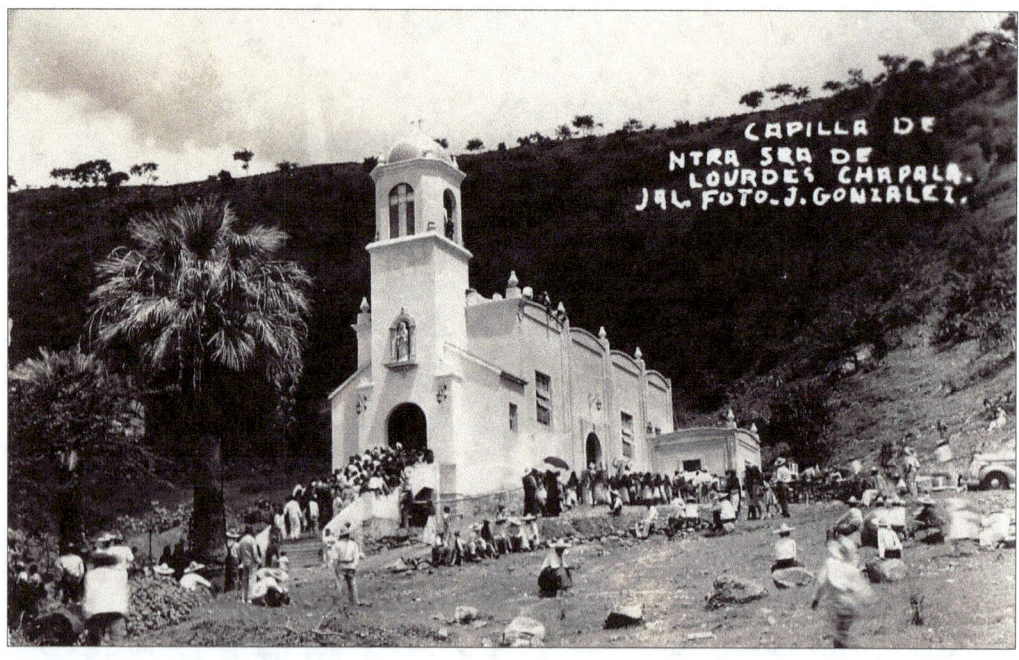

9.5. *Lourdes Chapel, c. 1943. J González.*
Most funding came from prominent Guadalajara families, many of them of French or German extraction, who had vacation homes in the village and appreciated its Lourdes-like spa water.

revamped Villa Montecarlo opened in 1964, and hosted, in quick succession, a lunch given by state officials for HRH Prince Philip, Duke of Edinburgh, and a working lunch of the executive board of People to People, a program founded by US President Dwight D Eisenhower to improve regional relations. Listening to keynote speaker Walt Disney at the latter lunch were President Adolfo López Mateos, former president Miguel Alemán and Jalisco governor Juan Gil Preciado.[5] In 1977, Villa Montecarlo was acquired by the Universidad de Guadalajara; the hotel and grounds comprise Chapala's only large-capacity conference venue.

The first stone of the Lourdes Chapel (Capilla de Lourdes) was laid in March 1940 and the chapel was consecrated in August 1941. The land had been donated by Walter Schnaider, who, with his late brother Joseph, owned La Perla, the largest brewery in Guadalajara.

Religious observances, often with an indigenous twist, have long been very important in personal and community life, but are rarely depicted on vintage postcards. One exception (figure 9.6) shows folk dances (*danzantes*) celebrating the Feast of the Immaculate Conception in the atrium of the parish church. Catholic churches throughout Mexico celebrate this day (8 December) annually with a variety of cultural festivities.

Inevitably, some festive occasions in Chapala have become far more touristy over the years. Carnival was a much smaller affair in the 1950s, when American author and illustrator John Russell Clift wrote this brief summary of pre-Easter activities in the town:

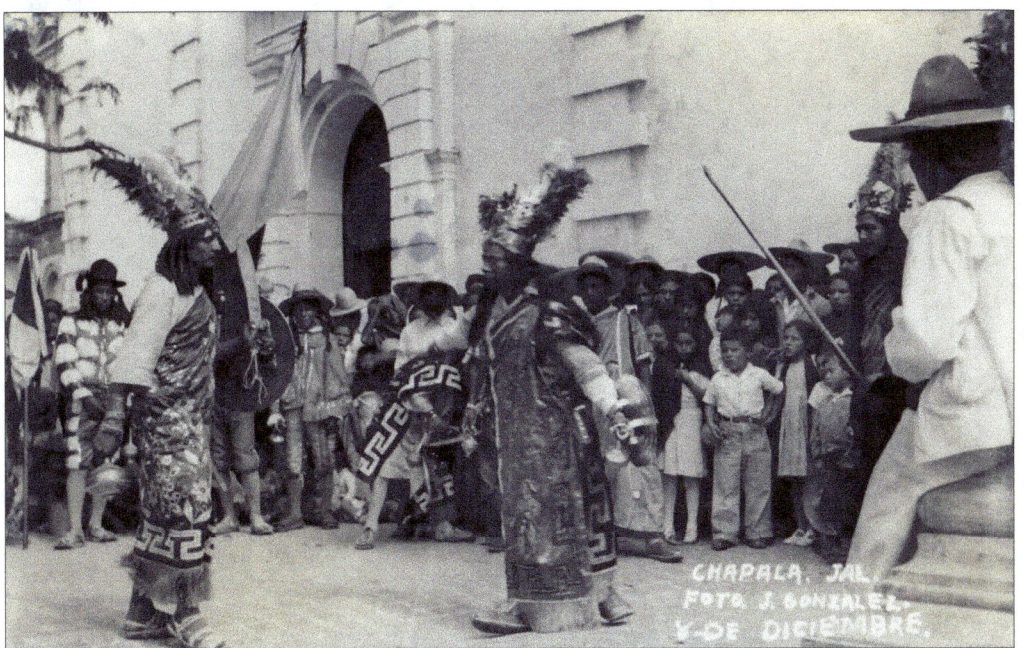

9.6. *Danzantes, Feast of the Immaculate Conception, c. 1945.* J González.

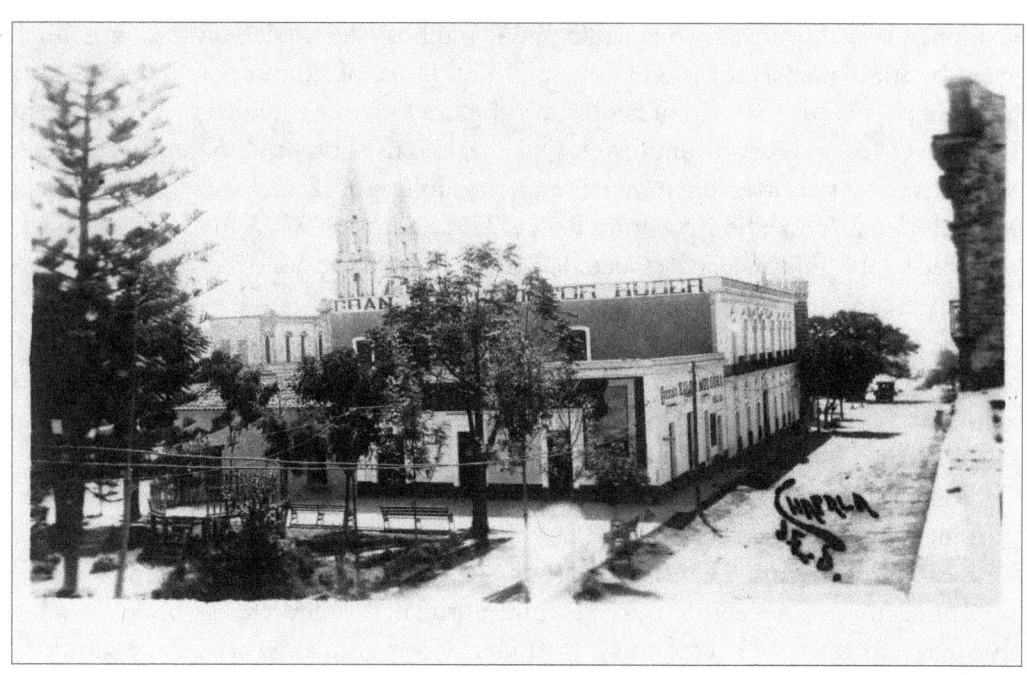

9.7. View from Old Municipal building, c. 1908. J E Sánchez.
The large two-story edifice fronting onto the jardín is the Gran Hotel Victor Huber. Behind it, barely visible, is the turret of the adjoining Villa Ana Victoria.

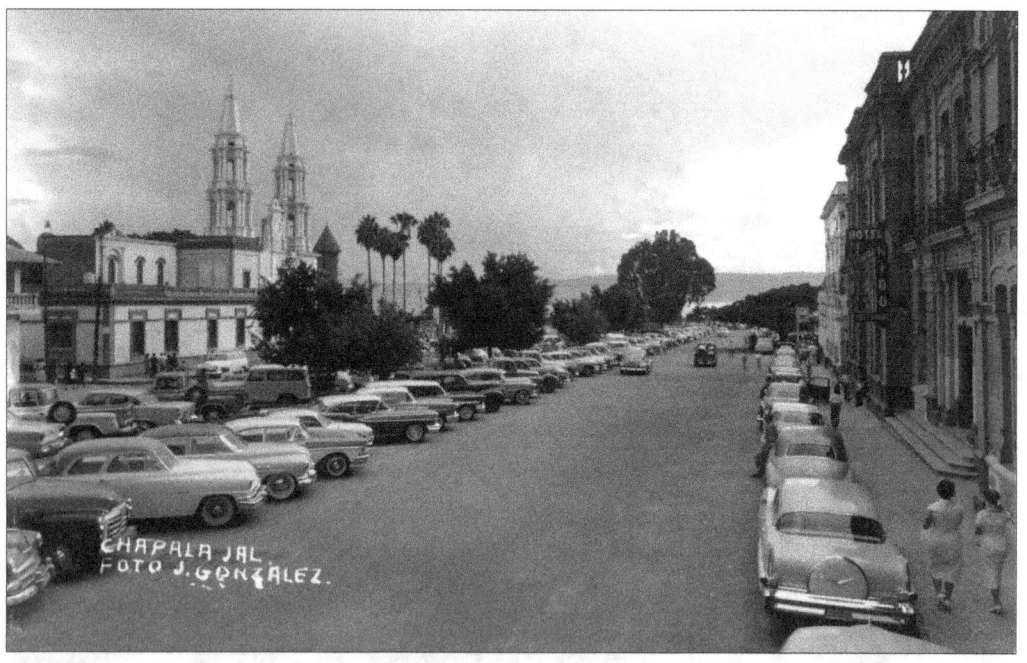

9.8. View from Old Municipal building, c. 1951. J González.
The southbound lanes of Avenida Madero, with the Hotel Nido to the right, are the direct route to the pier.

After Christmas and New Year's comes Carnival Time... For nine days preceding it there are bullfights twice a day in Chapala. A queen and her attendants are chosen. A dance and reception are held in the plaza and the tavern on alternating days. On Saturday of Holy Week a paper effigy of Judas is burned before the church, and the winter festival program is climaxed by Easter.

Today, Carnival in Chapala is a much larger, city-sponsored spectacle, with elaborate floats and parades designed to appeal not only to a local audience but also to tourists.

Clift visited Chapala during the state governorship of Jesús González Gallo (1947–1953), when a massive redevelopment of the town center was underway. The dramatic changes are shown by the two photographs (opposite), taken some forty years apart, of the view from the Old Municipal Building, at the intersection of Avenida Madero and Avenida Hidalgo.

The earlier photo shows where the village plaza (*jardin*) was originally located; the plaza was moved, and several buildings razed to the ground, to create Avenida Francisco I Madero with its central divide.

The creation of Avenida Madero was not the only change in downtown Chapala at this time. The road east from the jetty along Playa Chacaltita was also widened, and land was reclaimed from the lake for public gardens. A line of villas and homes built as lakefront properties suddenly found themselves well back from the lake. While they lost their views, they gained better protection at times when the lake was high.

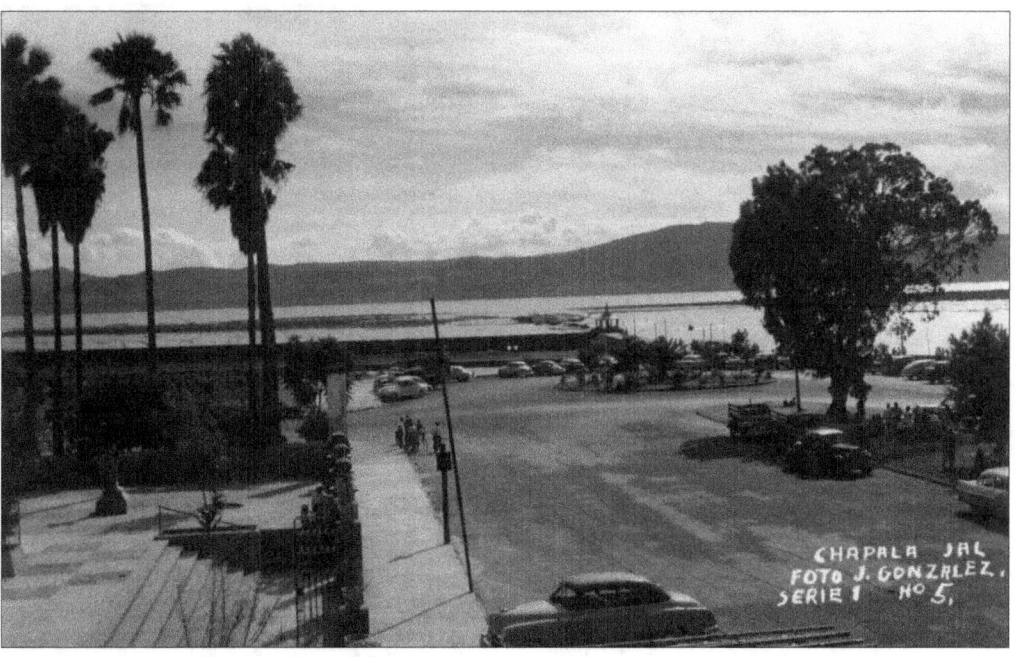

9.9. *Avenida Madero, c. 1950. J González.*
Car ownership was rising in Guadalajara and many city visitors preferred driving their own vehicle to Chapala for the day rather than relying on local buses.

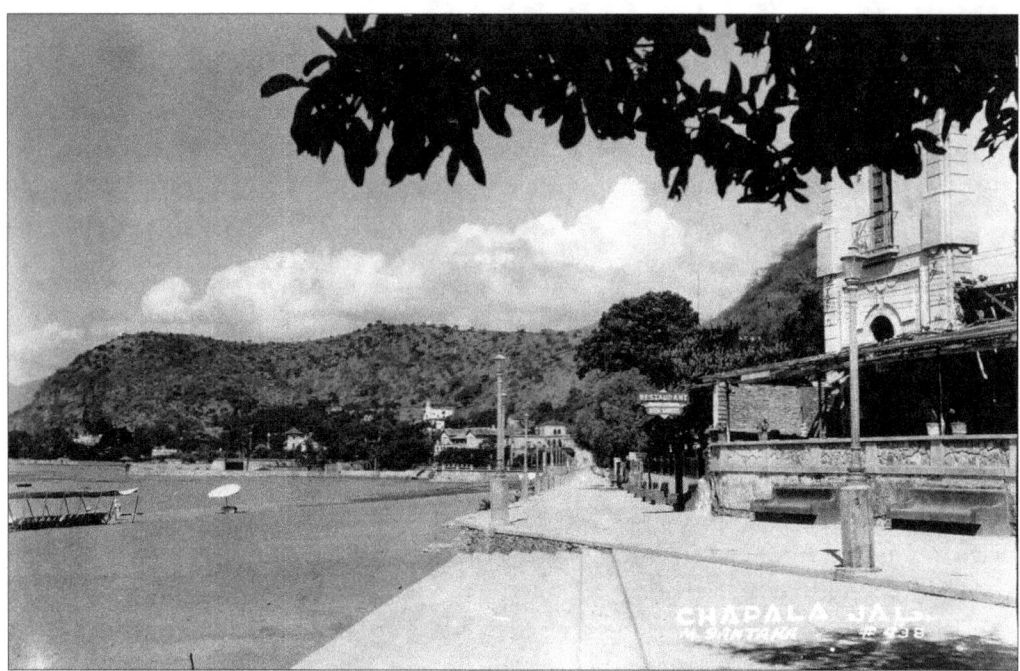

9.10. *Chapala malecón and Beer Garden, c. 1955? M Santana.*
The talented Guadalajara photographer María Santana is the earliest female photographer known to have taken postcard photos of Lake Chapala.

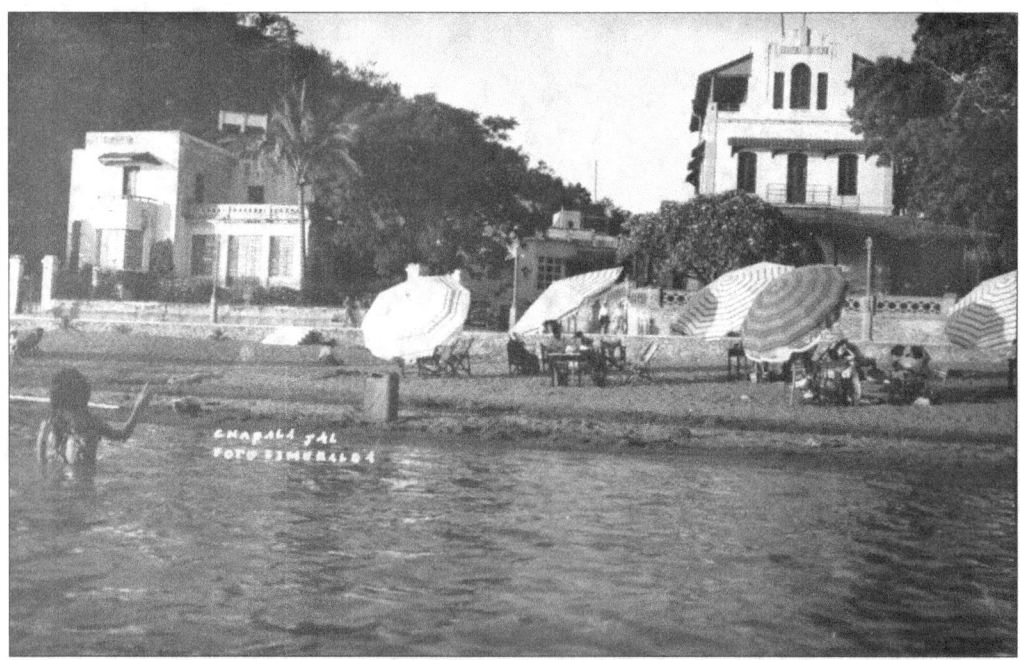

9.11. *Villa Aurora (left), Villa Ave María (back) and Casa Capetillo, c. 1950. Foto Esmeralda.*
Unlike the changes east of the pier, the narrow promenade constructed in front of these properties had little impact on their owners' views of the lake.

Plans to infill part of Playa Chacaltita had first been proposed in about 1920 by the Chapala Development Company, headed by Christian Schjetnan. Twenty years later, it was announced that a road would be built along the shoreline to connect to Avenida de la Estación, establishing access to a large new lakeside park.[6] By 1943, the project was well underway, relying on a mix of private and government funds. Several prominent local businesspeople, including Ramón Nido, Bohumil Hubička and María Pacheco, made substantial donations, in part because they agreed that their properties would immediately increase in value.[7]

But the major development came a few years later, in 1948, when the federal government conceded part of the shoreline for the construction of a wide new avenue. Even before the road was finished, a private club, Club Chacaltita, with shade trees, picnic tables, umbrellas, games, changing rooms, badminton courts and other amenities for visitors had sprung up three blocks east of the jetty. The first event advertised in the park was a US Independence Day picnic.[8]

Within a few years a promenade (*malecón*) had also been completed in front of the villas west of the jetty. Several of these villas had been significantly enlarged over the years, and some new ones added. Casa Capetillo, one of the oldest private homes in Chapala, had been significantly expanded. However, neighboring Villa Aurora, though much changed from its early days, had not yet been transformed into what is, today, the Lake Chapala Inn.

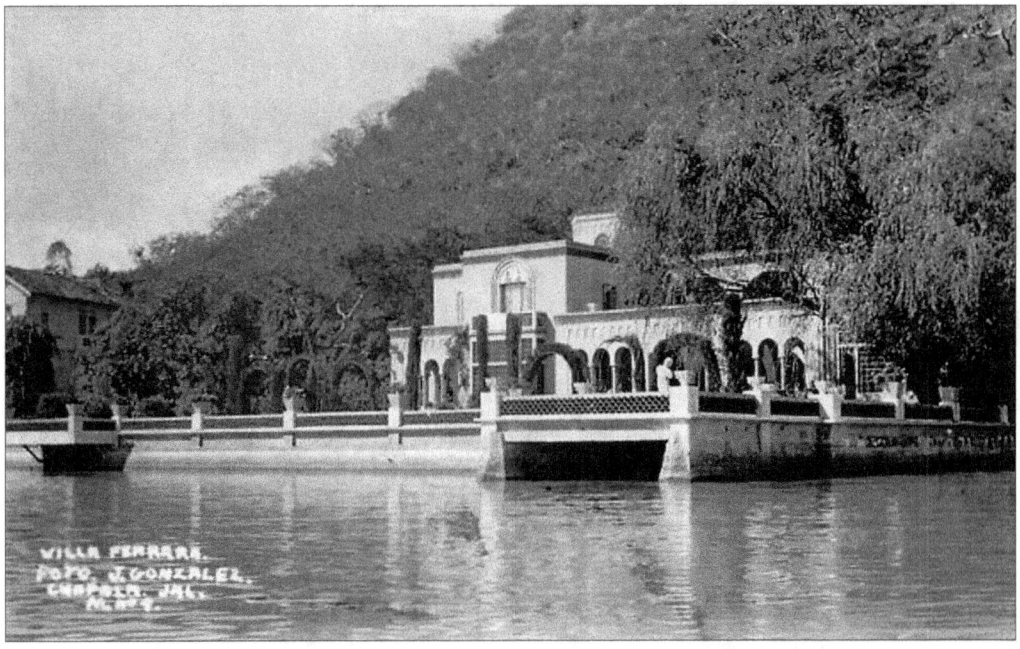

9.12. *Villa Ferrara. c 1945. J González.*
Villa Ferrara, designed by Pedro Castellanos Lambley, exemplifies Mexican modernism and is one of the crown jewels of the Escuela Tapatía de Arquitectura.

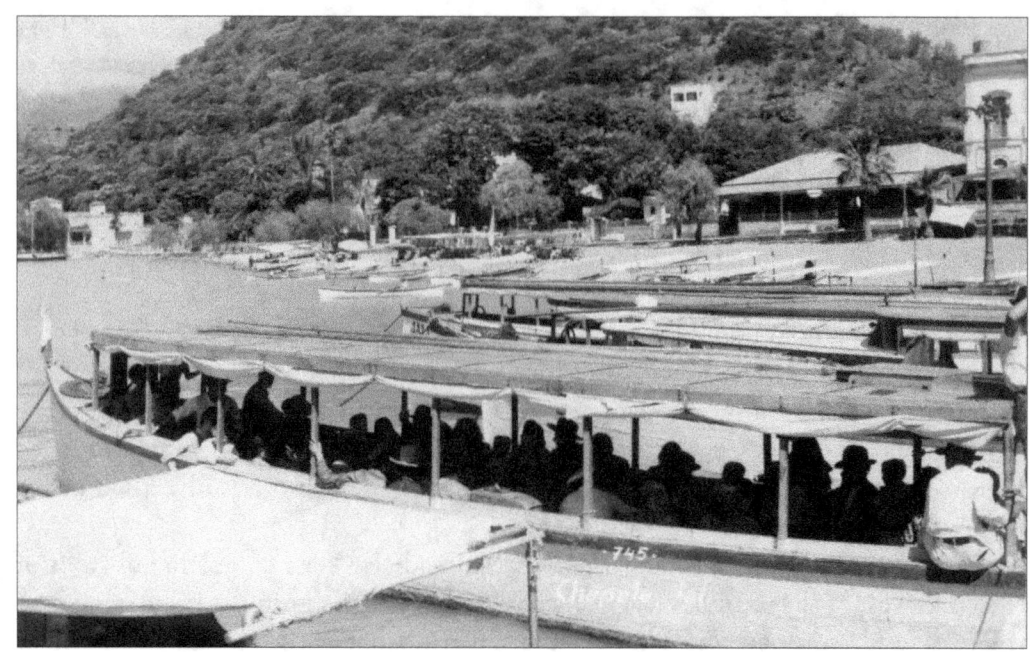

9.13. Tourist boat at Chapala, c. 1945? J González.
Boat rides along the shore or to a restaurant on nearby Scorpion Island (Isla de los Alacranes) were very affordable. Smaller boats could be hired for special individualized trips.

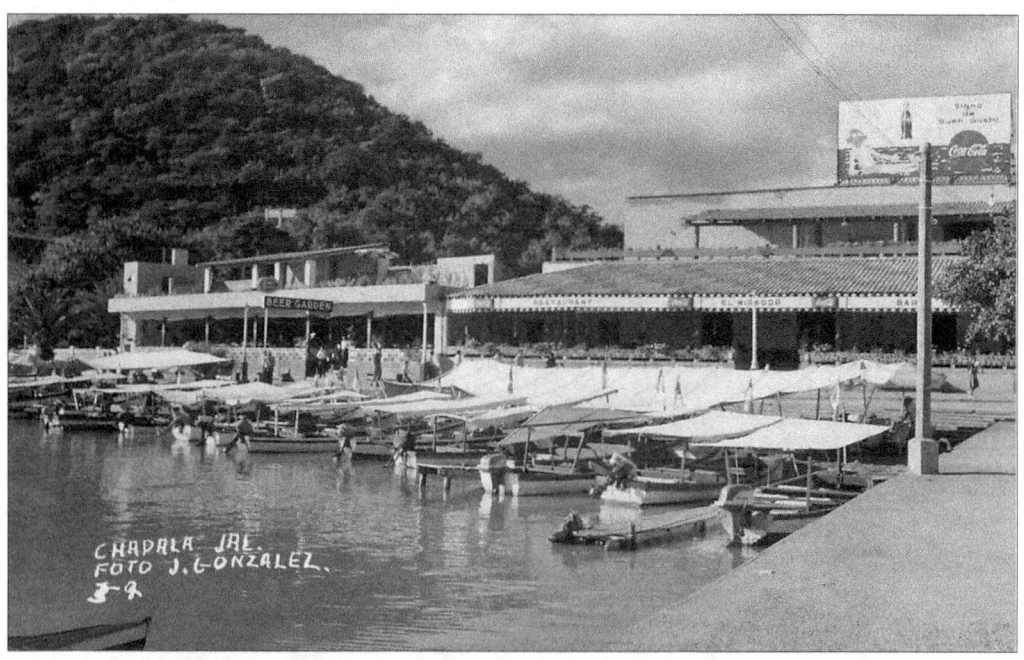

9.14. Beer Garden restaurant, Chapala, c. 1950. J González.
Next door to El Mirador (which had an upstairs section) was the Beer Garden, located on the site of Chapala's earliest lawn tennis court.

Further west, Villa Ferrara, built in about 1935, had rightly claimed its own place among the architectural gems of Chapala. Its architect, Pedro Castellanos Lambley, built or remodeled several fine residences in Chapala, but none in such a grand style as Villa Ferrara, commissioned by Tequila Cuervo heiress Lupe Gallardo González Rubio. Upgrades over the years have done nothing to diminish its original architectural integrity.

In the 1930s, well before the major revamp of the center of Chapala, a lakefront bar had been opened adjacent to the Hotel Arzapalo. From about 1940 it was managed by Chapala power couple Natalia and Luis Cuevas, and became known as the Beer Garden. It became a veritable institution, the preferred place to meet friends, sip beer and while away an afternoon to the music of Mike Laure. The bar appears in several movies, gets mentions in several books, and presidents, state governors, famous movie stars and foreign celebrities have all joined the regulars and visiting Tapatíos to down a tequila or two while looking out over the lake. The Beer Garden's precise location has changed more than once over the years; some later iterations have incorporated El Mirador, a ground floor section of the former Hotel Arzapalo.

The atmosphere in the Beer Garden was greatly enlivened by the liberal imbibing of tequila while trying to converse and cope with the cacophony of sound from competing mariachis. As an aside, some linguists believe that the word mariachi derives from the indigenous Coca language, spoken centuries ago at Lake Chapala.

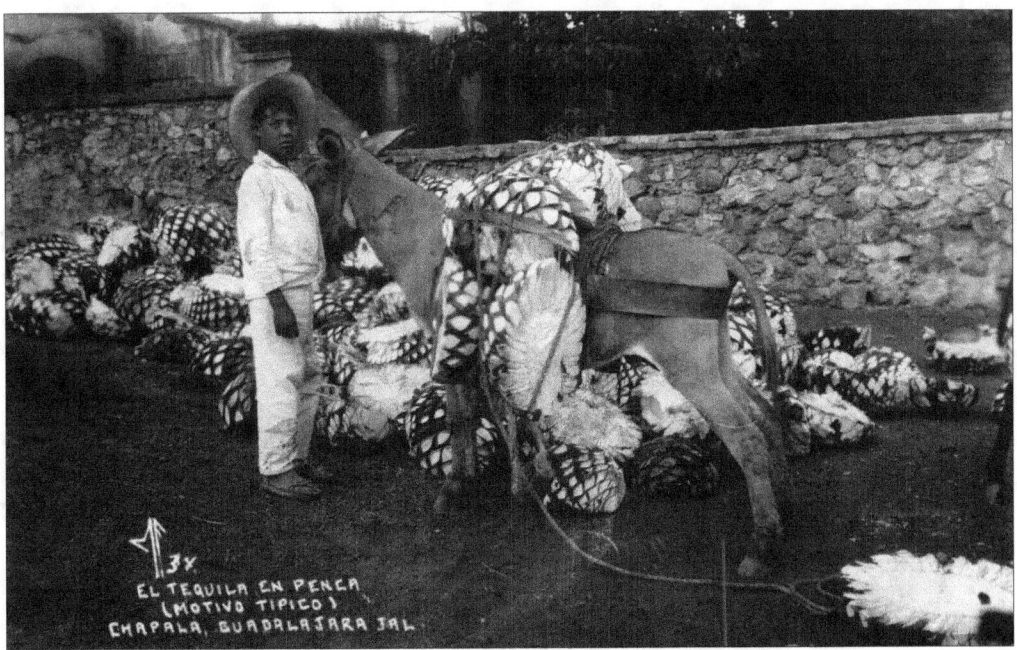

9.15. *Tequila piñas, Chapala, c. 1950. México Fotográfico.*
Tequila, Mexico's national drink, is made from these pineapple-like hearts or piñas *of a select specie of Agave. The caption mistakenly refers to them as* pencas *(leaves).*

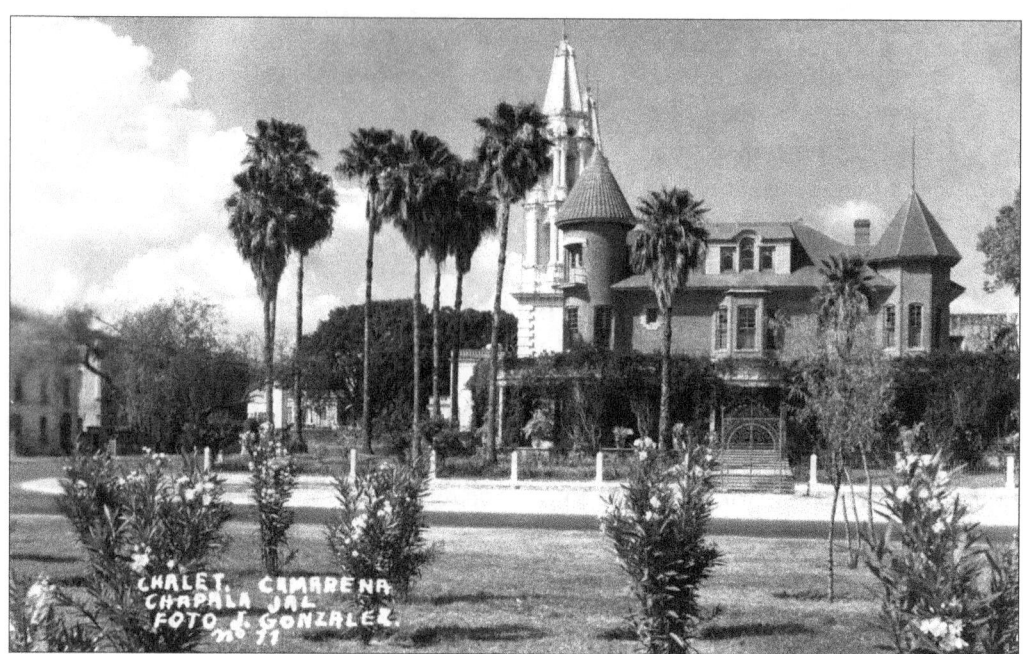

9.16. *Chalet Camarena (Casa Braniff), c. 1950. J González.*
Since the 1970s the ground floor has been a restaurant; patrons can still admire original wall coverings, stained-glass windows and period features.

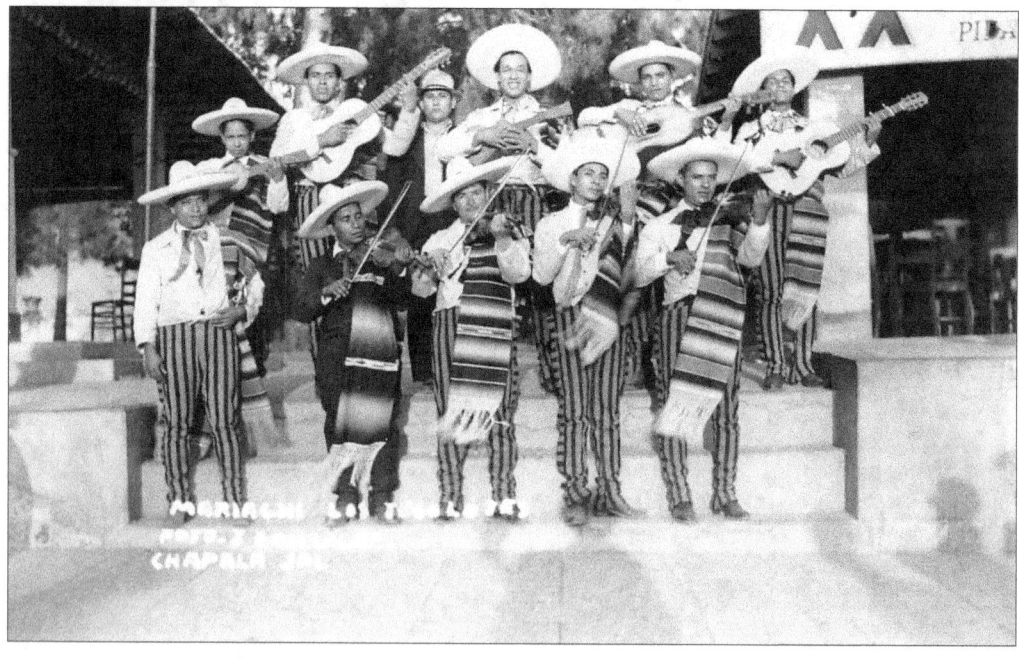

9.17. *Mariachi Los Tecolotes, c. 1950? J González.*
This traditional Guadalajara mariachi (string instruments only, no trumpets), was founded in 1942. Tecolotes (Owls) may refer to the musicians sleeping during the day before playing all night.

Of all the songs associated with the lake, the best known by far is "Chapala," the *ranchera* song composed by Pepe Guizar, and recorded by Mariachi Los Tecolotes in 1943. The words of the song refer directly to many of the more time-treasured alluring aspects of Lake Chapala: the fishing nets, fishermen, moonlit nights, sunrise, *canoas*, charales....

As for the Hotel Arzapalo itself, it had fallen into disuse by the time it was purchased in 1949 by Jesús González Gallo, state governor from 1947 to 1953. The building remains in his family; plans to revitalize it as a luxury hotel, with a swimming pool on an upper floor, have never been realized.

The Hotel Nido, next door to the Arzapalo, also changed management in the 1940s. After Ramón Nido died in 1945, the hotel was taken over by Roberto Cuevas, who ran it, with the help of other family members, for more than forty years, before it finally closed in 1994. The beautiful building, designed by Guillermo de Alba, was converted into the town hall (*presidencia municipal*) in 2001.

The foyer of the *presidencia* was originally the Hotel Nido dining room, where formally attired waiters served guests an inexpensive daily lunch menu (*comida corrida*) featuring local specialities such as whitefish and caldo michi.

The famous local whitefish, a delicacy found nowhere else in Mexico, was hailed in a Dane Chandos book as "one of the world's great eating fish... [with] so delicate a flavor and such firm soft flesh that it really needs no sauces or condiments. Lightly fried in a

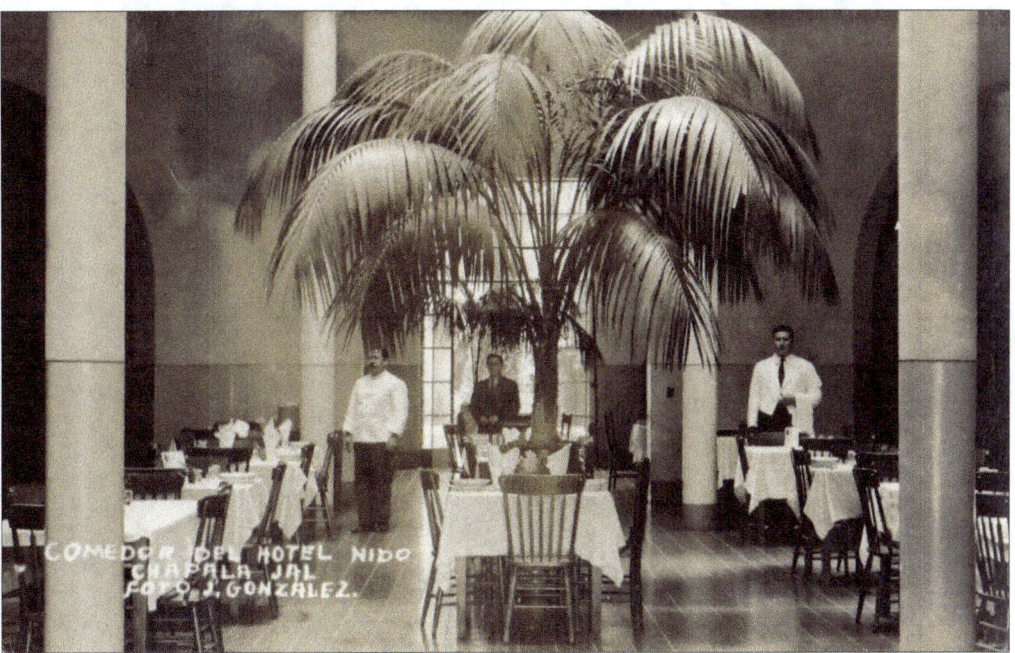

9.18. *Hotel Nido (formerly Hotel Palmera) dining room. c 1950? J González.*
This palm growing in the center of the Nido dining room harked back to the large central palm tree of the original Hotel Palmera forty years earlier.

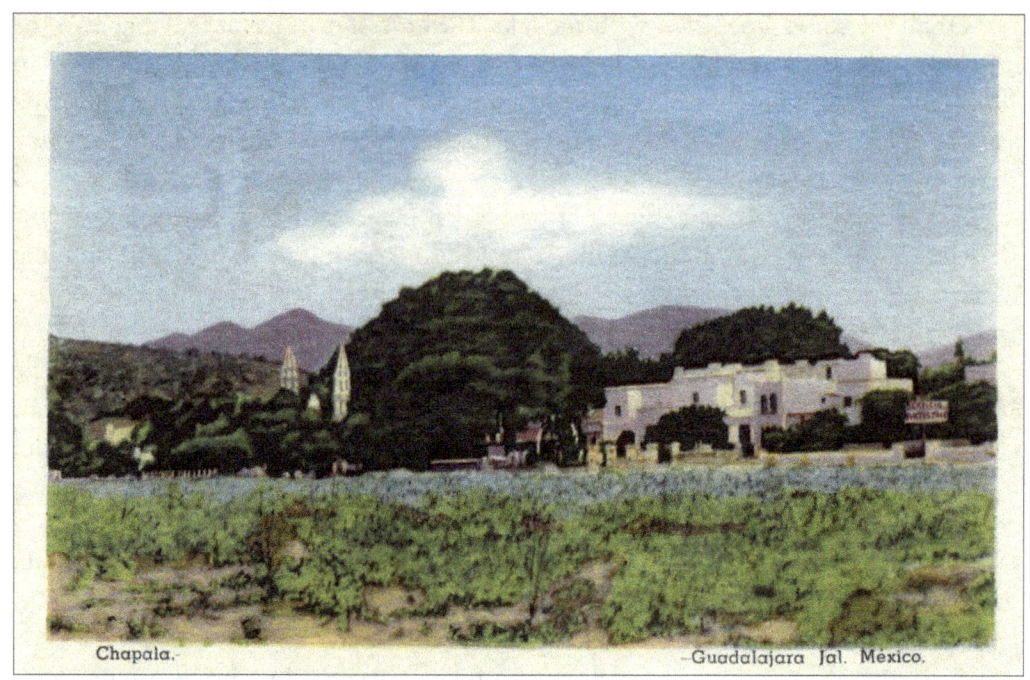

9.19. *Art card of Chapala, c. 1950? Alducin.*
The sign to the right of the modernist architecture proclaims "Servicio Artístico" (Artistic Service). The message on the reverse refers to a visit to Paricutín Volcano.

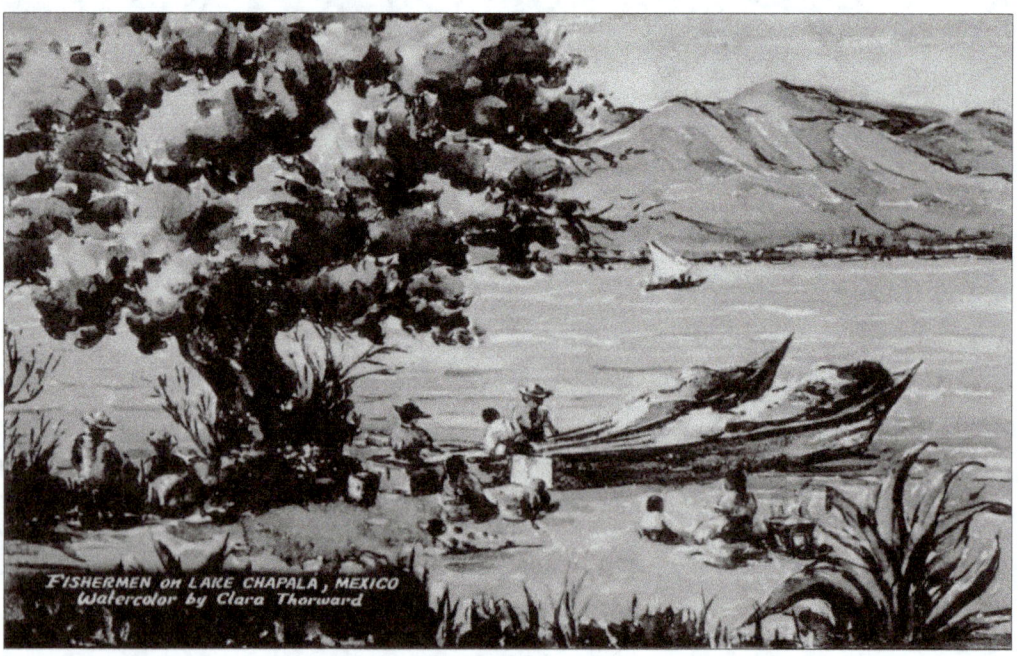

9.20. *Watercolor of fishermen and boats by Clara Thorward, c. 1958.*
This strong, evocative composition perfectly captures the cultural and aesthetic appeal of Lake Chapala, responsible for drawing so many talented artists to the area for more than a century.

thin envelope of beaten egg and with a squeeze of lemon juice, it is superb."[9] The Chandos authors, on the other hand, had nothing good to say about caldo michi, "a sloppy mess in which big lumps of fish and onion and tomato drown slowly in dishwater heavily seasoned with coriander."

The 1947 edition of *Terry's Guide to Mexico* told the world that "In both places [Ajijic and Chapala] there has also grown up in recent years an extensive artists' colony comprised of painters, sculptors, and writers. Many are Americans."[10]

Artists, attracted by the excellent light, reflections off the lake, colorful indigenous crafts, photogenic boats and fishing methods, and Mexican culture, have portrayed the lake and its surrounding in a myriad of different ways. Yet, despite long being famous as a haven of authors and artists, surprisingly few art postcards of the lake or its villages are known. The noteworthy early exceptions include the Kaiser reproduction of a landscape by Paul Fischer (figure 3.11).

The two art cards shown on the opposite page are from much more recent times. The unusual view showing Chapala from the lake was published by Mexico City firm Alducin, the brainchild of Rafael Alducin (1889–1924), founder of the city's *El Excelsior* daily. After his death, the company became a worker-owned cooperative which continued to publish newspapers, magazines and high quality postcards, including some using experimental techniques, into the late 1940s or early 1950s.

The scene of fishermen and boats by Clara Thorward (1887–1969) was privately produced by the artist for personal use. Thorward, a renowned watercolorist, held

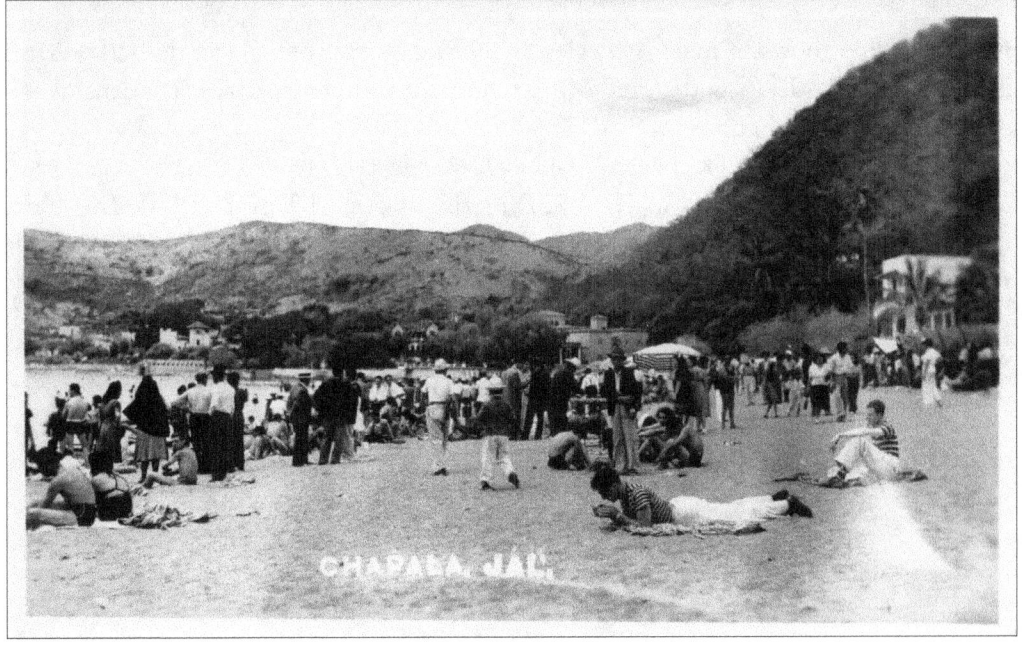

9.21. Chapala beach, c. 1958?
Whether wearing swimwear or formal attire, vacationers of all ages chatted and relaxed on the white sand beach of Chapala.

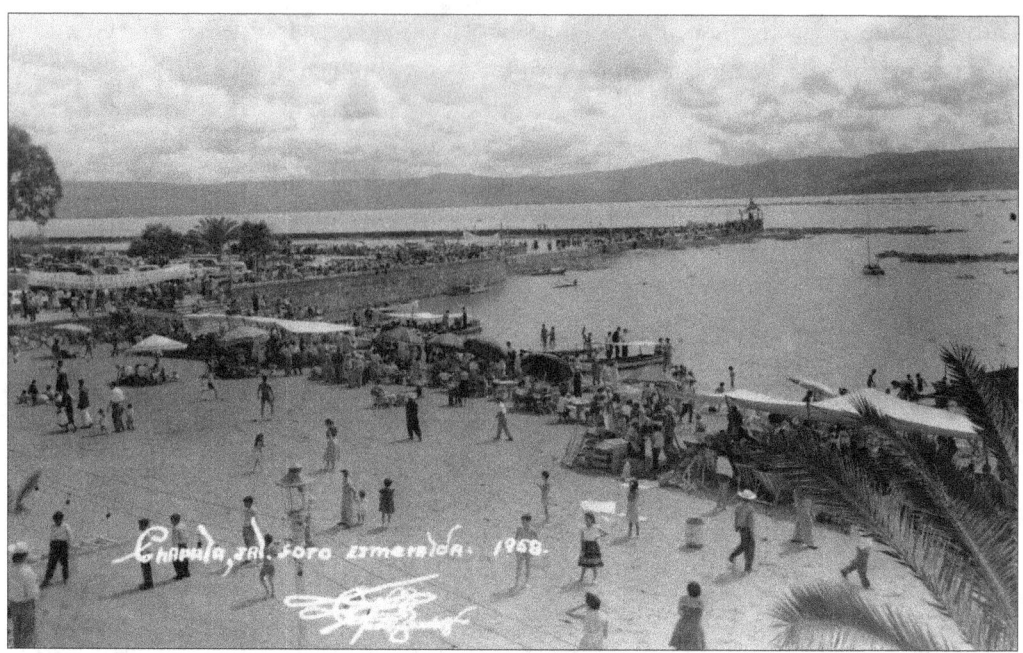

9.22. *Chapala beach and jetty, 1958. Foto Esmeralda.*
The park in the distance, east of the jetty, was a favorite place for families with young children. The banner on the extreme left reads "Demuestra tu cultura—Portate con dignidad y decencia" (Show your culture—Behave with dignity and decency), reminding visitors to be on their best behavior.

numerous solo shows in major galleries, including one at the Palacio de Bellas Artes in Mexico City in 1946, and visited Mexico numerous times to explore the central and southern parts of the country.

By 1960 the lake had recovered from its lowest level on record and the population of the town of Chapala had reached 7216, a rise of over 70% since 1940. The white sand beach of Chapala remained ever-popular. Visitors continued to enjoy a gentle stroll along the jetty to admire the boats and look back at the Chapala shoreline. The throngs of people every weekend on the jetty and waterfront at the end of the 1950s were testament to the long-standing and ever-enduring appeal of Lake Chapala.

10

Ajijic: favored by foreigners

In stark contrast to the town of Chapala, which enterprising entrepreneurs transformed at the dawn of the twentieth century into an important tourist destination—by adding hotels, steamships, fine residences, a yacht club and even a railroad—development in Ajijic began fifty years later.

The Mexican census of 1930 recorded a village population of 1882, with only a single foreigner—Alex von Mauch—then living in Ajijic. According to the 2020 census, Ajijic has become one of the most cosmopolitan settlements of its size in the world; 3090 of its 11,439 inhabitants were born outside Mexico. Members of the Ajijic-based Lake Chapala Society come from about 40 different countries. This explosive growth in

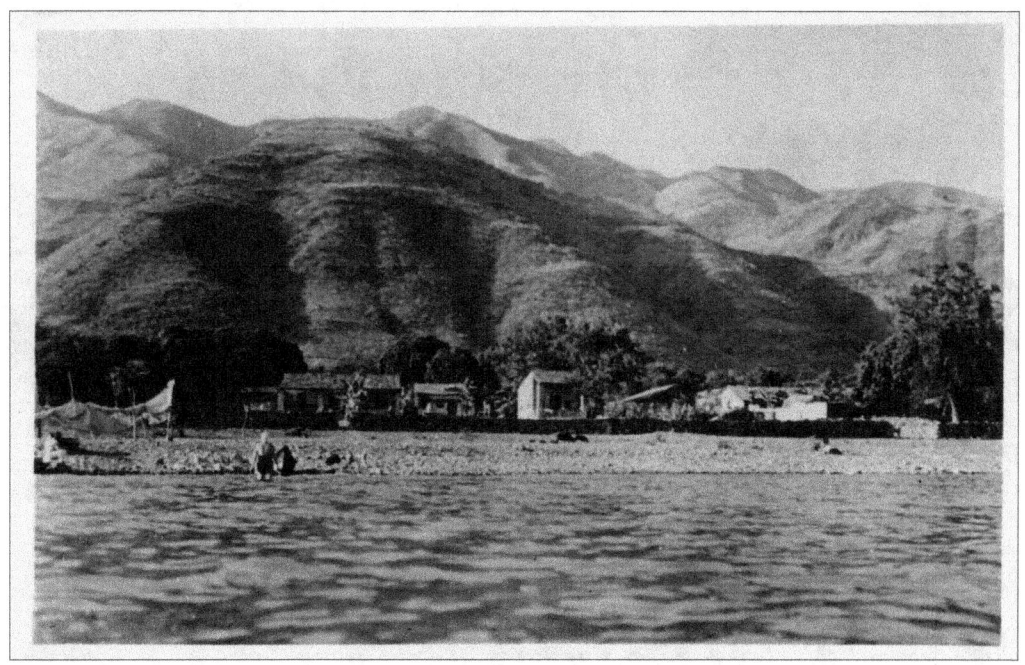

10.1. *View of Ajijic, c. 1945. H Johnson?*
On the shore left of center is Casa Heuer, the first hostelry in the village. The rustic inn was run by German émigré siblings Paul and Liesel Heuer from the mid-1930s to the late 1950s.

population has meant that modern housing subdivisions now stretch far up the slopes behind Ajijic and on either side of the former village.

In 1940, when Ajijic was still a tiny, dusty village of farmers and fishermen, only a handful of hardy foreigners had taken up residence in the village. They included Zara (La Rusa), with her dance partner, Holger Mehnen, and her mother; British author Nigel Millet and his father; recently arrived British engineer Herbert Johnson and his wife, Georgette; and the oddball German siblings Paul and Liesel Heuer. So it is not surprising that the earliest postcard of Ajijic dates back only as far as the mid-1940s.

Tourist interest in Ajijic began after the second world war, mushroomed during the 1950s (marked by a series of fine postcards), and exploded thereafter. Postally used examples of postcards of Ajijic are rare; the postcards were bought mainly as mementoes, not as a means of communication.

Prior to 1950 there were very few lakefront homes in Ajijic; most village homes were built a block or more back from the lake to avoid the risks of insect-borne diseases and floods. Among the foreigners who fell in love with the scenic shoreline and snapped up waterfront real estate at rock bottom prices were Paul and Liesel Heuer, whose inn attracted many international visitors, and Herbert and Georgette Johnson, who fled France for Ajijic just as the second world war erupted. Herbert is thought to be the photographer responsible for figure 10.1, the view of the Ajijic shoreline.

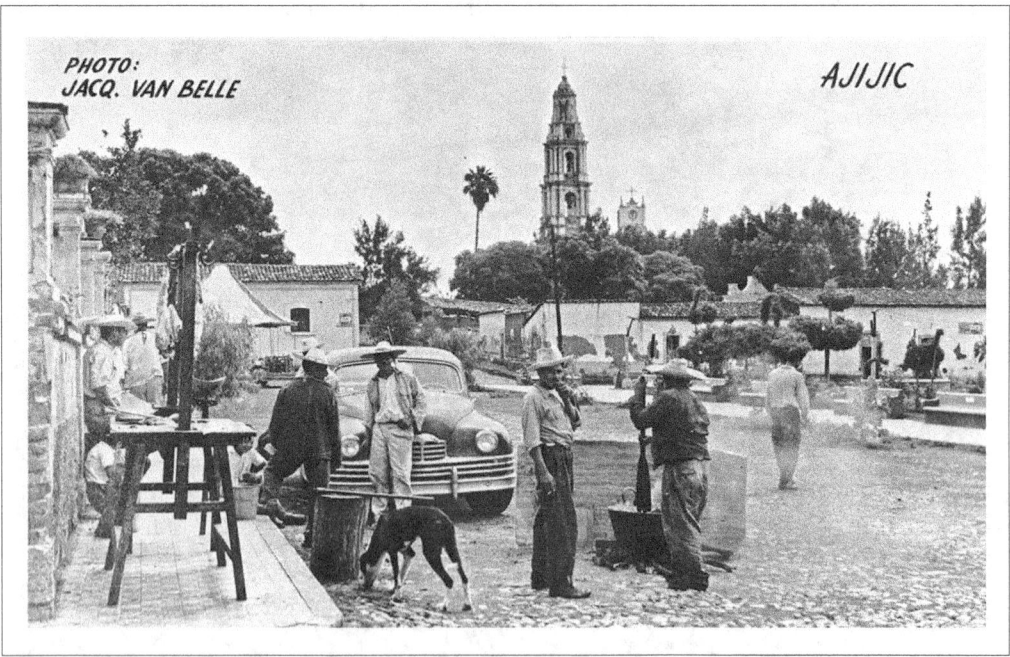

10.2. The north side of the plaza, looking east, c. 1957. J Van Belle.
In quieter times, with no foreign residents or tourists in sight, the single-story buildings allowed open views across the plaza to the church. Driving to Ajijic from Chapala was a perilous ordeal prior to the 1950s, particularly during the summer rainy season.

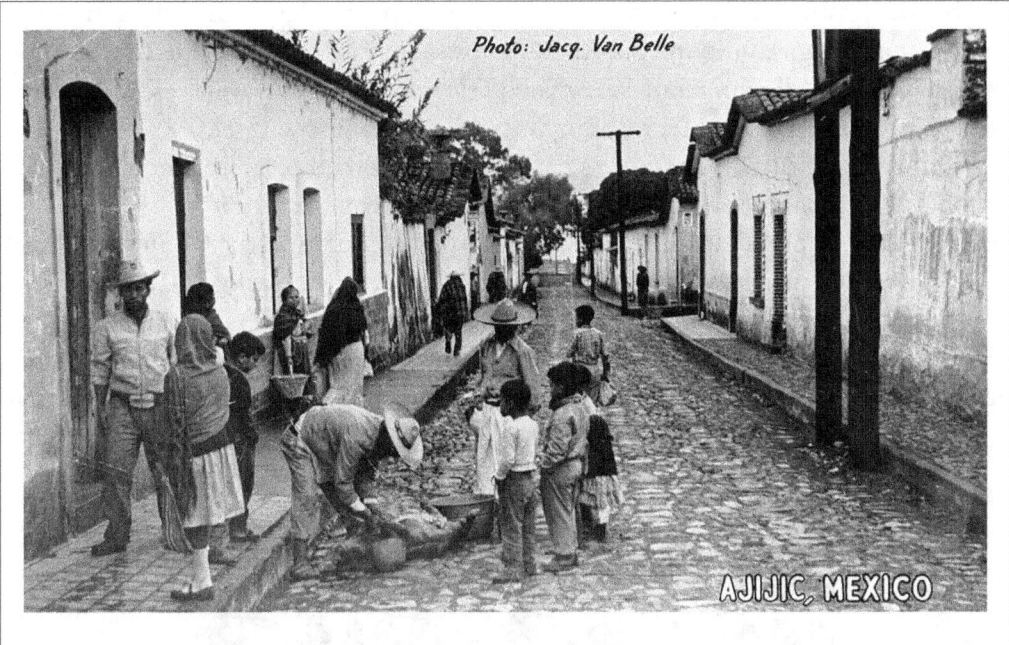

10.3. Meat day, c. 1957. J Van Belle.
The dearth of refrigeration in the village, even in the 1950s, meant that it was difficult to store any perishable foods. Hanging a red rag outside your home indicated that you had fresh meat available. A white rag indicated that a property was for rent.

English author Nigel Stansbury Millett and his father stayed at Casa Heuer for a few weeks in the late 1930s before moving to the Hacienda El Tlacuache, a lakefront property, alongside the pier, belonging to Casimiro and Josefina Ramírez. The Milletts persuaded their hosts to change its name to Posada Ajijic and allow them to run it as an inn. It was a village institution for more than half a century before closing in 1990. Using the nom de plume Dane Chandos, Nigel Millett and Peter Lilley co-wrote *Village in the Sun* (1945) and *House in the Sun* (1949), which brought Ajijic to the attention of the English-speaking literary public.

Electricity was installed in Ajijic in the late 1940s; prior to that households that wanted power had to rely on their own generators. Similarly, only in the 1950s did the village begin to supply potable water direct to homes. Previously, residents obtained their water from the lake, a spring in upper Ajijic, or from a communal holding tank in the plaza.

Ajijic was home to several adventurous artists in the 1940s. By the end of the decade the village had its own art gallery and offered art classes for international visitors. In the early 1950s two enterprising Englishmen—Peter Elstob and Arnold Eiloart—teamed up as Peter Arnold to run art vacations based at the Posada Ajijic.

A series of advertisements north of the border proclaimed that it was perfectly possible to live in Ajijic on $150 a month.[1] Similar advertisements, albeit it with upwardly revised figures, continued to appear for several years.

Besides hosting art groups, the Posada also became the center of social activity for the growing foreign community in Ajijic. Renovations in the 1960s helped attract more foreign tourists. All manner of Hollywood celebrities stayed in Ajijic, especially after former actor and restauranteur Booth Waterbury became manager.[2]

Only months after Waterbury's death in 1974, serendipity brought a Canadian couple—Judy and Morley Eager—to the hotel. They reopened the hotel the following year and never looked back.[3] In 1978, Morley helped organize the community's first chili cooking event which later morphed into the Mexican National Chili Cookoff, now a major fund raiser for local non-profits.[4] For many villagers the Posada was an important stepping stone to opening their own businesses; many of the shopkeepers and craftsmen of Ajijic started out by working in the Posada kitchen, bar or restaurant.

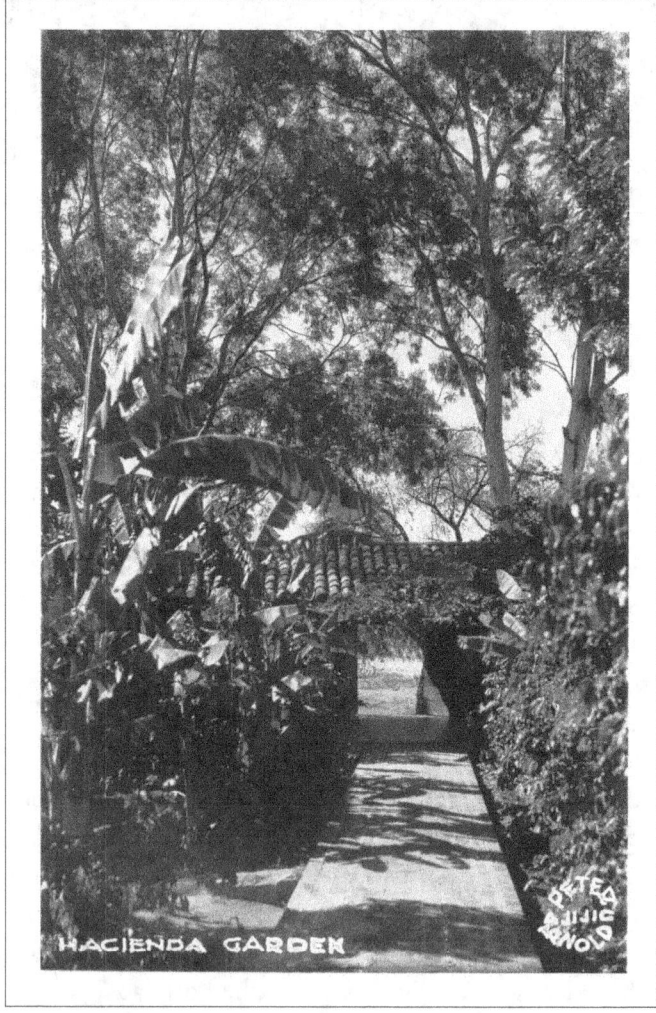

10.4. *Posada Ajijic, c. 1951. P Arnold.*
This publicity photo, aimed at the US market, showcased the tropical gardens of Posada Ajijic, the ideal venue for art and vacation stays.

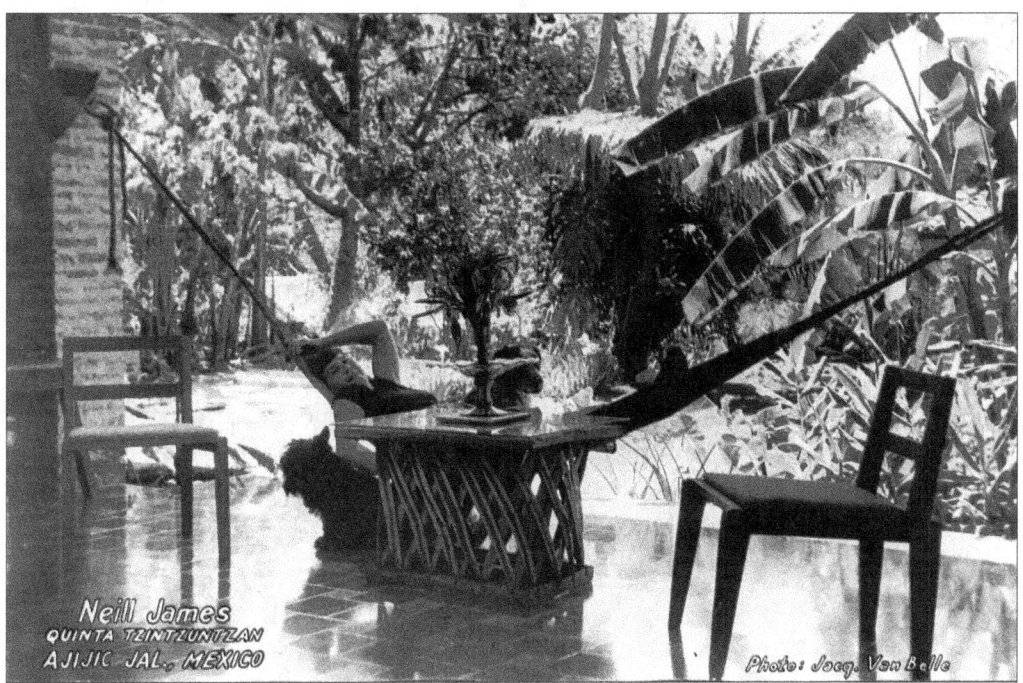

10.5. Neill James relaxing in her hammock at Quinta Tzintzuntzan, c. 1957. J Van Belle. James built Quinta Tzintzuntzan in 1948, five years after first arriving in Ajijic.

In 1990 the Eager family closed the Old Posada and opened La Nueva Posada on a lakeshore lot three blocks further east. By a strange twist of fate, it was on property once owned by Paul Heuer, who had started Ajijic's earliest, much more modest, lodging establishment at the other end of the village in the 1930s.

The single most influential foreigner to settle in Ajijic was American author Neill James (1895–1994), who made many positive contributions to the local community. When James first arrived, Ajijic had no electricity and only a single telephone. James established several businesses employing women, including the embroidery of cotton blouses and towels, Ajijic's first gift shop, and a clothing and weaving business, using cotton, wool, and locally produced silk. She also opened two children's libraries where, as an incentive for reading and studying, children were given free art classes. This was the start of the Children's Art Program, which stimulated so many talented youngsters to become professional artists, and which continues to this day.

In the 1970s, James proposed improving the village's appearance by adding murals of Mexican scenes. Though not immediately implemented, this was the genesis of the numerous, and remarkably varied, public murals that adorn Ajijic today. They include a colorful mural by Jesús López Vega in the Ajijic Cultural Center on the northern side of the plaza. It tells the story of mythological fish-princess Teomichicihualli, who, if angered, sucks up water from the lake, creates a water spout, and then dumps it onto nearby mountains, fields and homes.

The Ajijic artistic community today is comprised of a healthy mix of Mexicans and non-Mexicans, working in a wide variety of different media. There are numerous art studios and galleries open to the public, as well as frequent exhibitions in hotels, restaurants and the cultural center.

Neill James also donated buildings to the village for a health clinic, and gifted Quinta Tzintzuntzan, the home she built for herself in 1948, to the Lake Chapala Society a few years before she died. The Lake Chapala Society, with its extensive English language library, is a thriving hive of expat activities, from discussion groups, health check-ups and lectures to charitable events and exercise classes.

In about 1957 the Dutch-born professional photographer Jacques Van Belle produced a series of Ajijic postcards portraying life in Ajijic at the time.[5] Van Belle can only have visited for a few weeks at most, but took some captivating images of the village. The high proportion of images related to Neill James and her businesses suggests that the cards were commissioned by the American author for sale in her store.

With the arrival of more and more foreign settlers and tourists in Ajijic, many local businesses were established to support their needs and desires. The Chapala-Ajijic area was sufficiently well-known by 1957 that it was the subject of a photo-article in *Life* magazine, and featured in dozens of newspaper articles. The following year, Ajijic

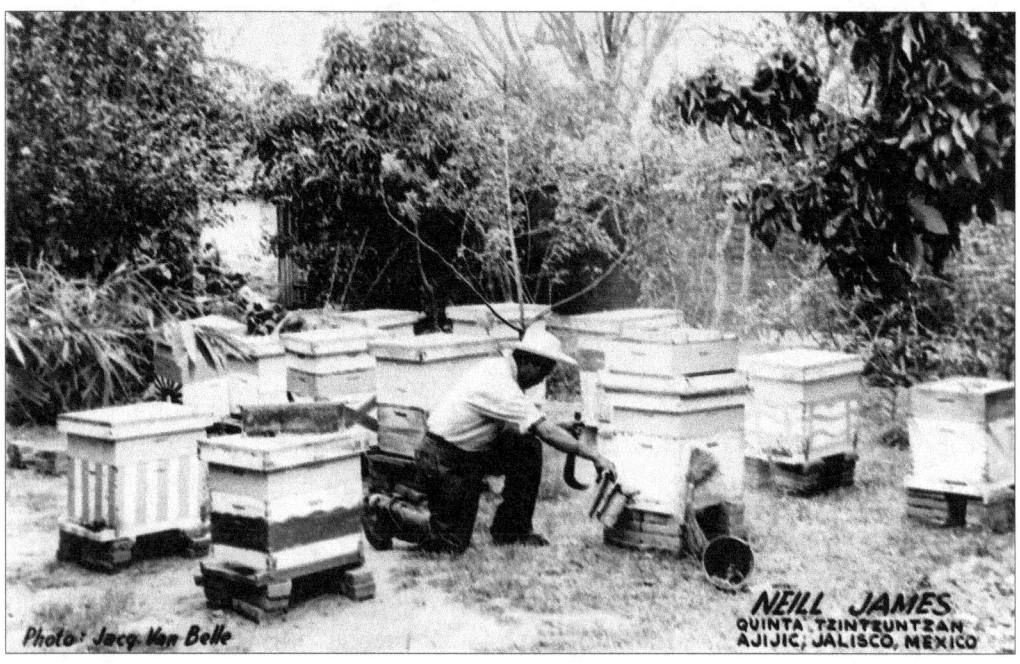

10.6. *Beekeeping, c. 1957. J Van Belle.*
Neill James kept twelve colonies of honey bees in Ajijic for about a decade. Honey production proved to be more of a hobby than a business and was never very profitable, exactly as Austrian musician Alex von Mauch had found in the 1930s, when he had maintained beehives at his ranch in western Ajijic.

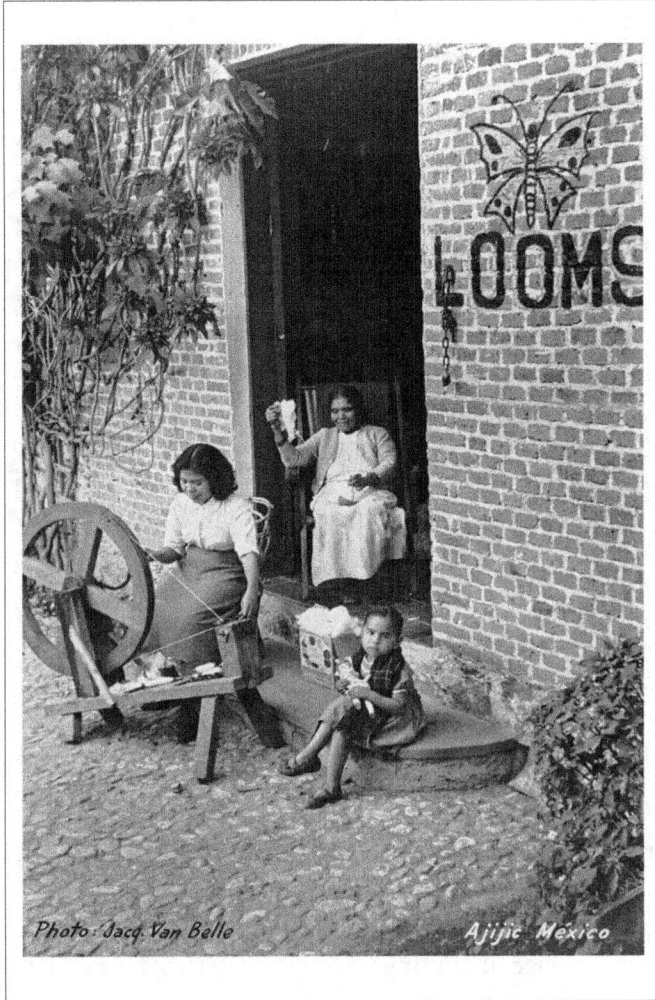

10.7. *Neill James - Looms, c. 1957. J Van Belle.*
Neill James started her looms business in the early 1950s in direct competition with Ajijic Hand Looms.

starred in a 30-minute TV documentary about Lake Chapala titled *The Expatriates*. Among those interviewed on camera was Helen Kirtland, of Ajijic Hand Looms.[6]

Ajijic Hand Looms, the village's first large-scale weaving business was begun in 1950 by American designer Helen Kirtland and her artist-writer husband, Mort Carl. Neill James started her own smaller-scale weaving business shortly afterwards. Ajijic Hand Looms gained an international reputation for the quality of its textiles and clothing items. The business, later known as Telares Ajijic, continued into the early 1990s.

Much of village life in the 1950s revolved, as it had done for centuries, around fishing and farming. It was common to see long fishing nets strung out along the beach to dry, a picturesque sight depicted by numerous photographers and artists. The invariable costume of Ajijic fishermen was "white trousers rolled to the knee,

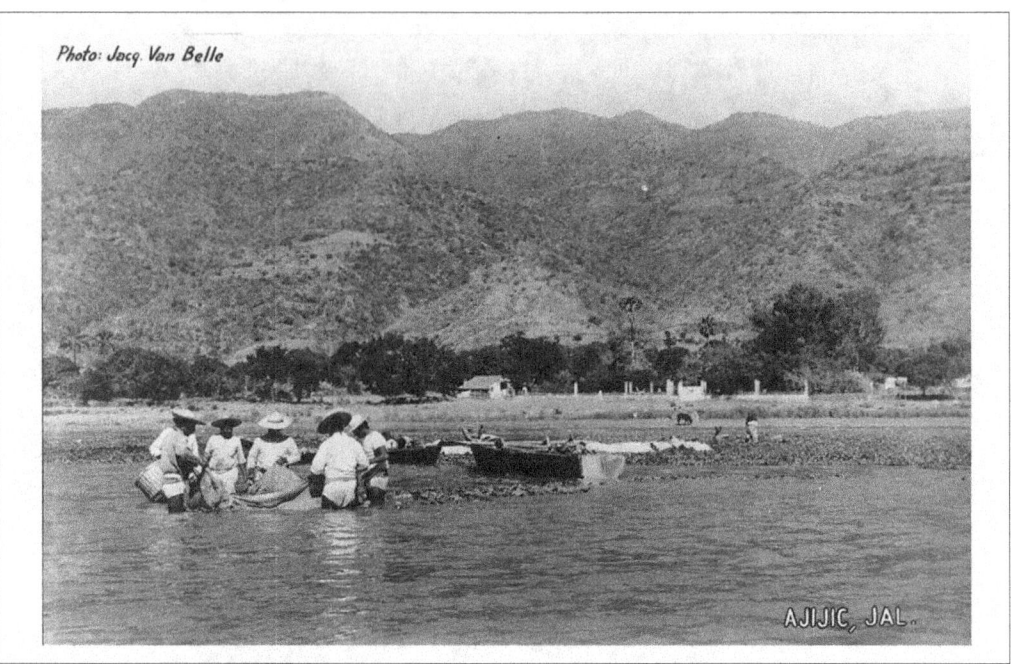

10.8. Fishing, c. 1957. J Van Belle.
The lakeside home in the middle of this photograph, taken in the western part of Ajijic, is, following the severe drought of 1955, much further from the water than normal. Behind it rise the steep slopes of Sierra El Travesaño.

faded blue shirts open to the diaphragm and knotted at the waist, and flat, white sombreros."[7]

In addition to Casa Heuer and Posada Ajijic, several other hotels of note opened mid-century in the village, including Quinta Mi Retiro, Posada Rancho Santa Isabel, and Hotel Laguna.

Quinta Mi Retiro, at Calle 16 de Septiembre 34, was owned from the mid-1940s by retired Mexican general José de Jesús Ahumada Alatorre and his wife, Remigia. Travel writer Mabel Knight told her readers in 1952 that "The General's House or Quinta Mi Retiro," had several elegant lake view bungalows, which, given that the hotel did not offer any meals, were "designed for Mexican families with maids."[8] A second article a few years later described the "Gran Hotel del General" as the most luxurious hotel in the village.[9]

An eccentric Englishman, the self-styled Dr Bernard Lytton-Bernard, rented part of Quinta Mi Retiro in the 1950s to establish the first health spa at Lake Chapala. Lytton-Bernard had previously published several popular books in the US on topics such as diet, sex and marriage. A former Olympic wrestler, who stood barely five feet tall, he was subsequently convicted of mail fraud for a scheme promoting a height increasing apparatus! Lytton-Bernard was an ardent advocate of vegetarianism and, during his time in Ajijic, actively promoted the health benefits of papaya. Towards the end of the 1950s, Lytton-Bernard closed his Ajijic spa to open the Río Caliente health spa in the Primavera Forest, a short distance west of Guadalajara.

The Posada Rancho Santa Isabel was built on a lakefront lot at the eastern edge of Ajijic in 1956 by Chapala-born Isabel Hunton and her husband, Carlos Zeiner. According to *Terry's Guide to Mexico*, it was a pleasant, informal, cottage-type establishment with ten units, a fair dining room and cocktail service. Double rooms, with private bath and veranda, were $9.60 a night, meals included.[10] By the time Posada Rancho Santa Isabel closed in March 1975, three small motels were operating in Ajijic: La Carreta on the village plaza, and Las Calandrias and Las Casitas on the main highway.[11]

The relatively short-lived Hotel Laguna, a block west of the plaza on Calle Juárez, was the forerunner of the Hotel Anita, "the hot spot in town" in the early 1960s, when the bar was "a classic watering hole for the rich and semi famous… and anyone else who wandered in."[12] The property ceased to be a hotel in about 1970.

During the 1960s, Ajijic was 'discovered' by hippies. These politically active youngsters descended in droves on the village, where many experimented with marijuana and ever-stronger consciousness-changing drugs, such as LSD. The hippie lifestyle openly challenged traditional Mexican attitudes and drew the ire of many villagers. Following a series of purges of 'undesirables' by authorities, some degree of order was restored.

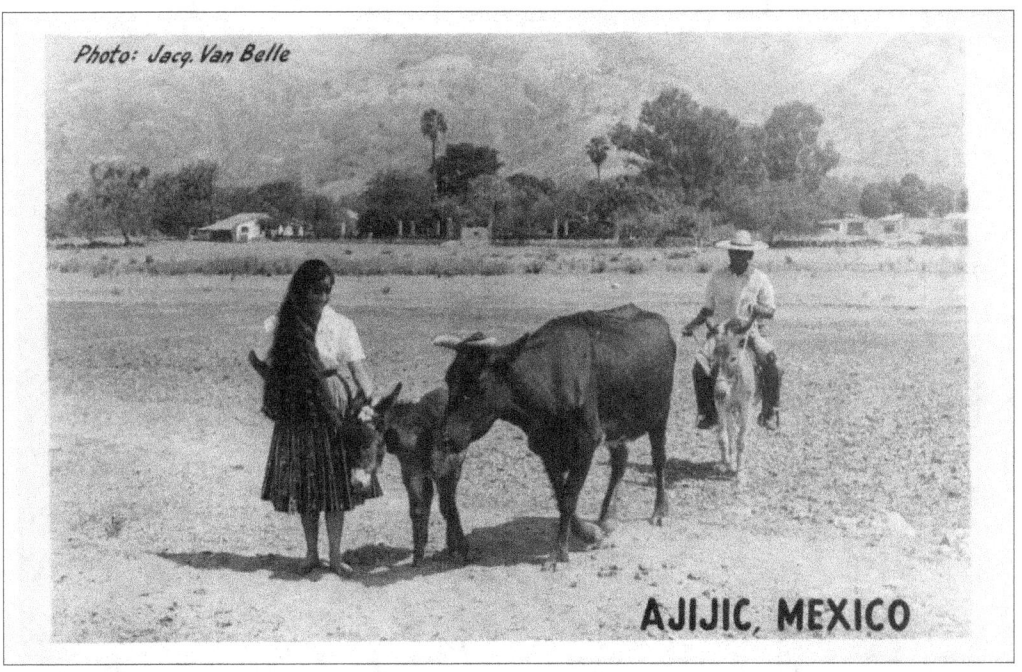

10.9. *Leading the animals to water, c. 1957. J Van Belle.*
Taken in the vicinity of the previous photograph, the effects of the 1955 drought are evident, shown by the wide expanse of former lakebed still exposed. The line of trees marks the normal shoreline. The lake recovered after the bountiful rainy season in 1958.

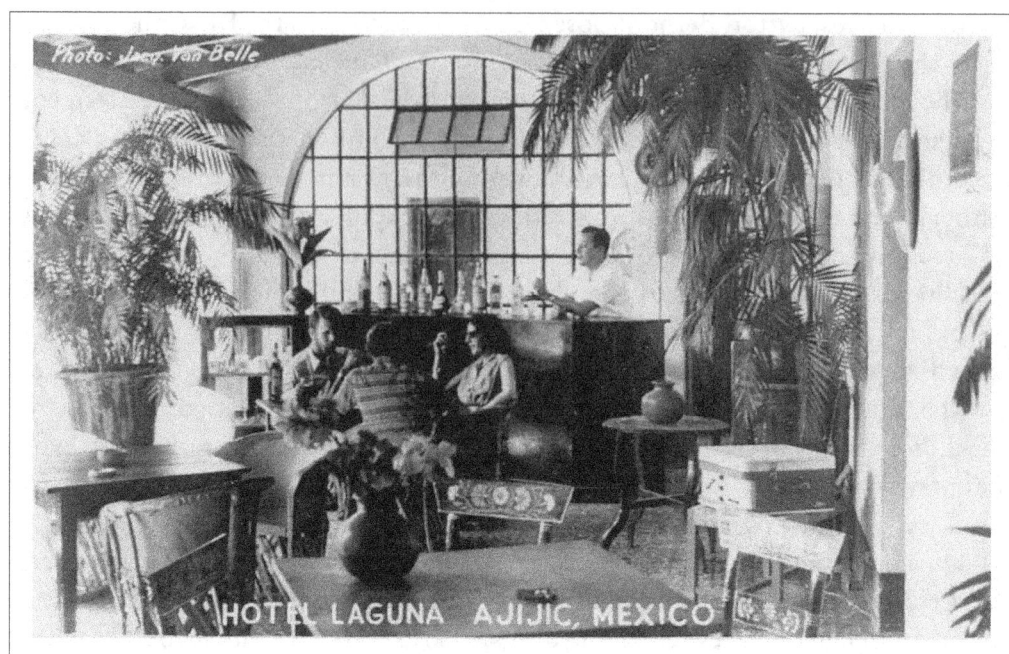

10.10. Hotel Laguna, c. 1957. J Van Belle.
The bar of the relatively short-lived Hotel Laguna was, for a time, the 'in' place to drink and relax.

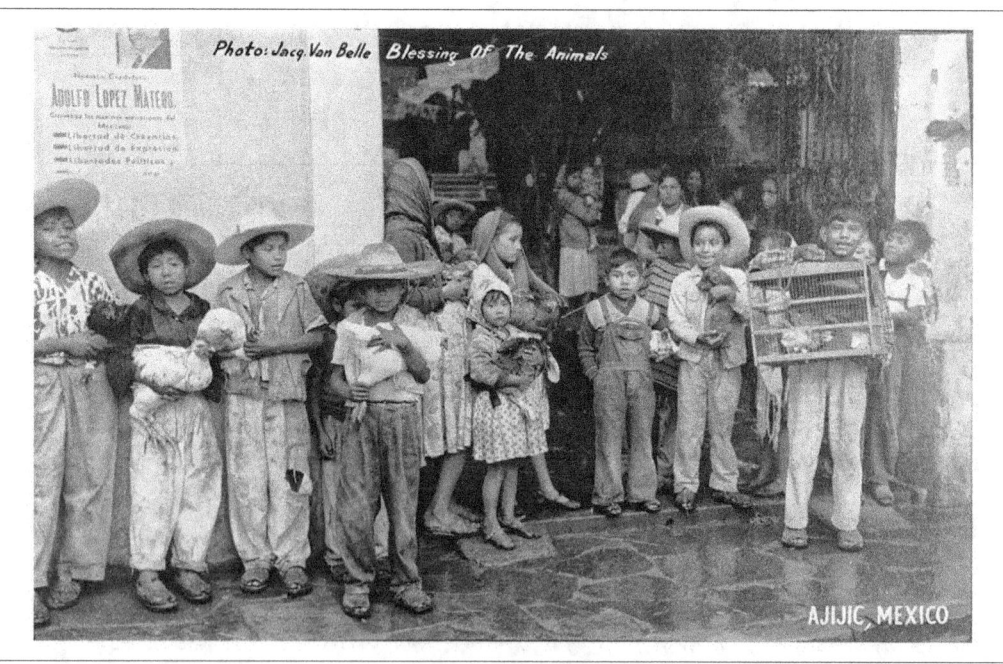

10.11. Blessing of animals, c. 1957. J Van Belle.
Children wait patiently to have their pets blessed by the local priest. The political poster on the wall dates this image to 1957.

Among the many annual events long celebrated in Ajijic is the Blessing of Animals on 17 January, the Fiesta of St. Anthony the Abbot (San Antonio Abad). This eloquent description comes from 1951:

> Every animal in the village, from bulls to pet doves, from pigs to cats to burros, to goats, are bathed and sprayed with perfume. Some of the animals are lovingly painted with color and always they are bowed in great satin pink and red ribbons. The animals are then led under the wall of the church where the priest stands, reading to them an imposing text, and scattering over their sweet heads his liquid dispensation. Things often get a trifle out of hand, as bulls start bellowing, armadillos run away, and spoiled cats climb up the priest's robe.[13]

Less blessed are the bulls selected for local bullfights and some of the horses ridden by matadors in the bullring.

Other annual festivities include the nine-day fiesta in honor of San Andrés at the end of November, which has all the usual fairground amusements accompanied by music, folkloric dancing and plenty of fireworks, and the Ajijic Easter celebration, now one of the most extravagant in the country, when local farmers, fishermen, shopkeepers and tradespeople reenact the trial and crucifixion of Christ. The costuming and open-air sets are magnificent and this is a real must-be-seen-to-be-believed occasion.

When Neill James first arrived in 1943, Ajijic had "six streets which parallel the lake, cut by six others extending from lake to the sierras."[14] By about 1960 the village

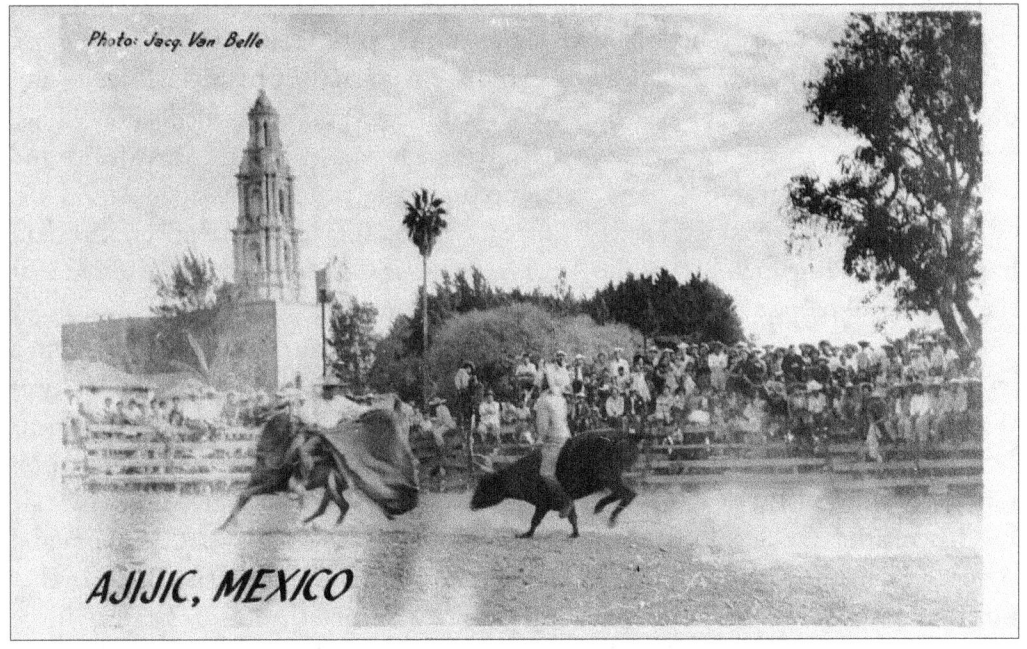

10.12. Bullfight. Matador on horseback teases a bull, c. 1957. J Van Belle. In the background is the parish church of San Andrés, dating from 1749.

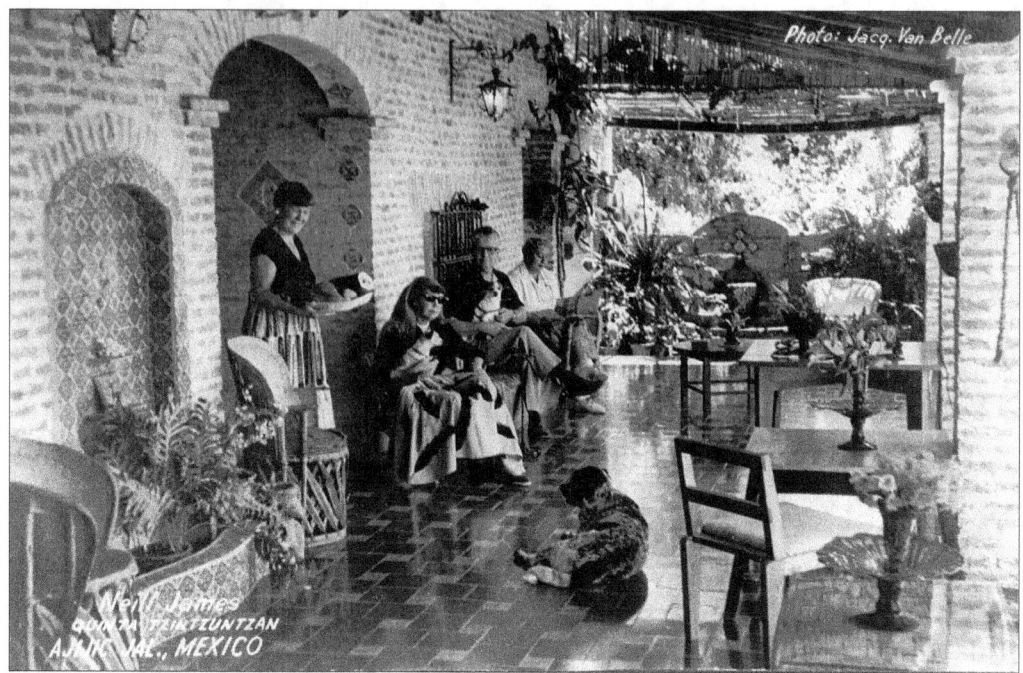

10.13. Neill James entertains guests at Quinta Tzintzuntzan, c. 1957. J Van Belle. Ajijic benefactor Neill James (standing) serves guests at her home. Shortly before she died, James gifted this property to the Lake Chapala Society.

extended four or five blocks in each direction from the plaza, with the eastern edge of the village more or less coinciding with Calle Francisco I Madero.

Urban sprawl changed Ajijic for ever in the 1970s when the massive La Floresta subdivision was constructed, with its broad, cobblestone streets and decidedly non-village feel. It was the first major tourist-residential integrated complex anywhere in Mexico and included a luxury Camino Real hotel, later purchased by the Universidad Autónoma de Guadalajara and renamed Hotel Real de Chapala. The development certainly had its critics, including members of the Ajijic Indigenous Community who asserted that they had never relinquished their rights over the property.

Ajijic also expanded rapidly westwards. The Hotel Danza del Sol, also now owned by the Universidad Autónoma de Guadalajara, was built in the early 1970s. Many of the subdivisions further west were built on land amassed by Buffalo-born entrepreneur Louis Wertheimer, who first arrived in Ajijic in about 1960 and gained a reputation for unscrupulous land dealings. Rural properties developed by Wertheimer include La Cristina, Las Salvias, Piedra Rayada, Tio Domingo, Alceseca, La Canacinta and Arroyo Colorado. Were she still alive, Neill James would be disheartened to learn that a plethora of subdivisions in recent decades has now turned the former fishing village of Ajijic into an almost continuous amorphous urbanized mass stretching from La Canacinta to San Antonio Tlayacapan.

11

West end: Jocotepec and Roca Azul

The earliest postcards of Jocotepec all appear to date from the 1950s and none identifies the photographer or includes any date or formal publisher imprint on the reverse. Given the variety of styles and typefaces used for captions, it seems likely that they were self-published, perhaps by more than one photographer. Very few postally used examples of these postcards are known. As was the case in Ajijic, the majority of the postcards were probably purchased by visitors and hotel guests as mementos of their stay in Jocotepec.

When the Spaniards arrived in the early sixteenth century, they moved the settlement of Xilotepec (place of the tender corn) and renamed it San Francisco Xocotepec

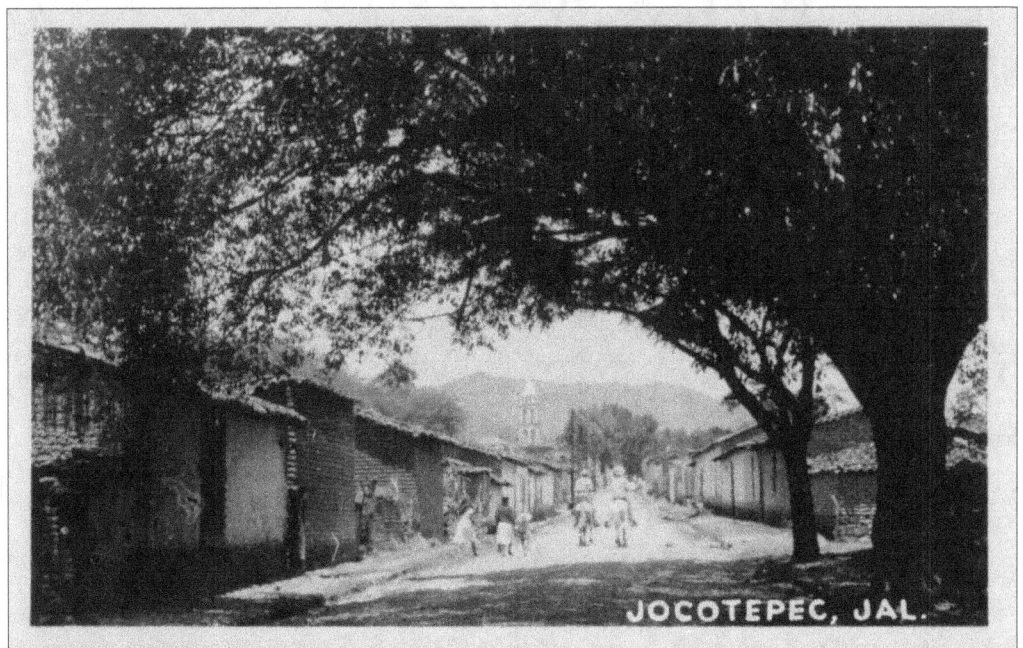

11.1. Calle Miguel Arana, looking west towards the plaza, c. 1955. R Whipple?
The plaza, which had large trees at the time, is in the distance, to the right of the multi-tiered steeple of the San Francisco church.

(place of the guavas), which in time became simply Jocotepec. Today, in terms of fruit, Jocotepec is best known for producing raspberries, primarily for export.

The original sixteenth-century church was destroyed in a storm; its replacement, remodeled several times, dates from some two hundred years later. The last major reconstruction of the church was at the end of the nineteenth century, and was overseen by Miguel Arana, priest of the parish from 1866 to his death in 1888. Arana, who is remembered today in the name of one of the town's main streets, initiated the fiesta of La Virgen del Refugio which takes place in early July each year.[1]

In Arana's time, the main route, or *camino real,* through Jocotepec from Ajijic ran along Calle Morelos, before continuing west past the town cemetery and along Calle

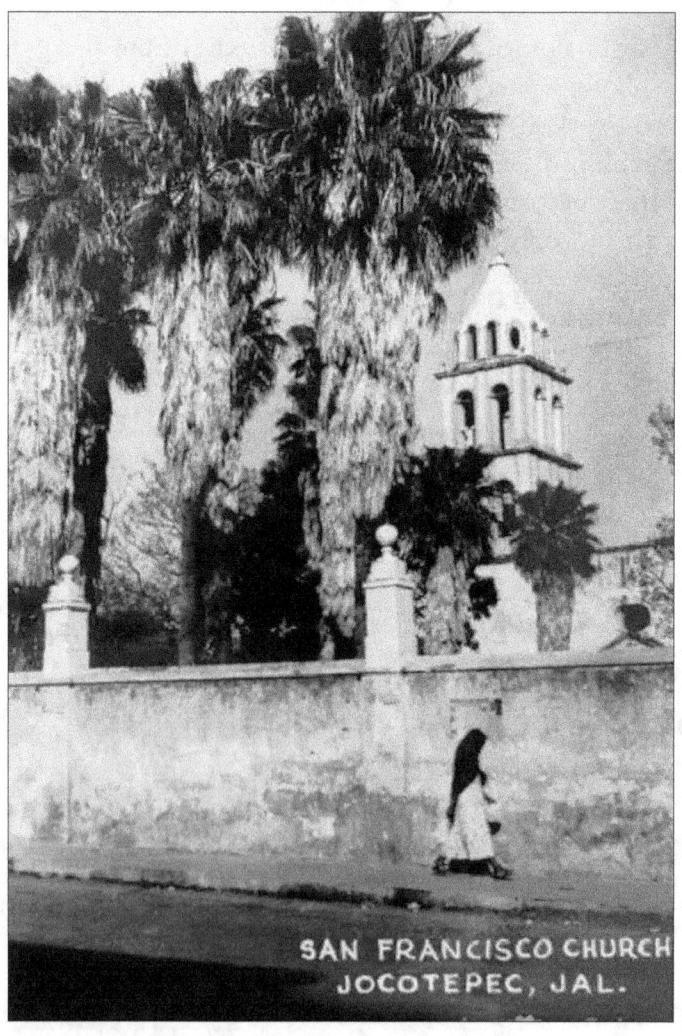

11.2. San Francisco Church, Jocotepec, c. 1955. R Whipple?
The parish church, with its distinctive steeple, looks benevolently over the town plaza; visitors to Jocotepec's main church have a good chance of witnessing a first communion, baptism or marriage ceremony.

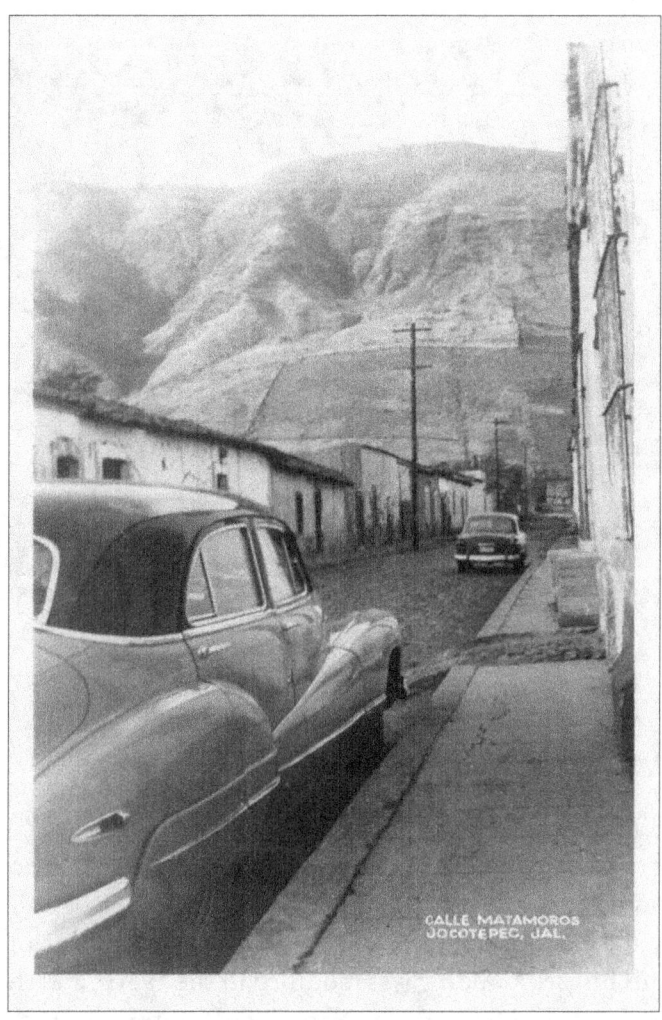

11.3. Calle Matamoros, looking north, c. 1955. R Whipple?
The prominent steep hill in the background, Cerro Los Agraciados—verdant green in the rainy season and tones of brown the rest of the year—forms a wonderfully scenic backdrop to Jocotepec.

Anima Sola. A different route was chosen in the mid-twentieth century for the first paved highway through the town. It followed the street (now called Calle Miguel Arana) one block south of Morelos as far as the plaza, and then turned south along Calle Hidalgo before heading west to meet Highway 15, the main Morelia-Guadalajara highway.

Prior to the 1980s, Jocotepec was a town of predominantly single-story adobe dwellings with tile roofs. Since then the fashion for concrete buildings, with multiple stories, has completely transformed the look of the town. Unlike Ajijic and Chapala, Jocotepec has not been enhanced by any homes designed by regionally famous architects.

Years before the advent of tourism in Chapala, the Hotel La Quinta served merchants and travelers as their last overnight stop on their way to Guadalajara from Mexico City and Morelia. La Quinta first opened its doors to visitors in 1824 and has

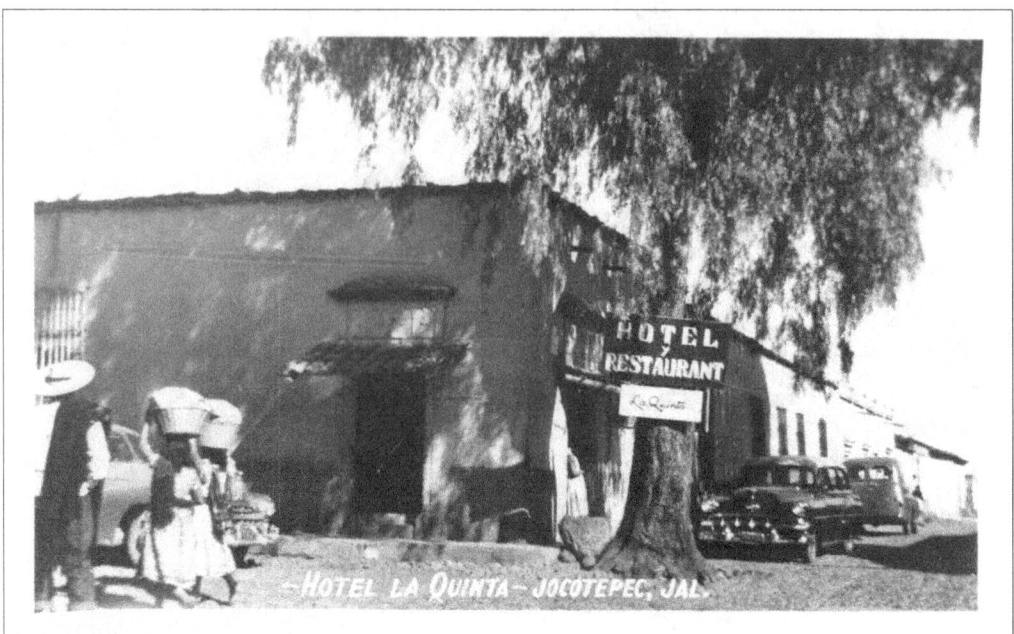

11.4. Entrance to Hotel La Quinta, c. 1955. R Whipple?
La Quinta briefly hosted French troops in 1864 and famous revolutionary Francisco "Pancho" Villa allegedly slept in the inn in 1915, before fighting (and winning) the Battle of Sayula.

one of the most interesting histories of any lakeside building. By 1970 it was billed as the "oldest public hostelry in continuous operation in Western Mexico."[2]

La Quinta occupied the north-east corner at the intersection of Calle Miguel Arana and Calle Matamoros. Lamentably, in an act of wanton destruction of the town's cultural heritage, this historic building was modified in the 1980s, and then demolished.

Formerly known as El Mesón de los Naranjitos (for its orange trees), the inn was very close to the nineteenth-century stagecoach route from Mexico City and Morelia to Guadalajara. After an overnight stop it could take ten hours or more to ride into Guadalajara. The *camino real* connecting Mexico City to Guadalajara was also used by mule and burro "trains" of up to 100 animals at a time.

Walled corrals, where horses and pack animals could be fed and watered, once surrounded the inn. To ensure that the benefits of this passing trade were maximized, the hotel had strict rules including "No se permite que entre pastura" (Guests are not allowed to bring hay), meaning that only the hotel could furnish any traveler's exhausted animals with feed. All this through-traffic guaranteed a regular income not only to the hotel but also to the town's ladies of the night and others. After the completion of the railroad between Mexico City and Guadalajara in 1888, Jocotepec drifted into quieter times, even though stagecoaches continued to run through the town until about 1920.

The hotel was a typical adobe building with a tile roof, shuttered windows and wrought-iron work. Inside, it was built one room deep around three patios. Entering was like stepping into a tropical garden: "Banana trees with bunches of bananas on them, orange trees..., bougainvillea... gorgeous geraniums, filled the patios."[3]

Among the many owners of La Quinta over the years was Allen W Lloyd, who arrived in the early 1950s and married Martha O'Rourke Manjarrez, a Mexican widow with four children. He offered guests advice about automobile insurance and investments in Mexico, which led to him starting his own eponymous firm in Guadalajara a few years later.

Lloyd also claimed some responsibility for reviving Jocotepec's traditional sarape industry. Older guide books refer to the town's famous white sarapes, though the traditional sarapes were never entirely white, but had subtle black or grey designs or colored flower motifs.

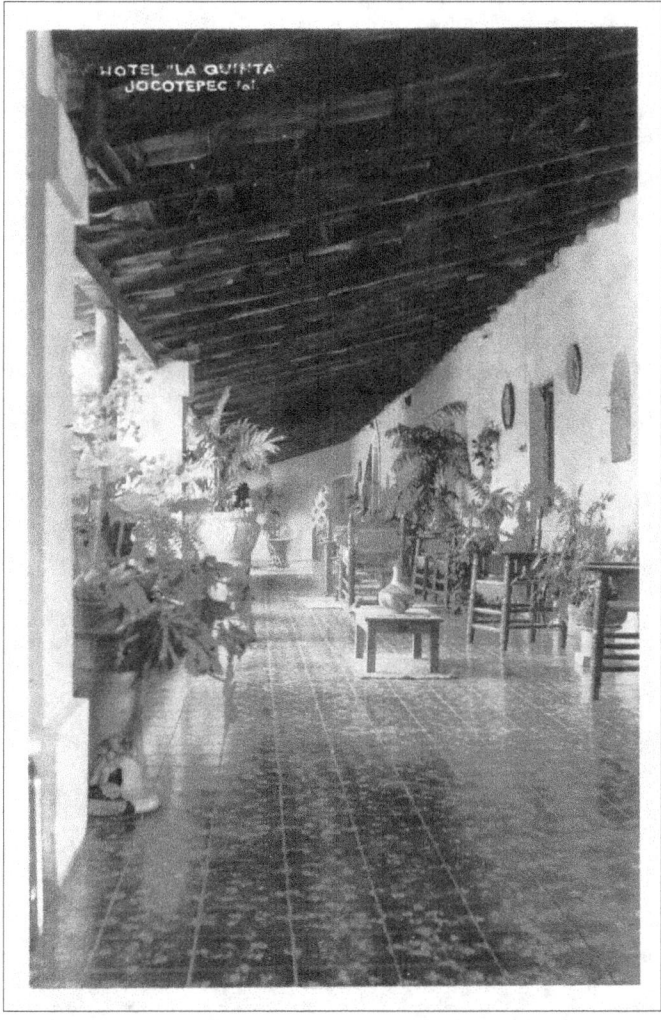

11.5. Tile-floored passageway in La Quinta. c. 1955. R Whipple?
Long galleries with tiled floors were hung with colorful Mexican handiwork. A table and chairs were provided for the private use of the occupants of each room.

The town's reputation for fine sarapes goes back a long time. In 1923, D H Lawrence was so taken with the craftsmanship of Jocotepec artisans that he traveled by boat from Chapala to Jocotepec to commission a special sarape, which he collected a few days later. Witter Bynner, who accompanied Lawrence, later wrote a poem titled "A Weaver from Jocotepec." Excellent woven blankets, sarapes, and wall-hangings are still produced on hand looms in the town.

The owner of La Quinta from about 1958 to 1976 was Robert (Bob) Whipple Jr (1928–1991), a former archaeology student who had served as a chief radio technician in the US Navy, and had just come into a small inheritance. A 1958 reviewer boasted of having found "the most charming old inn, La Quinta, right in the middle of a primitive little fishing village alive with children, burros and nut-brown old women in black shawls."[4]

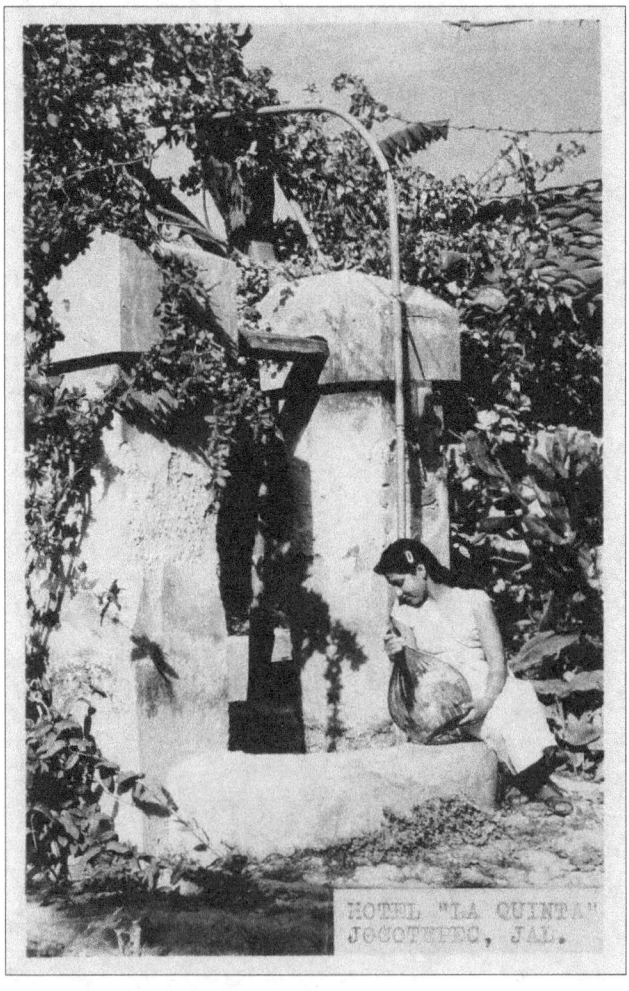

11.6. *Well at Hotel La Quinta, c. 1955. R Whipple?*
La Quinta obtained its water from two private wells. The original well, which dated back to mid-nineteenth century, was still functional into the 1970s.

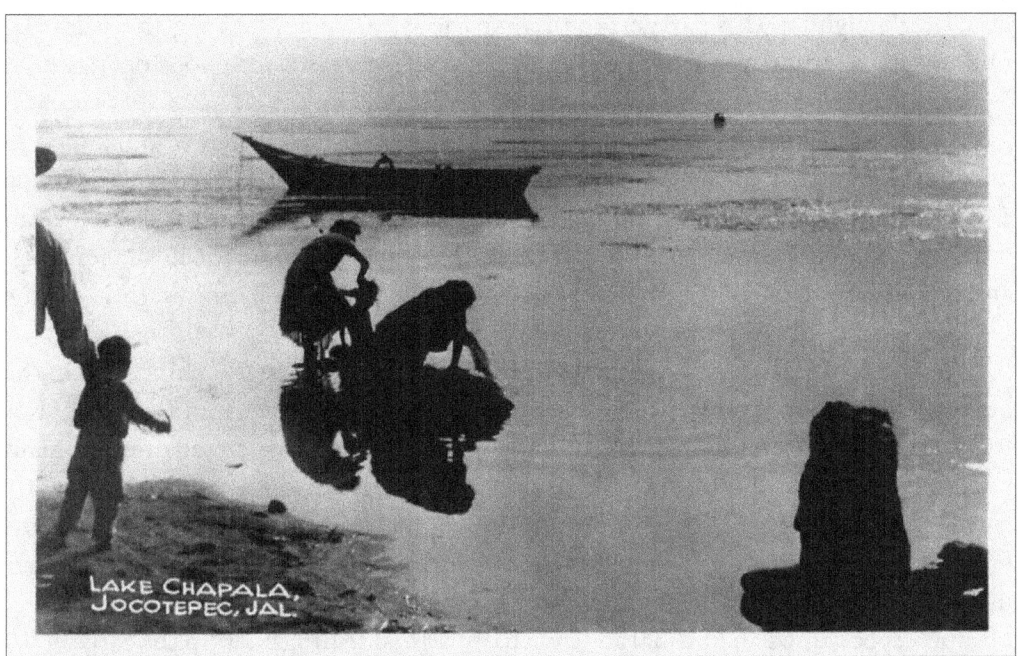

11.7. Lakeside scene, c. 1955. R Whipple?
A mother is bathing a child while a second woman is doing her washing in the lake. The aquatic weeds in this photo are masses of water hyacinth (lirio).

Most of the postcards in this chapter are believed to be the work of Whipple, who welcomed all manner of guests to La Quinta. Lady Bird Johnson did not stay overnight but did visit her brother and his wife who stayed for several days each year.[5] Whipple recalled that the Lord Mayor of Edinburgh, famous international artists and writers, Vincent Price, aristocrats and judges, tequila manufacturers and foreign correspondents all spent time at La Quinta. When Mexican President-elect Adolfo López Mateos visited the hotel in 1958, he arrived by way of Chapala; paving the final stretch of the Chapala–Jocotepec road had been completed only a few hours earlier.

After a decade running the hotel, Whipple decided to sell, and installed Peter and Nancy Spencer as interim managers. Whipple accepted a down payment for the hotel from Al Matthews, a flamboyant California-based trial lawyer, and La Quinta re-opened under new management in September 1965 with an extravagant party attended by former president Miguel Alemán and local dignitaries.

However, the purchase fell through after Matthews installed his "son" as manager, and ran La Quinta as "the place to stash his hot clients." Mexican immigration officials swooped in and arrested the manager and an accomplice—it turned out that both were wanted by the FBI—as they tried to flee the country, and handed them over to US authorities.

Whipple finally succeeded in selling La Quinta in 1976, this time strictly for cash, to a group of local Jocotepec businessmen. One member of this group, Ignacio

Jara, later bought out his partners to become the sole owner. Not long afterwards La Quinta's extraordinary run as the oldest public hostelry in continuous operation in Western Mexico came to an end.

In 1979 the property was rented by Morley and Michael Eager, who planned to install a new kitchen and open it as a restaurant, even as they worked to get Posada Ajijic back on track. Not long afterwards, Canadian Howard Fryer and his Mexican wife, Yolanda, took over, gave La Quinta back its original name of Los Naranjitos, and established a gift shop and Jocotepec's first pizzería on the premises. In 1984, the Fryers moved the Los Naranjitos restaurant to Ajijic.[6]

After a spell as a dance-hall, and in the absence of adequate maintenance, the building fell into disrepair. The interior was drastically remodeled in the mid-1980s for use as a discotheque. The luxuriant La Quinta garden was concreted over, the main patio lost its stone columns, and the former open courtyard was given an unsightly corrugated metal roof. Then, in the early 1990s, the remaining historic parts of the building, including its largely intact exterior, were demolished to make way for a hideous modern store and open air car park.[7] May it rest in peace.

Jocotepec gained an unusual addition to its regular fishing boats in the early 1970s when the *Reina Guadalupe*, a faux side-wheeled paddle steamer under construction for use as a vehicle and passenger ferry between Ajijic and Puerto Corona, was set free from its moorings in Puerto Corona and drifted across the lake. It was advertised in

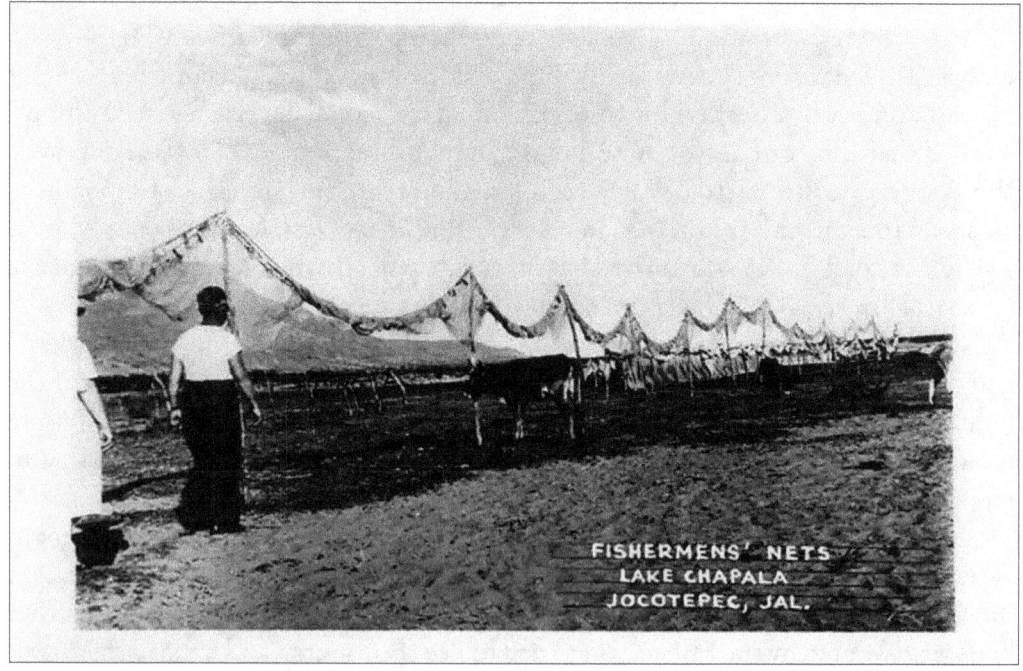

11.8. *Fishermen checking their nets. c. 1955. R Whipple?*
Nets this long, used for commercial fishing when fish were more plentiful, required the close cooperation of several boats and fishermen.

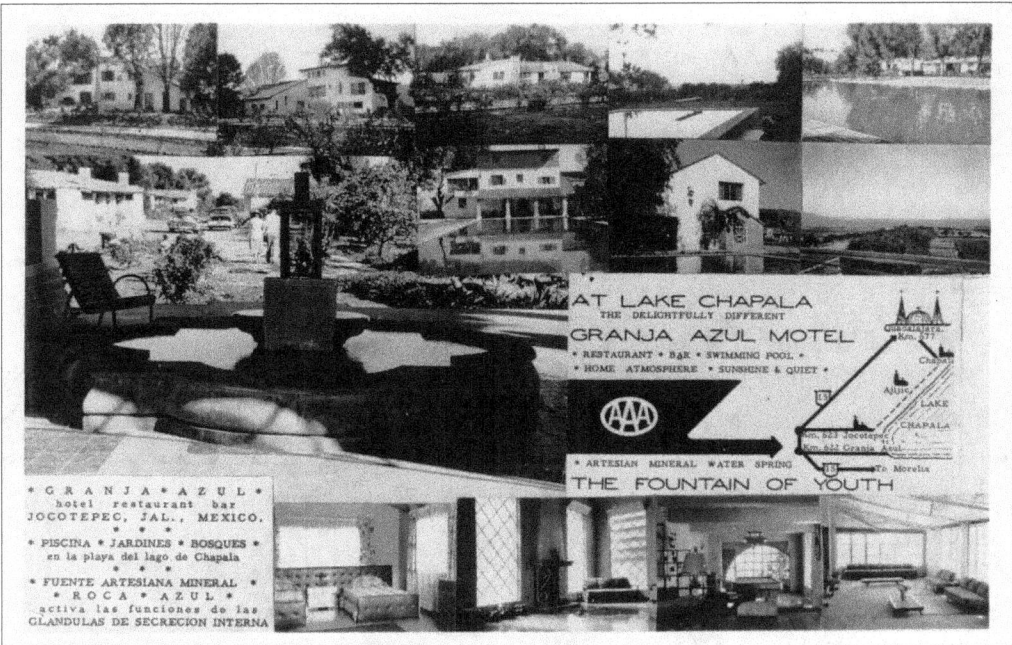

11.9. Granja Azul Motel, c 1956.
The small photos on this promotional postcard for the Granja Azul Motel, on the southern outskirts of Jocotepec, show the accommodations, restaurant, bar, and country homes comprising the subdivision now known as Roca Azul.

1977 as the venue for a restaurant-bar and a floating center for dances, with rentals supervised by Carlos Rodríguez, the then mayor of Jocotepec.[8] After a few years, the business failed, the boat was abandoned, and its stripped-out hull left to rust on Jocotepec beach. It was eventually sold for scrap.[9]

Mexico's first Centro de Estudios Tecnológicos en Aguas Continentales (Center for Freshwater Technological Studies) was established in Jocotepec in the 1980s. Its students take academic courses alongside vocational training in fields such as aquaculture, environmental science and food production.

Roca Azul, adjacent to Jocotepec, was best known, prior to its subdivision in the mid-1950s, for commercializing mineral water from a spring named Agua Santa (Holy Water). The original plans for Roca Azul included a lighthouse, yacht club and communal areas, as well as an extensive residential area. The first regatta for the Roca Azul Cup (Copa Roca Azul) was held in August 1971,[10] when property in this section of the lakeshore sold for only about $3.20 a square meter. Those were the days! Sadly, by the end of the decade, a shortage of investors, and the shallow depth of that portion of the lake, had ended hopes for a viable yacht club. Despite the failure of the yacht club, Roca Azul remains a focal point for attractive private homes, and continues to provide a mix of tourist services, including an RV park, sports facilities and restaurant, to this day.

Acknowledgments

Most of the postcards chosen for this book come from the author's private collection, which includes several cards generously donated by Sylvia Fein, Dr RB Brown and Margarita Manzo viuda de González. I am very grateful to the following individuals for their kindness in supplying and allowing me to use additional images:

Ing. Mario González García (figures 5.7, 5.25, 7.2, 7.12, 7.18, 9.10)
Gustavo Barriga Maldonado (figure 8.12)
Raymond Crump (figure 10.10)
Mto. Manuel Flores Jiménez (figure 11.1)

The original negatives for almost all of the postcards by Jacques Van Belle (chapter 10) are in the possession of Ajijic photographer Xill Fessenden. I am very grateful to Xill for allowing them to be digitized for use in this book. Regrettably, efforts to contact Van Belle's family to formally request permission for their use have proved unsuccessful. I hope the family will consider their inclusion here as a well-deserved tribute to a fine photographer. Every effort has been made to locate all copyright holders. Any errors or omissions in this regard will gladly be corrected in subsequent editions.

I am also very grateful to the following for their willingness to share information and expertise: Francisco G Montes Ayala, Presidente of the Asociación de Cronistas Jalisco–Michoacán, supplied the population figures used for La Palma, Michoacán; Mona Lang brought the letter written at Villa Montecarlo by artist Nils Dardel to my attention, and kindly supplied a translation; Trevor Burton gave expert advice regarding image enhancement; Gwen, Marisa and Celia Burton all offered valuable comments on early drafts.

In response to a wide range of queries, a number of good friends—Jorge Varela Martínez Negrete, Rogelio Ochoa Corona, Katie Goodridge Ingram, John Burdett Frost, Milagros Sendis, Michael Eager and the late Loy Strother—went above and beyond in sharing additional insights which have greatly enhanced this book.

Appendix 1. Dating early postcards

Only a small number of vintage postcards have any precise date printed on them. It made no commercial sense for publishers to include dates since most postcards remained on sale for years, in some cases decades. The dates given for the cards reproduced in this book are estimates. The use of "c. 1905" indicates that the publication date is thought to be within five years of 1905; "c. 1905?" is indicative of a wider time range.

In cases where the identity of the photographer is known, knowledge of their life may establish when they had the opportunity to photograph a specific subject or location. Equally—as in the case of figure 1.2—a detailed knowledge of the subject and location may help narrow down a time frame.

Dating the image is not the same as dating the publication of the card. Some publishers used the same image multiple times over a period of many years. Precise dates have been established for when some specific postcard publishers were in business; for those in operation for only a short period of time, this helps limit the time frame for some cards. Several of the more prominent publishers submitted postcards for formal registration with the federal authorities. These requests (and approval if granted) were published in the *Diario Oficial*. Where it is possible to ascribe, with certainty, the numbers, captions or the brief descriptions in the requests to a particular postcard, this establishes the card's minimum age.

For postally used cards, the minimum possible age for a card can also be determined in many cases by the postage stamp and postmarks on the card. During the first decades of the twentieth century it was customary to handstamp cards with location, date and time at both the post office where the card was mailed and the receiving office. Messages written on some cards can also offer valuable clues to to their date.

The paper and format used for postcards can also help date them. As mentioned near the start of the book, postal regulations were revised by 1907 to allow illustrated cards to have a divided back. This change (approved a year or two earlier in some European countries) took effect in the US on 1 March 1907, and is an easy way to separate pre-1907 cards from those published later.

In a few cases, the brand of paper used can help establish the earliest possible date when an individual postcard was printed. Major manufacturers of photographic paper were continually making improvements and expanding their range of products, some of which were only produced for a very limited time. For example, Kodak's ARTUR paper—used by Chapala hotelier Antonio Mólgora and others—was only made between 1911 and 1921, while the particular version of the same manufacturer's VELOX paper used by Dwight R Furness, son of the owner of the Hotel Ribera Castellanos, was limited to 1907–1909.

Cards formatted with a white border around all four sides of a centered image generally date from between about 1915 and 1930, though there are some notable exceptions.

The use of color on postcards is generally not a reliable indicator of when a card was produced, though, in cases where there are monochrome and color versions of the same image, the monochrome version (whether gray, sepia, blue or green) is normally earlier. Note that the many attractive early color postcards of Lake Chapala were not based on color photographs but were lithographs or engravings with colors added by hand or machine.

Appendix 2. Index of photographers and publishers

Alba y Fernández 2.8, 2.11, 5.10, 5.11, 5.12, 5.14, 5.15, 5.23, 5.26, 6.6, 6.8, 6.9, 8.10
Alducin 9.19
Altamirano, S 7.1, 7.3, 7.8, 7.9, 7.10
Andrade 2.4
Arnold, Peter 10.4
Brehme, Hugo 5.20, 7.19
Buedingen Art Publishing Co. 4.2
Calpini y Cia 5.6
Compañía Fotográfica Mexicana 8.9
de Alba, B[enjamín?] 5.18, 7.11
de la Torre, A. 5.3
de Obeso, J. 2.8, 5.26
Exclusivas Julio 8.11, 8.17
Fischer, Paul 3.11
Fot B.A. 5.12
Foto Esmeralda 4.1, 9.11, 9.22
Furness, Dwight R. 6.1, 6.3, 6.4, 6.5, 6.6, 6.7, 6.9, 6.10
García, Librado V. 5.11, 8.10
González, Jesús 2.7, 5.25, 8.1, 8.2, 8.4, 8.13, 8.16, 8.18, 8.19. 9.2, 9.3, 9.4, 9.5, 9.6, 9.8, 9.9, 9.12, 9.13, 9.16, 9.17, 9.18
Granat, Jakob 5.1
Granja Roca Azul 11.9
Hernández, Manuel 2.5, 2.9, 3.9, 5.8, 5.13, 5.16, 5.21, 5.24; Hernández Sucr 5.14, 5.15
Iturbide Curio Store 3.5
Johnson, Herbert 10.1?
Kaiser, Juan 1.2, 1.8, 2.2, 2.3, 3.1, 3.6, 3.10, 3.11, 5.4, 5.7, 5.17, 5.20
La Joyita 2.12
Latapi & Bert 1.3
Lotería Nacional 8.12
Lupercio, José María 1.8, 2.1?, 2.5, 2.9?, 3.3, 3.7, 3.9?, 3.10?, 5.4, 5.8, 5.9, 5.13, 5.16, 5.17, 5.21, 5.22, 5.24
Magallanes, Pedro 5.10, 5.23, 6.8
Márquez, Luis 8.8
Martin, F[elix] 7.16
Mexican Consulate, Milan, Italy 1.4, 1.5, 1.6
México Fotográfico 7.13, 7.14, 9.15
Mólgora (Antonio?) 5.5
MTB (full name unknown) 1.4, 1.5, 1.6
Pellandini, Claude 2.10
Publicaciones Fischgrund 8.8
Romero 7.1, 7.2?, 7.3?, 7.8?, 7.9?, 7.10?
Ruhland & Ahlschier 1.1, 3.2, 3.3, 3.4, 3.7
Sánchez, José Edmundo 5.2, 7.5, 7.6, 7.7, 7.12, 7.15, 8.3, 9.7
Santana, María 9.14
Schwidernoch, T. 2.1, 2.9, 5.9
Scott, Winfield 1.1, 1.2, 1.9, 2.12?, 3.2, 5.1, 5.19?, 6.2
Sonora News Company. 5.19, 6.2
Thorward, Clara 9.20
Van Belle, Jacques 10.2, 10.3, 10.5, 10.6, 10.7, 10.8, 10.9, 10.10, 10.11, 10.12, 10.13
Waite, Charles Betts 3.1?, 3.5, 3.6
Whipple, Robert 11.1-11.8 inclusive?
Yáñez, Mauricio 2.6, 8.5, 8.6, 8.7

Endnotes

AHMC: Archivo Histórico Municipal de Chapala.
CMAC: Catastro Municipal del Ayuntamiento de Chapala.

Introduction

1. They include: J Jesús González Gortázar. 1994. *Aquellos tiempos en Chapala / Past Times in Chapala* (bilingual). Guadalajara: Editorial Agata; and Manuel Galindo Gaitán. *Estampas de Chapala*. Guadalajara: Ediciones Pacífico, SA, Vol 1 (2003) and Vol 2 (2005).
2. This book extends the work of the late Dra Brigitte Boehm Schoendube. "El Lago de Chapala: su ribera norte. Un ensayo de lectura del paisaje cultural," in *Relaciones de historia y sociedad*, vol XXII #85 (2001), 57-83. Zamora, Michoacán: El Colegio de Michoacán.

Chapter 1. Wish you were here: picture postcards in Mexico

1. A few illustrated cards, with images unrelated to Mexico, were circulating in Mexico by the 1890s.
2. *Jalisco Times*, 10 April 1908.
3. Malagón Girón, *Winfield Scott*.
4. Carson, *Mexico: the wonderland*, 349–354.
5. Gregorio Torres Q. 1908. "Los Mapas Pintorescos." *La Enseñanza Primaria*, 15 April 1908, 310.
6. One noteworthy exception was those using invisible ink sent home by soldiers during wartime. See Francisco Montellano. 1998. *Charles B Waite: la época de oro de las postales en México*. Mexico: Consejo Nacional para la Cultura y Las Artes, 10–11.
7. *El Tiempo Ilustrado*, 28 November 1909, 19.
8. Ruben Dario. 1913. "La Tarjeta Postal." *El Imparcial*, 10 December 1913, 6.

Chapter 2. By boat, stagecoach and train

1. Carson, *Mexico: the wonderland*, 349–354.
2. AHMC: unpublished timeline, entries for 25 April 1898; 15 September 1898.
3. Angulo Supulveda, *La Navegación de antaño*, 58.
4. Embree, *A Dream of a Throne*, 179, describes a boat carrying firewood from Tizapán for a lime kiln in Ajijic.
5. Talavera Salgado, *Lago Chapala*, 71.
6. *Daily Alta California*, Volume 18, #7024, 18 December 1866, 1.
7. AHMC: Unpublished timeline, entry for 2 June 1868.
8. AHMC: Unpublished timeline, entry for 30 July 1881.
9. Tweedie, *Mexico as I Saw It*, 249–250.
10. Terry, *Terry's Mexico Handbook*, 152.
11. Caballero, *Primer almanaque histórico*, 191.
12. AHMC: Untitled document in "Box: Ind y Com de Chapala 1884–1998"; *Jalisco Times*, 16 September 1904; *El Correo de Jalisco*, 9 January 1907.
13. Szyszlo, *Dix mille kilomètres*, 242–244 (translation by Marie Josée Bayeur).
14. James Charlton. 1891. "Mexico Revisited, 1890." *The Newcastle Weekly Chronicle Supplement* (UK), 14 March 1891, 5.

15. Francisco Montes Martínez, "La industria textil en Jalisco", en *La ingeniería en Jalisco*. Guadalajara: Gobierno del Estado de Jalisco, 1990, 263–280; and Sergio Valerio Ulloa. 2002. *Empresarios Extranjeros en Guadalajara Durante el Porfiriato*. Guadalajara: Universidad de Guadalajara.
16. Romero, *Apuntes de un lugareño*, 148. Burton, *Lake Chapala Through the Ages*, chapter 41.

Chapter 3. Chapala at the end of the nineteenth century
1. Rogers, *Mexico? Sí, señor*.
2. De Alba, *Chapala*, 125.
3. For details of these and other historic buildings in Chapala, see Burton, *If Walls Could Talk*.
4. *TimesDemocrat* (New Orleans), 5 January 1896, 13.
5. *El Nacional*, 24 April, 1897.
6. *The Mexican Herald*, 4 August 1903. Crowe's contribution to developing tourism in Chapala is discussed in Burton, *If Walls Could Talk*.
7. Marie Robinson Wright. 1897. *Picturesque Mexico*. Philadelphia: J B Lippincott, 271.
8. *The Mexican Herald*, 13 May 1899, 5; 15 March 1898, 4; 2 December 1899, 1.
9. *The Mexican Herald*, 11 January 1899, 5.
10. *El Paso Herald*, 7 December 1899.

Chapter 4. South shore: Tizapán el Alto and la Palma
1. Nicolás Antonio de Ornelas Mendoza y Valdivia. 1719–1722. *Crónica de la provincia de Santiago de Xalisco*. Modern edition: 1962 Guadalajara: Instituto Jaliscience de Antropología e Historia.
2. Bárcena, *Ensayo estadístico*.
3. Angulo Supulveda, *La Navegación de antaño*, 58.
4. Bárcena, *Ensayo estadístico*.
5. *London Evening Standard*, 11 April 1903, 8.
6. Embree, *A Dream of a Throne*.
7. *The Dayton Herald* (Dayton, Ohio) 10 April 1902, 10.
8. *Arizona Republican*, (Phoenix, Arizona) 17 August 1919, Section 2, 5.
9. *El Continental: revista popular jalisciense*, 13 January 1895, 3.
10. *St. Louis Globe Democrat* (St. Louis, Missouri), 13 February 1905, 2.
11. *San Antonio Express* (San Antonio, Texas), 25 September 1908, 9.
12. *New York Times*, 8 October 1930.
13. *The Mexican Herald*, 12 Dec 1896, 5.
14. Montes & Montes, 2008, 1, quoted in Pedroza Gutiérrez, Carmen and Jaime Chavolla. 2018. "Conviviendo con la escasez. Cultura y adaptabilidad pesquera en el lago de Chapala." *Perfiles Latinoamericanos*, 26(51) 2018, 89–121.
15. Kingsley, *South by west*.
16. Christian Reid. 1894. *The Land of the Sun: Vistas Mexicanas*. New York: Appleton.
17. Angulo Supulveda, *La Navegación de antaño*.
18. Francisco G Montes Ayala, personal communication, October 2021.
19. Pedroza Gutiérrez, Carmen and Jaime Chavolla. 2018. "Conviviendo con la escasez. Cultura y adaptabilidad pesquera en el lago de Chapala." *Perfiles Latinoamericanos*, 26 (51) 2018, 112.

Chapter 5. Chapala 1900–1920: the golden age of tourism
1. *El Imparcial: diario ilustrado de la mañana*, 19 April 1908.
2. *The Daily Express* (San Antonio, Texas), 19 June 1906, 8.
3. Terry, *Terry's Mexico Handbook*, 152.
4. Gillpatrick, *The man who likes Mexico*, 159.
5. *El Correo de Jalisco*, 12 April 1907; de Alba, *Chapala*, 116.
6. *Jalisco Times*, 30 April 1904.
7. AHMC: unpublished time line, entry for 27 November 1897.

8. Gillpatrick, *The man who likes Mexico*, 159.
9. E W Nelson. "A Winter Expedition into Southwestern Mexico." *National Geographic*, Sept. 1904.
10. *The Mexican Herald*, 11 April 1897.
11. *The Mexican Herald*, 9 April 1900.
12. *Jalisco Times*, 12 March 1904; 18 June 1904; 3 September 1904.
13. *Jalisco Times*, 8 September 1907, 5.
14. Burton, *Lake Chapala Through the Ages*, 25.
15. AHMC: unpublished time line, entry for 29 May 1899.
16. *Jalisco Times*, 18 June 1904; CMAC: historial catastral for Villa Aurora.
17. *The Mexican Herald*, 29 October 1902, 5; AHMC: unpublished time line, entries for 1 April 1903 and 30 September 1903; *Jalisco Times*, 2 January 1904.
18. G W Baylor. 1902. "Lovely Lake Chapala." *El Paso Herald*, 1 November 1902.
19. *El Tiempo*, 21 April 1908.
20. Cristina, *El Chapala de Natalia*, 15; AHMC: 2016. "Las Limonadas de los Pérez Arce."
21. AHMC: unpublished timeline, entries from 15 February to November 1910.
22. Carson, *Mexico: the wonderland*, 349–354.
23. de Szyszlo, *Dix mille kilomètres*, 235–236, translation by Marie Josée Bayeur.
24. *Jalisco Times*, 6 March 1908.
25. *El Informador*, 15 September 1918, 2.
26. Terry, *Terry's Mexico Handbook*, 152.
27. *El Pueblo*, 28 February 1916, 1; 1 March 1916, 1, 8.
28. *Jalisco Times*, 23 January 1904; 16 January 1904; 17 April 1908; *El Tiempo*, 21 April 1908.
29. *El Informador*, 20 March 1920, 7,
30. *El Informador*, 14 March 1919, 2.
31. For a fuller account, see Burton, *If Walls Could Talk*, chapter 42.

Chapter 6. East end: Ocotlán and Hotel Ribera Castellanos

1. Ángulo Sepulveda, *La navegación de antaño*.
2. *Jalisco Times*, 30 August 1907.
3. *The Mexican Herald*, 18 February 1902, 3.
4. *El Abogado Cristiano Ilustrado*, 24 December 1903, 16. Furness' 1917 US passport application.
5. Martin, *Mexico's Treasure House*, 243–244.
6. *The Mexican Herald*, 21 May 1902, 2.
7. *The Mexican Herald*, 31 May 1902, 4.
8. *Arizona Republic* (Phoenix, Arizona) 24 July 1902, 4.
9. *The Mexican Herald*, 7 May 1904; 4 November 1904; 8 November 1907; 17 January 1908.
10. *The Mexican Herald*, 4 January 1907; *The Mexican Herald*, 13 May 1907.
11. *The Mexican Herald*, 27 September 1907. *The Mexican Herald*, 27 September 1907, 8; 5 June 1909.
12. (a) Reau Campbell. 1899. *Campbell's New Revised Complete Guide and Descriptive Book of Mexico*. Chicago: Rogers & Smith Co. (b) Mrs James Edwin Morris. 1902. *A tour in Mexico*. The Abbey Press.
13. E W Nelson. "A Winter Expedition into Southwestern Mexico." *National Geographic*, Sept. 1904.
14. Percy Martin. 1907. *Mexico of the Twentieth Century*. London: Edward Arnold, vol II, 67–68.
15. *Jalisco Times*, 29 March 1907.
16. *Jalisco Times*, 1 May 1908.
17. *The Mexican Herald*, 5 September 1909, 3
18. *The San Bernardino Sun*, 4 December 1909.
19. *The Mexican Herald*, 27 June 1910, 5.
20. *The Mexican Herald*, 24 August 1911, 7.
21. For example, *El Mundo Ilustrado*, 5 October 1913.
22. Witter Bynner, *Journey with Genius*, 125.

23. Lawrence, *The Plumed Serpent*, chapter 5.
24. *Los Angeles Times*, 19 October 1923.

Chapter 7. Chapala 1920–1940: after the Revolution

1. *El Informador*, 20 March 1920, 7.
2. Chente García, "Chapala," in Álvarez del Castillo, *Arquitecto Guillermo de Alba*.
3. Advertisement in *El Informador*, 10 November 1920.
4. Chente García, "Chapala," in Álvarez del Castillo, *Arquitecto Guillermo de Alba*.
5. *Reading Times* (Reading, Pennsylvania), 31 August 1926, 1.
6. (a) David C Bailey. 1974. *Viva Cristo Rey!: The Cristero Rebellion and the ChurchState conflict in Mexico*. University of Texas. (b) Emma Lindsay Squier, in *Gringa: An American Woman in Mexico* (1934), explains how "the bloodthirsty bandit who had attacked and set fire to a passenger train" was the same captivating man riding a black horse who had previously helped her change a tire in the middle of nowhere.
7. *El Informador*, 2 March 1934, 1, 2.
8. *El Informador*, 30 March 1923; 8 April 1923, 5; 25 March 1925, 8.
9. *El Informador*, 8 May 1930, 6.
10. *El Informador*, 16 June 1937, 3 (editorial).
11. Bynner, *Journey with Genius*, 93.
12. Letter dated 3 May 1923 to Kai Gotzsche and Knud Merrild, quoted in Knud Merrild's, *A Poet and Two Painters: A Memoir of D.H. Lawrence*.
13. Lawrence, *The Plumed Serpent*, chapter 9.
14. CMAC: historial catastral for the property.
15. *El Informador*, 24 April 1932; 29 April 1934.
16. *El Informador*, 2 July 1931, 2.
17. Jack McDonald, "Inn's Charming Hostess." *Guadalajara Reporter*, 29 June 1968, 12.
18. *El Informador*, 12 December 1924, 4, 6.
19. *East–West*, Vol. 2 #4 (May–June 1927); Vol 4 #3, (November–December 1929).

Chapter 8. Fishing and environmental change

1. Hansen, 220.
2. Barbour, C D. 2002. "Chirostoma contrerasi (Atherinopsidae, Menidiinae) a new species from Lago de Chapala, Mexico," p 23–33 of LozanoVilano, M L (ed). *Libro Jubilar en Honor al Dr Salvador Contreras Balderas*. Universidad Autónoma de Nuevo León.
3. Edna Mae Stark. 1937. "Discovering Mexico," *Modern Mexico*, July 1937, 19 23.
4. Pauncefote, Hon. Maud. 1900. "Chapala the Beautiful," *Harper's Bazar*, 29 December 1900.
5. Luisa Paré. 1989. *Los Pescadores de Chapala y la Defensa de su Lago*. Guadalajara: ITESO, 54, ftnt 10.
6. Chandos, *Village in the Sun*, 159–160.
7. Chandos, *Village in the Sun*, 49.
8. Luisa Paré. 1989. *Los Pescadores de Chapala y la Defensa de su Lago*. Guadalajara: ITESO.
9. R Moncayo Estrada, C Escalera Gallardo, V Segura García. 2003. "Los pescados blancos del lago de Chapala. Características generales." *Historia y Avances del Cultivo de Pescado Blanco*. Instituto Nacional de la Pesca, 51–67.
10. Witter Bynner, *Journey with Genius*, 119.
11. Rogelio Ochoa Corona, personal communication; Lawrence, *The Plumed Serpent*, chapter 12.
12. *New York Times*: 28 October 1951, 104.
13. Supulveda, *La Navegación de antaño*, 62.
14. *El Agricultor Mexicano*, Vol XX, #3 (September 1905), 78.
15. *San Francisco Chronicle*, 9 October 1905, 1.
16. *Caras y caretas* (Buenos Aires, Argentina), 3 June 1905, 7. Similar adverts appeared until at least 1907.

17. Daniel Llueh Belda, Laurence Irving and Michael Pilson. 1964. *Algunas observaciones sobre mamiferos acuaticos*. Mexico City: Secretaria de Industria y Comercio.
18. AHMC: unpublished timeline of major events, entry for 1 April 1948.
19. *Guadalajara Reporter*, 7 October 1967; 11 November 1967.

Chapter 9. Chapala 1940–1960: tourism and redevelopment

1. *New York Times*, 27 July 1947; 10 August 1947; 9 November 1947; 10 November 1947.
2. Mona Lang, personal communication.
3. Bashford, *Tourist Guide to Mexico*.
4. *Guadalajara Reporter*, 22 January 1977, 17.
5. *Guadalajara Reporter*, 22 October 1964; 29 October 1964. *El Informador*, 31 October 1964.
6. *El Informador*, 1 August 1940.
7. *El Informador*, 4 June 1943, 1, 7.
8. *El Informador*, 2 May 1948, 1; 4 July 1948.
9. Chandos, *Village in the Sun*, 49.
10. Terry, *Terry's Guide to Mexico*, 476.

Chapter 10. Ajijic: favored by foreigners

1. For example, *Los Angeles Times*, 14 October 1959, 55; *Esquire*, February 1960.
2. Trivia note: Booth Waterbury was a great grand-nephew of John Wilkes Booth, assassin of President Lincoln in 1865.
3. *Guadalajara Reporter*, 7 February 1976.
4. Dale Hoyt Palfrey. 2018. "Flashback to the birth of the Mexican National Chili Cookoff," *Guadalajara Reporter*, 15 February 2018, 9.
5. Almost all the postcards reproduced in this chapter are the work of Jacques Van Belle (1923–2012).
6. *The Desert Sun* (Palm Springs), 8 August 1960.
7. John Upton. 1950. "Ah-hee-heek: A Place to Loaf in Mexico." *San Francisco Chronicle*, 7 May 1950.
8. Mabel F Knight. 1952. "Ajijic - The Gem of Jalisco", *Pemex Travel Club magazine*, 1 February 1952.
9. Anon. "San Andres en Ajijic." *Club de Viajes Pemex*, 1 December 1956.
10. Terry, *Terry's Guide to Mexico*, 250.
11. *Traveler's Guide to Mexico*, Jan 1973, G10G11.
12. Loy Strother, personal communication.
13. Zoe Kernick. "Ajijic." *Mexican Life*, April 1951.
14. James, *Dust on My Heart*, 277.

Chapter 11. West end: Jocotepec and Roca Azul

1. Manuel Flores Jiménez, personal communication.
2. Jack McDonald, *Guadalajara Reporter*, 24 March 1973, 1.
3. *Delta-Democrat Times* (Greenville, Mississippi), 24 August 1958.
4. *Delta-Democrat Times* (Greenville, Mississippi), 24 August 1958.
5. Bob Whipple, interviewed at his home in Jocotepec in August 1989.
6. Howard Fryer. 2010. *El Nitty-Gritty*.
7. Tony Burton. 1990, 1992. "The Sad End to the Long History of La Quinta." *Chapala Riviera Guide*, volume 1, #3 (February 1990) and "Drastic Modifications to One of the Chapala Riviera's Most Historic Buildings: La Quinta, Jocotepec." *Chapala Riviera Guide*, volume 3, #9 (August/September 1992).
8. *Guadalajara Reporter*, 12 February 1977, 1.
9. Howard Fryer. 2010. *El Nitty-Gritty*.
10. *El Informador*, 13 August 1971, 3B.

Bibliography

Aguila Pérez, Aida and Miguel Chabolla. 2011. *Photo-history of Jocotepec, Jalisco*. Second edition.
Álvarez del Castillo, Jaime (coordinator). 2002. *Arquitecto Guillermo de Alba*. Agata/Fotoglobo.
Ángulo Sepulveda, Jose Maria. 1987. *La Navegación de antaño en el Lago de Chapala*. Guadalajara: Gobierno de Jalisco.
Arias Ibarra, José Guadalupe. Undated. *Jocotepec. Historia de un Pueblo*. Privately printed.
Bárcena, Mariano. 1888. *Ensayo estadístico del Estado de Jalisco*. Guadalajara: Gobierno de Jalisco, 1983.
Bashford, G. M.. 1954. *Tourist Guide to Mexico*. McGrawHill.
Bedford, Sybille. 1960. *A Visit to Don Otavio: A Traveller's Tale from Mexico*. London: Collins.
Burton, Tony. 2008. *Lake Chapala through the ages: an anthology of travelers' tales*. Sombrero Books.
____ 2020. *If Walls Could Talk: Chapala's historic buildings and former occupants*. Sombrero Books.
Bynner, Witter. 1951. *Journey with Genius: Recollection and Reflections Concerning The D.H. Lawrences*. New York: The John Day Company.
Caballero, Manuel. *Primer almanaque histórico, artístico y monumental de la República Mexicana 1884 y 1885*. Mexico / Nueva York: The Chas. M. Green Printing Co.
Carson, William English. 1909. *Mexico: the wonderland of the south*. New York: Macmillan.
de Alba, Antonio. 1954. *Chapala*. Banco Industrial de Jalisco.
Embree, Charles Fleming. 1900. *A Dream of a Throne: the Story of a Mexican Revolt*. Boston: Little, Brown and Company.
Ficke, Arthur Davison. 1939. *Mrs Morton of Mexico*. New York: Reynal & Hitchcock.
Gibbon, Eduardo A. 1893. *Guadalajara, (La Florencia Mexicana). Vagancias y Recuerdos*. 1992 reprint: Guadalajara, Jalisco: Presidencia Municipal de Guadalajara.
Gillpatrick, Owen Wallace. 1911. *The man who likes Mexico. The spirited chronicle of adventurous wanderings in Mexican highways and byways*. New York: The Century Co.
Kingsley, Rose Georgina. 1874. *South by west or winter in the Rocky Mountains and spring in Mexico*. London: W. Isibister & Co.
Lawrence, D H. 1926. *The Plumed Serpent*. London: Martin Secker Ltd.
Malagón Girón, Beatriz Eugenia. 2012. *Winfield Scott: retrato de un fotógrafo norteamericano en el porfiriato*. Mexico City: Universidad Autónoma Metropolitana, 2012.
Martin, Percy. 1906. *Mexico's Treasure House*. New York: The Cheltenham Press.
Parmenter, Ross. 1983. *Stages in a Journey*. New York: Profile Press.
Rogers, Thomas L. 1893. *Mexico? Sí, señor*. Boston: Mexican Central Railway Co.
Romero, José Rubén. 1932. *Apuntes de un lugareño*. Translated by John and Ruth Mitchell as *Notes of a Villager: A Mexican Poet's Youth and Revolution*. 1988. Kaneohe, Hawaii: Plover Press.
Scofield, Sandra. 1996. *A Chance to See Egypt*. New York: Cliff Street Books.
Szyszlo, Vitold de. 1913. *Dix mille kilomètres a travers le Mexique, 1909–1910*. Paris: PlonNourrit et Cie.
Talavera Salgado, Francisco. 1982. *Lago Chapala, turismo residencial y campesinado*. Mexico City: INAH.
Terry, Thomas Philip. 1909. *Terry's Mexico Handbook for Travellers*. México City: Sonora News Company and Boston: Houghton Mifflin Co.
____ 1947. *Terry's Guide to Mexico*. Hingham, Massachusetts.
Tweedie, Mrs Alec (Ethel Brilliana Harley). 1901. *Mexico as I Saw It*. New York: Macmillan; London: Hurst and Blackett.

Index

accidents 17, 19, 53, 60, 85
Adams, Frederick Upham 69
agriculture 36, 37, 38, 40, 82, 87, 132
Agua Caliente 50, 51, 52
Ahumada Alatorre, José de Jesús 126
Ajijic 2, 13, 52, 85, 86, 88, 93, 97, 117, 119-130, 134, 138
Ajijic Hand Looms 125
Ajijic Indigenous Community 130
Alducin, Rafael 117
Alemán, Miguel 107, 137
Anisz, Enrique 72
Anzino, Alberto 7, 32
Arana, Miguel 131, 132, 133, 134
Arroniz, Carlos Ochoa 29
artists 33, 95, 97, 105, 116, 117, 121, 123, 125, 137
Arzapalo, Ignacio 22, 31, 42, 44, 49, 51, 55, 58
Atequiza 21, 22, 33
authors 1, 19, 24, 33, 38, 79, 89, 105, 107, 117, 120, 123-4,
Avenida Hidalgo, Chapala 52, 109
Avenida Madero, Chapala 101, 108, 109

Bárcena, Mariano 99
Barragán, Juan José 72
Barragán, Luis 72, 82
bathing huts 43, 44, 45
Bedford, Sybille 85, 105
Beer Garden 104, 110, 112, 113
Benson, William Townsley 33
Blessing of animals 128, 129
boats 2, 4, 5, 10, 12, 13, 15, 16, 18, 19, 24, 31, 32, 35, 37, 38, 40, 45, 47, 55-57, 61-4, 66-8, 80, 82, 86, 88, 94, 96-101, 104, 105, 112, 116-8, 138
Braniff family 47, 58, 64, 79, 98
Brehme, Hugo 55, 86
bullfights 109, 129

buses 59, 70, 73, 81, 109
Bynner, Witter 74, 76, 79, 85, 136

caldo michi 43, 77, 115, 117
Calle de la Pesquería, Chapala 79, 80
Calle de San Miguel, Chapala 7, 30
Calle Juárez, Chapala 48, 127
Calle Matamoros, Jocotepec 133, 134
Calle Miguel Arana, Jocotepec 131, 133
cameras 4, 5, 12, 18, 83, 103, 125
Cameron, Duncan 19, 38
canoas 15, 18, 37, 39, 87, 94, 99, 115
Capetillo, Manuel 19, 29, 44, 49, 76
Carden, Lionel 19, 31, 47, 55
Carmichael and Cox 3
Carnival 107, 109
Carranza, Venustiano 55
Carson, William 7
Casa Albión 2, 4, 26, 28, 29, 30, 31, 55, 56
Casa Braniff 7, 25, 27, 29, 46, 47, 48, 49, 74, 78, 79, 81, 85, 99, 114
Casa Capetillo 2, 26, 29, 49, 50, 54, 56, 76, 77, 81, 94, 110, 111
Casa Galván 49, 50, 60, 81, 94
Casa Heuer 119, 121, 126
Casa Pérez Verdía 29
Castellanos family 3, 21, 34, 61, 62, 64, 67-8
Castellanos Lambley, Pedro 82, 111, 113
Cerro San Miguel 7, 27, 30, 51, 52, 53, 54, 55, 83, 100, 101
Chacaltita 26, 27, 29, 48, 81, 82, 109, 111
Chalet Paulsen 29, 30, 51, 56, 82, 94
Chandos, Dane 89, 92, 115, 121
Chapala (song) 115
Chapala Development Company 72, 74, 111
Chapala Railroad 60, 72, 73, 101, 102
charales 88, 89, 91, 92, 115
Charlton, James 23
Chili Cookoff 122, 150

INDEX

Christmas 9, 31, 109
church 4, 6, 7, 25, 27, 29, 41, 42, 43, 46, 47, 48, 54, 78, 101, 102, 107, 109, 120, 129, 131, 132
Clift, John Russell 107-8, 109
climate 27, 32, 33, 36, 64, 65, 89
Cojumatlán 36, 38, 40
Collignon, Eduard 29, 46, 47, 57
Compañía de Navegación del Lago de Chapala y Río Grande 18
Corona, Ramón 19, 46, 82
Corsi, Angelo 8, 57, 58, 105
costumbrista images 68, 93, 97
cotton manta clothing 95
Cristero War 75
Crowe, Septimus 28, 30-31, 47, 55, 78, 102, 147
Cuesta Gallardo family 47, 57, 83
Cuevas family 76, 113, 115
cuisine 59, 68, 104

dancing, *danzantes* 77, 86, 107, 129
Dardel, Nils 105
Darío, Rubén 9
de Alba, Guillermo 42, 49, 60, 71, 72, 74, 82, 83, 115
de Ávalos, Alonso 35
de la Mora, Roberto and Manuela 29
de Szyszlo, Vitold 22, 148
Día de la Marina 105
Díaz, Porfirio 5, 19, 31, 47, 49, 52, 57, 58, 59, 60, 82, 95, 97, 98
Díaz Morales, Ignacio 82
Disney, Walt 107
Dollero, Adolfo 7
drought 17, 101, 102, 126, 127
ducks 89
Duke of Manchester 59

Eager family 122, 123, 138
Easter 31, 42, 57, 59, 71, 75, 76, 107, 109, 129
Echauri, Joaquín Fermín de 35
Eiloart, Arnold 121
Eisenhower, Dwight D 107
Eisenmann, Carlos 31
El Castillo 21, 22, 23, 24
El Fuerte 62, 66, 67, 70
Elizaga, Lorenzo 47, 57, 58, 59
El Salto 23, 82
Elstob, Peter 121

Embree, Charles 33, 36, 37
Enríquez, Manuel 44, 45

Feast of the Immaculate Conception 107
federal concession zone 102
Fermín de Echauri, Joaquín 35
Ficke, Arthur Davison 85, 151
fiesta 129, 132
firewood 16, 17, 18, 90, 146
Fischer, Paul 33, 34, 117
fish 33, 43, 87, 88, 89, 91, 92, 99, 115, 117, 138
Fisher, Frances Christine 39
fishing, fishermen 4, 11, 13, 15, 17, 18, 27, 40, 70, 75, 79, 87, 88, 89, 90, 91, 92, 93, 95, 96, 97, 98, 99, 100, 101, 115, 116, 117, 120, 125, 129, 139, 137, 138
floods 73, 75, 101, 102, 120
Franck, Harry 68
friary 27, 47
Fryer, Howard and Yolanda 138
Furness, Dwight 62-5, 68, 69
Furness, Dwight R (son) 65, 142

Galván, Gabriela 49
Gillpatrick, Owen Wallace 42, 45, 147, 151
González, Jesús 6, 11, 104
González Gallo, Jesús 109, 115
González Hermosillo, Aurelio 51, 57, 78
Gran Hotel Chapala 59, 76, 101
Guanajuato 62, 63, 64, 69
Guizar, Pepe 115

haciendas 40, 61, 87
    Hacienda Buenavista 29
    Hacienda San Francisco 35, 36, 38
health spa 126, 127
Hermosillo, Aurelio González 51
Hernández, Manuel 10
Heuer, Liesel and Paul 119, 120, 123
hippies 127
Hotel Arzapalo 2, 3, 4, 7, 9, 11, 21, 31, 32, 33, 34, 42, 43, 44, 47, 54, 59, 62, 65, 71, 74, 75, 76, 77, 79, 81, 83, 113, 115
Hotel Danza del Sol 130
Hotel Laguna (Hotel Anita) 126, 127, 128
Hotel La Quinta 133, 134, 136, 137
Hotel Nido 77, 108, 115
Hotel Niza 76
Hotel Palmera 42, 58, 71, 73, 76, 77, 115

Hotel Real de Chapala 130
Hotel Ribera 3, 21, 34, 59, 61, 62, 63, 64, 65, 66, 67, 68, 69, 70, 82
Hotel Victor Huber 22, 32, 42, 43, 52, 59, 76, 101, 108
Huber, Victor 22
Huichol people 98
Hunton family, 83, 85, 127

Irapuato 20, 21, 22, 23, 25, 61, 63
Ixtlahuacán de los Membrillos 29

Jalisco Development Company 51, 55, 60
Jamay 19, 64, 65, 68
James, Neill 85, 123, 124, 125, 129, 130
Jocotepec 2, 35, 101, 131-139
Johnson, Herbert 120
Johnson, Willard 76
Juanacatlán 22, 23, 83

Kaiser, Juan 3, 4, 10, 69, 117
King, George Edward 31, 47, 58, 85
Kingsley, Rose Georgina 38
Kirtland, Helen 125
Knight, Mabel 126
Kodak 4, 5, 142

La Barca 19, 20, 37, 75
Laboratorios Julio 11
La Canacinta 130
La Capilla 51, 72, 73, 74
La Floresta 130
Lake Chapala Agricultural and Improvement Company 64
Lake Chapala Society 124, 130
Langenscheidt, Enrique 65, 69
Laure, Mike 113
La Palma 17, 19, 24, 35, 37, 38, 39, 40, 68, 88
La Quinta 133-138
Las Delicias 50, 51
Lawrence, D H 59, 70, 74, 76, 77, 79, 80-82, 97, 136
level of the lake 49, 75, 101
lighthouse 97, 139
Lilley, Peter 121
Limantour, José Yves 67
lirio, see water hyacinth
Lloyd, Allen W 135, 137
López Mateos, Adolfo 107, 137

López Portillo y Weber, José 66
López Vega, Jesús 123
lottery 96
Lourdes Chapel 106, 107
Loweree Brothers 20
Lupercio, José María 3, 10, 26, 46
Lytton-Bernard, Bernard 126

Magallanes López, Pedro 67
malaria 65, 69
mariachi 77, 113, 114
marijuana 127
markets 35, 36, 53, 63, 81, 122
Márquez Romay, Luis 93
marriage 18, 67, 126, 132
Martin, Winifred 68
Matthews, Al 137
Mehnen, Holger 86, 120
Mexcala 65, 98, 99
Mexican Central Railway 20, 21, 22, 24, 25, 41, 51, 61, 65, 67
Mexican Revolution 6, 38, 58, 69
Mexico City 3, 9, 20, 21, 24, 31, 37, 38, 47, 57, 59, 60, 61, 64, 69, 74, 75, 79, 82, 98, 117, 118, 134
México Fotográfico 81, 82
Michoacán 38, 39, 40
Millet, Nigel 120, 121
mineral water 32, 52, 63, 93, 139
mining 4, 18, 31, 63
Mi Pullman 49
Mólgora, Antonio 6, 7, 76, 142
Morales, Ignacio Díaz 82
murals 123
murder 69

National Geographic 67, 93
Nelson, Edward 45, 67, 147, 148
nets 11, 79, 87, 88, 90-3, 96, 97, 115, 125, 138
New Orleans 31, 57
New York 77, 86, 97, 105
Nido, Ramón 76, 77, 111, 115
Norwegian 51, 60, 72, 76, 78
Nuño, María Guadalupe 74

Obregón, Álvaro 70, 75
Ochoa Arroniz, Carlos 29
Ocotlán 3, 13, 17, 19, 21, 23, 24, 34, 35, 37, 40-42, 57, 59, 61-67, 69, 72, 75, 82, 98, 99

O'Rourke, Martha 135
Palacio Municipal, Chapala 53
Paricutín Volcano 116
Paseo Ramón Corona, Chapala 82
Paulsen, Ernesto 30, 51, 55
Pauncefote, Maud 89
Pérez Arce, Salvador 52
Pérez Verdía, Luis 47, 79, 98
petroleum 37
photography, photographers 3, 6, 9, 10, 24, 59, 65, 67, 69, 75, 86, 92, 110, 120, 124, 131
pier 2, 12-15, 17, 29, 31, 33, 37, 40, 43-9, 55, 56, 57, 60, 67-8, 96, 99-102, 104, 110
pirates 38
plaza 23, 52, 53, 68, 77, 93, 95, 97, 109, 120, 121, 123, 127, 130, 131, 132, 133
political refugees 103
Posada Ajijic 121, 122, 126, 138
Posada Doña Trini 32, 43
Posada Rancho Santa Isabel 126, 127
power boats 64
Prince Philip, Duke of Edinburgh 107
promenade 96, 110, 111
prostitution 52
Purnell, George and Idella 76

Querétaro 49
Quinta Mi Retiro 126
Quinta Tzintzuntzan 123, 124, 130

railroad 3, 5, 8, 20, 21, 23, 24, 25, 33, 38, 51, 53, 61, 63, 65, 73, 74, 76, 119, 134
Ramírez, Casimiro and Josefina 121
reclamation of beach 84
redevelopment of town center 109
regatta 58, 60, 105, 139
Revolution 6, 9, 38, 40, 55, 58, 59, 69, 71, 98
Río de la Pasión 37
River Lerma 20
River Santiago 22, 23, 61, 99
River Zula 23
Roca Azul 131, 139
Rogers, Thomas 27, 30
Romay, Luis Márquez 93
Romero, José Ruben 24
Romero Rubio, Carmen 31
rowing 5, 15, 18, 49, 105
Rubio, Carmen Romero 31

Ruhland and Ahlschier 2, 3
sailboats 12, 15, 16, 17, 36, 62
San Antonio Tlayacapan 2, 52, 130
Sánchez, José Edmundo 6, 74, 83
San Luis Soyatlán 88
Santana, María 110
Sayula 95, 134
Schjetnan, Christian 51, 60, 72, 73, 111
Schnaider family 31, 55, 107
Scorpion Island 7, 88, 99, 112
Scott, Winfield 2-4, 24, 26, 58, 62, 65, 67, 69
Seimandi, Antonio 7, 33
Somellera, Andrés 71
stagecoach 4, 13, 19-22, 33, 43, 134, 135
Stark, Edna Mae 88
steamships 15-21, 23, 24, 37, 40, 41, 42, 51, 61, 62, 67, 72, 98, 99, 119, 138, 139
    Chapala 19
    Libertad 18, 19, 38, 98
    Viking 72
Stephenson, Ana Victoria 29, 47
storms 37, 38, 96, 97, 132
Strange, Charles 30, 59
Switzerland 32, 58

tequila 22, 74, 113, 137
Terry, J Phillip 20, 79, 117, 127
textile factory 23
Thorward, Clara 116, 117
Tizapán el Alto 19, 35, 36, 37, 38, 88, 99
tourists 5, 22, 33, 54, 59, 61, 62, 76, 81, 83, 93, 97, 104, 109, 120, 122, 124
Townsend, Cora Alice and family 31, 57. 58
trains 19, 20-24, 41, 42, 62, 65, 67, 70, 73-75, 98
Tuxcueca 19, 37
Twardowicz, Stanley 97
Tweedie, Mrs Alec 19
typhoid 76

Van Belle, Jacques 124
Villa Ana Victoria 4, 6, 27, 29, 33, 41, 47, 52, 57, 59, 76, 77, 101, 108
Villa Aurora 50, 51, 60, 81, 110, 111
Villa Ave María 60, 110
Villa Carmen 6, 26, 29, 48, 49
Villa El Manglar 55, 57-60
Villa Elena 71, 83
Villa Ferrara 111, 113
Villa, Francisco "Pancho" 134

Villa Josefina 2, 4, 28, 29, 31, 55, 56, 71
Villa Montecarlo 10, 29, 30, 31, 51, 52, 55, 57, 58, 71, 77, 78, 94, 105, 106, 107
Villa Niza 60, 71
Villa Ochoa 29
Villa Paz 26, 29, 51, 54, 56, 82
Villa Reynera 55, 85, 86
Villa Robles León 80, 82
Villa Tlalocan 2, 4, 19, 28, 29, 30, 31, 47, 51, 55, 82, 83, 94, 104
Villa Virginia 83, 84, 85, 86
von Mauch, Alex 119, 124

Waite, Charles Betts 3, 28
Waterbury, Booth 122
water carriers 4, 93, 94
water hyacinth 50, 96, 99, 101, 102, 137
watersports 105
weaving 123
Wertheimer, Louis 130
Whipple, Robert (Bob) 136, 137
whirlpool 40
whitefish 43, 88, 115
winds 37, 97, 99
Winsnes, Birger 72, 76
wood, woodsellers 15, 16, 17, 18, 19, 92
Wright, Marie Robinson 31

yachts, yachting 17, 31, 48, 58, 59, 72, 119, 139
Yáñez, Mauricio 92
Yogananda, Paramahansa 86

Zara (La Rusa) 85, 86, 120
Zeiner, Carlos 127

Author

Tony Burton, born and educated in the UK, taught, researched, lectured and guided specialist cultural and ecological trips in Mexico for eighteen years. A three-time winner of ARETUR's travel-writing competition for articles about Mexico, he has written extensively about Mexico to bring its ecology, history, economics, tourism and geography to a wide audience for more than thirty years.

His previous books on Mexico are *Western Mexico: A Traveler's Treasury* (fourth edition, 2014), *Lake Chapala Through the Ages, an Anthology of Travelers' Tales* (2008), *Mexican Kaleidoscope: myths, mysteries and mystique* (2016), *If Walls Could Talk: Chapala's historic buildings and their former occupants* (2020), and *Foreign Footprints in Ajijic* (2022). He also coauthored, with Dr Richard Rhoda, the landmark volume *Geo-Mexico, the Geography and Dynamics of Modern Mexico* (2010). His original articles and maps have appeared in numerous magazines, journals and books in Mexico, Canada, the US, Ireland and beyond.

Tony and his wife, Gwen, live on Vancouver Island in Canada and revisit Mexico as often as they can.

Other books by this author

Western Mexico: A Traveler's Treasury (4th edition, 2014)
The author departs from "the stock formula found in conventional guides. He adheres to a more organic approach, drawing on personal experience and meticulous research to divulge the virtues and peculiarities of every destination." —Dale Palfrey, *The Guadalajara Reporter*

Lake Chapala Through the Ages, an Anthology of Travelers' Tales (2008)
"Intermingled with the firsthand accounts of the area in different eras, Burton provides snippets of background history to give some larger context.... Burton is a consummate scholar whose writing is also enjoyable to read." —novelist Robert Richter

Geo-Mexico, the Geography and Dynamics of Modern Mexico (2010) (coauthored with Dr Richard Rhoda) "Geo-Mexico illustrates both the richness of geography as a field of study and the spectrum of cultural, economic, and environmental anomalies that make Mexico so eternally fascinating." —Felisa Rogers, *The People's Guide to Mexico*

Mexican Kaleidoscope: myths, mysteries and mystique (2016)
"In this lively interweaving of history, cuisine, culture, tradition and superstition, Tony Burton brings the reader refreshing and often startling insights into the forces that shaped Mexican culture." —author Dr. Michael Hogan

If Walls Could Talk: Chapala's historic buildings and their former occupants (2020)
"Tony Burton's thoroughly researched and utterly fascinating book takes us through the surprising and richly textured history of Chapala's past from the mid-eighteen hundreds onwards.... a wonderful historical gift to the people of the village." —Rita Pomade, *MexConnect*.

Foreign Footprints in Ajijic: decades of change in a Mexican village (2022)
The author does "a masterful job of revealing the role of foreigners in Ajijic's story. It's a great legacy, filling an enormous gap in accounts of local history. Besides that, a brilliantly written chronicle that will surely captivate readers." —journalist Dale Palfrey